D0065268

Institutions of Economic Growth

INSTITUTIONS OF
ECONOMIC GROWTH

A Theory of Conflict
Management
in Developing Countries

BY JOHN P. POWELSON

PRINCETON UNIVERSITY PRESS

PRINCETON, NEW JERSEY

1972

This book has been composed in Linotype Caledonia

Printed in the United States of America
by Princeton University Press, Princeton, New Jersey

To Mary Powelson and Lydia Roberts,
and to the memories of John A. Powelson
and Byron T. Roberts

Contents

Preface

WHY, in some countries, is economic growth stopped by internal quarrels and mistrust? Why, in others, do competitors not only control their conflicts but *use* them to promote growth? In addressing this question, the present volume develops a broad-based theory of institutions. Growth depends, among other things, on a national capacity to build institutions to manage conflicts. This capacity, furthermore, requires national consensus on an economic and a political ideology. These ideologies are defined as the ways in which individuals envisage the economic and political systems—how they operate, and how just they are. Ideological consensus in turn is fostered by a popular nationalism, which therefore plays a positive role in growth rather than the negative one usually attributed to it by economists. In sum, the chain is as follows:

| Popular nationalism | → | Ideological consensus | → | institutions Effective | → | Economic growth |

Capital and entrepreneurial capacity are frequently cited as principal bottlenecks in economic growth. We add a third: the effectiveness of institutions in managing conflict. Furthermore, the kinds of institutions that will be most effective depend on the particular ideology on which consensus is formed. No one ideology is inherently superior to another. Thus, for example, if President Nyerere is successful in persuading the Tanzanian people to believe in African Socialism, his own doctrine which holds that capitalism is unjust, then nationalized enterprises and cooperatives may be the most effective institutions of production in that land. But if his partner in the East African Community, President Kenyatta, succeeds in interpreting African Socialism in Kenya to have a strong flavor of private enterprise, then a mixture of government- and private-owned business is likely to be more effective in that setting.

We do not concern ourselves with how consensus is formed, whether by a long march of history (as would seem to be the case in Mexico) or by a flamboyant personality (as in Cuba). Our theory does not encompass how growth begins, but only the process by which it is sustained. Indeed, many countries show a high growth rate confined to a small geographical or cultural segment (Brazil? Kenya?) before ideological consensus is achieved. But consensus must ultimately emerge (as in Mexico?) or growth will falter (Argentina?).

This theory requires measurable definitions of institutional effectiveness and of economic and political ideology, as well as a taxonomy of institution types from which choices are made. All this is attempted here. In sum, we develop a general theory of institution-building for economic growth, which includes the following:

1. The principles by which emerging nations select and form institutions to handle the problems of economic growth.

2. A taxonomy of institutions, or institutional dimensions, by which the potential choice is depicted among uniform types.

3. A concept of institutional effectiveness applicable to all institutions and distinct from efficiency, which applies only to those producing a measurable output on which its evaluators agree.

4. A theory relating institutional effectiveness to economic growth.

The theory is summarized in the first chapter.

I am indebted to Kenneth Boulding, Bert Hoselitz, Wilbert E. Moore, Gilbert White, Kenneth Hammond, Raymond Mikesell, Clarence Boonstra, Gottfried Lang, Joseph Lazar, Kent Geiger, Joseph Colosi, Donald Warwick, Richard Jessor, David Summers, Monroe Miller, Tom Steward, and Ragaei El Mallakh, who all read the entire manuscript or significant parts of it and offered their encouragement and advice. Peter Boyle and Margaret Marshall programmed and carried out the computer simulation of Chapter 3. My greatest debt goes to my students. The idea for the theory was born four years ago in a graduate seminar on economic growth in Latin America at the University of Colorado. Edith Miller and John Hansen made significant contributions to its early formulation. Subsequently, Suzanne Gardner, Karen Friden, and William Loehr made suggestions on both clarity and content. As the manuscript approached its final version, it was also critically read by Ayhan Copur, Visuth Kanchanasuk, Christina Wu, Ronald Beaton, Christopher Dowswell, Robert Moseley, and William Schust. Robin Bowler typed it several times over before it reached publishable form, and my wife, Alice R. Powelson, assisted in the proofreading. I should also like to thank my children, Kenny and Carolyn, for alphabetizing the index.

PART I

A Theory of Institutions

CHAPTER 1

Introduction and Summary

What Is a Theory of Institutions?

NATIONS experiencing rapid economic growth require new institutions —both formal organizations and informal modes of interpersonal behavior. Especially is this so if growth has increased, become continuous, or recently come to be regarded as a national goal.

How do such nations choose their new institutions? Which institutions are discarded? Is there indeed a choice, in that different institutions might alternatively perform the *same* functions? Are there any common trends, or similarities, in the institutions that one nation selects to perform *different* tasks? How can such similarities be classified? How can the effectiveness of institutions in performing their assigned tasks be measured?

It is to these and similar questions that *Institutions of Economic Growth* addresses itself. We attempt to set forth the role of institutions in growth, to establish the principles by which selection is made, and to determine institutional classifications and ways of measuring effectiveness.

The resulting theory ought to be useful in understanding the process of growth. It should also help policy-makers in exercising choice over institutions. But more than that, it should shed light on some of the more puzzling questions of growth that have not been adequately resolved: What is capital absorptive capacity, and what causes it to increase? What is the role of administrative and management capacities in economic growth? Are they substitutable for capital investment, complementary to it, or sometimes one and sometimes the other? Is there any relationship between a nation's capacity for political stability and for smoothly functioning enterprise? Under what circumstances do these contribute to or detract from economic growth?

An obvious example of alternative institutions is private versus government enterprise. In some nations steel mills are privately owned, in others they are nationalized, and in still others government and private influence over them is subtly mixed. Why? Do nations that have opted differently have the same goals, or different? Assuming economic growth to be the common goal, is one choice universally "better" than the others, are some nations "correct" and others "mistaken"? Or do some nations have different basic characteristics from others which make one choice logical for them but less logical for the others? If so, what are those characteristics? All these are questions with which institution theory is concerned.

But the options are not limited to that between private and government enterprise. They relate also to families (is the nuclear family universally more effective for economic growth than the extended?), to friendship (is growth promoted if friends are made primarily through occupation rather than through school or the family?), and to kinds of civic organizations and businesses (authoritarian, personalistic, formal, hierarchical, etc.).

Finally, does a selection made in one field influence subsequent selections in another? Does the fact that the national president is elected by secret ballot make it easier for a business to choose its directors through an election by stockholders? Is it hard to have a decentralized government if there is an authoritarian family? Is there a national ideology concerning institution types that transcends traditional categories? If so, does such an ideology promote growth by facilitating the selection of institutions, or does it hinder it by artificially narrowing the field of choice?

Strategy of Presentation

The book is divided into two parts. Part I presents a theory of institutions, while Part II considers some of its ramifications, leading to the question of where we go from here?

This chapter is the introduction and summary. In the following section, some elementary concepts are presented. The final section contains a complete summary of the theory. Any reader who wants only a survey of its essential elements may stop after the first chapter. Subsequent chapters elaborate on the summary; they repeat parts of it, as appropriate, but not all of it. The reader who wishes for suspense and a denouement is not favored; he would be ill advised to skip the summary.

The second chapter deals with conflict. It reviews the works by both sociologists and economists on those elements of conflict theory that I believe are necessary to the theory of institutions. In brief, economic growth generates conflict, and institutions are the means by which conflicts are controlled and diverted into growth-inducing channels.

The third chapter again deals with concepts and definitions, including values, norms, institutions, consensus, and the difference between constructive and destructive conflicts. It introduces the concept of *institutional effectiveness*, or the measurement of an institution's capacity to identify the conflicts within its jurisdiction so that all contestants understand them, to establish clear-cut rules of resolution or management, and to command the consensus of all persons concerned that the institution is more appropriate than any feasible alternative.

The general theory of institutions is developed in the fourth and fifth chapters, which should be considered the heart of the book. The fourth deals with micro-theory and the fifth with macro-theory. The micro-theory covers the principles by which an individual institution is selected at a moment of time. The macro-theory describes the development of an overall system of institutions over time. In the micro, national values are taken as constant, and an institution is selected to conform to them. In the macro, a path of successive selection is traced, in which national values are themselves altered.

Part II is introduced by Chapter 6, which illustrates the theory through a consideration of planning in Latin America. Drawing largely on my own experiences as consultant to planning and financing institutions, this chapter points to specific instances where institutional effectiveness would probably rate high or low in conflict-management capacity.

Chapter 7 relates the theory of institutions to modern growth theory. It reviews the status of this theory in both sociology and economics, and suggests that the concept of institutional effectiveness may be a bridge between sociological and economic models which would lead toward an interdisciplinary model of growth. We do not, however, cross that bridge. It is not one of the purposes of this book to create an interdisciplinary model of growth but only to give some indications of how the theory of institutions may be useful in developing such a model in the future.

Only in Chapter 8 do we turn primary attention to more developed countries. Here we question whether there are limits to economic growth, and if so, what their impact will be on institutional effectiveness. We speculate whether the beginning of growth (takeoff) and its end (landing) are symmetrical in that national goals are upset in each period, conflicts abound, and institutional effectiveness diminishes. We ask whether the United States is perhaps approaching the landing pattern.

As with any work of this type, the subject-matter had to be limited to what was necessary to advance the thesis to a certain point. The scope of the work may be defined as follows.

1. This is a theory of institutions and not a theory of economic growth. While the potential contributions of the former to the latter are outlined in Chapter 7, they cannot be actually made without empirical investigation that has not yet been done.

2. The empirical investigation will be extremely difficult, not so much because of technical limitations as because of the sensitivity of the subject. Both government and business officials may not relish having their institutions tested for effectiveness. While this statement applies to more and less developed countries alike, it is all the more strong when the suggestion originates in a more developed country for application in a less developed.

The sensitivity is twofold. First, the belief is strong in less developed countries that failure to achieve satisfactory growth is caused by factors external to the present generation: either by archaic systems inherited from the past which cannot be readily changed, or by foreign pressures, including colonialism, unfair pricing of primary products, and a refusal to allow equal bargaining power in foreign investment. The theory of institutions suggests, on the contrary, that deficiencies may also be internal—that they may lie in the inability of national groups to collaborate adequately with each other in pursuit of growth. This suggestion is not likely to be popular, and empirical investigation of it is likely to be resisted. Secondly, the measurement of effectiveness in any one institution always implies the possibility that deficiencies will be revealed on the part of its management, which is the very group that must decide whether the measurement is to be permitted.

3. I believe that the possibility of empirical measurement will be enhanced if the reasons for it have already been published and discussed. Perhaps it will not then appear to be so much of an

ogre. Progressive officials may even be eager to uncover ways of improving the effectiveness of the institutions they manage, on the assumption that the deficiencies belong to their underlings and not to themselves. It is primarily these hopes that have led me to the decision that the theory should be published now.

4. The illustrations in this book are drawn primarily from Latin America, for two reasons. First, Latin America as a whole is more advanced in economic growth than are Asia and Africa. Growth institutions have had more opportunity to develop there; hence they are more susceptible to meaningful analysis. Secondly, Latin America has been the area of my own experience. I have found it difficult to comment with authority on institutional effectiveness where I have not myself been involved in the institutions, though from time to time I refer to the experiences of others (e.g., Pye on Burma; see Chapter 3). To some critics, this limitation may suggest bias. To me, it has seemed more reasonable to formulate my theory on the basis of my own experiences and to leave it to others to confirm or deny its applicability to other areas.

Fundamental Concepts

The summary of the theory will be more intelligible if certain fundamental concepts are defined and explored first. These are treated below.

ECONOMIC GROWTH AND ECONOMIC DEVELOPMENT

Economic growth is a state of increase in the national product, without reference to income distribution. Per capita economic growth occurs when the percentage increase in national product is greater than the percentage increase in population. *Economic development,* on the other hand, is economic growth combined with the nurture of those culture objects (norms, institutions, and values) necessary to make growth continuous. Often consensus on some income distribution is necessary to sustain the appropriate culture objects. The adjective "economic" indicates that the theme centers on an economic object, gross national product (or gross domestic product, in the terminology of many countries). The acquisition of culture objects is thus included in *economic* development.

GROWTH SENSITIVITY

A growth-sensitive individual is one whose system structure ("everything that is dear to him") would collapse if *national* economic growth (not necessarily his own income) were to stop or substantially slow down. The threshold at which a previously nonsensitive person becomes sensitive is not clear, but some individuals are obviously on one side of it and others on the other. The member of a primitive society who has been on the edge of starvation for generations is not growth sensitive. He belongs to a community whose output per capita has not substantially changed over time, even though other social changes (sometimes radical) may have been occurring. In more developed countries, on the other hand, per capita income must increase over time or it will go down. There is no such thing as its remaining constant. The middle-class homeowner in the United States is growth sensitive. If growth did not occur, his job, the education of his children, his financial security, and his entire way of life, would be put into jeopardy.

Growth sensitivity does not imply awareness or desire. The growth-sensitive person may be content with his income or even willing to settle for less. Not being a student of economics or sociology, he may not be aware of how stability in the other elements of his system are dependent on a growing *national* product. Conversely, he may not be aware of the costs that growth imposes upon him, such as resource pollution, which might otherwise alter his perspective. Thus the term, "growth sensitive," and not "growth conscious" or "growth desiring," conveys the idea we wish.

I confess to some uncomfortableness about the concept of growth sensitivity, which I believe cannot be more precisely defined until some research is done on it. How is an individual's growth sensitivity rated? One might perhaps list his aspirations, such as employment, power over others, home, and neighborhood, education for children, and so on, and determine the likelihood of these being fulfilled given different rates of growth of national income. Clearly scales, trade-offs, estimates of likelihood of fulfillment, and correlations would have to be worked out. Some subjective judgment will doubtless be necessary. I defend the use of the concept by an observation that I take as axiomatic: that there are some people in this world to whom it does not personally matter if the economy around them is not growing, while there are others to whom it does. If the theories within this book are accepted, social scientists must some day work out ways of measuring the difference between the two and of establishing a graded scale from one to the other.

"Growth sensitivity" may also be applied to groups. Like individuals, groups also have system structure. Military officers, businessmen, government technicians, teachers, farmers, all may or may not be growth sensitive as groups. Here, however, the problem of definition is compounded. Not only is the threshold unclear, but the groups must have identity. Some segments of the military, for example, may be growth sensitive, while others may not be. The distinction can be made only by delineating the factions according to their principal goals and by demonstrating how these goals are or are not affected by national economic growth.

ECONOMIC GROWTH AS A DOMINANT GOAL

Economic growth is a dominant goal of growth-sensitive individuals and groups. Dominance, of course, must be interpreted according to common sense. We do not mean that economic growth would be selected if it conflicted, let us say, with the goal of saving one's own life. But it is selected over virtually all other competing goals. The individual or group need not consciously make the selection in favor of growth; he may even be unaware that it is being made. Nevertheless, the sum total of individual and group actions will be such as to promote economic growth if it is a dominant goal.

Once again, nothing is implied about the *desirability* of growth. It may be that the individual or group does not want increased material possession and would like to be out from under its yoke; he feels "trapped in the system." There is evidence, indeed, that many in the United States are now in this position. Though content with present possessions and incomes, they nevertheless strive for more, because if they did not they would not live up to the expectations of others and severe calamities might befall them. If they do not strive for more themselves, they may still depend on the fact that others do. This thought is by no means Marxian; rather, it is Galbraithian. Marx argued that "the system" impels economic growth because capitalists are enchanted with increased material possessions. In seeking them, they cannot escape exploiting the proletariat. Neither of these ideas is inherent in our concept of growth as a dominant goal. On the other hand, the concept does not exclude those who desire increased possession; indeed, they are probably the most usual.

Finally, economic growth may conflict with such social goals as the development of integrated personalities, military or personal security, or the avoidance of tension. If a society opts for these other goals rather than for economic growth, then growth is not a dominant goal, and our theory does not apply to it. Or the theory may apply only partially, to the extent that the society opts for economic growth as a secondary goal subject to the constraint of a dominant, conflicting goal.

TAKEOFF

We find "takeoff" a useful concept, though our definition differs from that of Rostow.[1] Takeoff, which may be short or lengthy, covering a decade or a century, separates two historical periods. The pre-takeoff period is one in which economic growth is not a dominant social goal, and growth-sensitive groups are not pervasive or in political power. There may (and likely will) be strong and effective institutions, but they are not designed to manage the conflicts of growth.

Takeoff is a period in which growth-sensitive groups form and obtain power. This power is not only political (i.e., in government), but also in business, the family, clubs, and informal social functions. Early-forming growth-sensitive groups may be those that have been "put upon" (cf. Hagen),[2] entrepreneurial types who develop a need for achievement (cf. McClelland),[3] persons who have migrated (cf. Hoselitz),[4] persons subject to the demonstration effect because they have traveled abroad or met foreign visitors in their own country, persons subject to the exhortation of demagogues, persons persuaded through education of the virtues of growth, government functionaries hired for planning ministries or development corporations whose jobs

[1] W. W. Rostow, *The Stages of Economic Growth: A Non-Communist Manifesto* (New York: Cambridge University Press, 1960).

[2] Everett E. Hagen, *On The Theory of Social Change* (Homewood, Ill.: Richard D. Irwin, 1962).

[3] David C. McClelland, *The Achieving Society* (Princeton, N.J.: Van Nostrand, 1961).

[4] Berthold F. Hoselitz, *Sociological Aspects of Economic Growth* (Glencoe, Ill.: Free Press, 1960).

depend on successful growth, and the like. The formation of some growth-sensitive groups gives rise to others dependent on the first, such as politicians who represent them, suppliers who sell to them, and professors who teach them. We do not believe there is a single, universal cause of the formation of growth-sensitive groups. Clearly, however, they interact, and they try to persuade other groups of the virtues of growth. It is only as these groups grow proportionately within a society that consensus on growth as a dominant goal is achieved.

The takeoff period is one of tension, as growth-sensitive groups vie with growth-resistant groups for support. The danger of violence lies in the fact that social institutions have not been formed to cope with this type of conflict. Sometimes growth-sensitive groups select coercive instruments in order to eliminate an opponent who would otherwise not join in the consensus. If he is eliminated completely (e.g., executed or permanently exiled), this ploy may be successful. The principal problem of violent revolution, however, is that it is impossible to eliminate *all* opponents completely. Revolution often divides people more than it unites them, making their absorption into the consensus even more difficult later.

Takeoff is further complicated by conflicts among growth-sensitive groups, principally over how political power and increments of national product will be shared. Inability to resolve or manage these conflicts lengthens the takeoff period, preventing or delaying the formation of post-takeoff values and institutions. Inflation, for example, usually connotes a lack of efficient conflict-managing institutions: contestants have thrown their potential for compromise to the wind and let natural forces take hold.[5]

Successful completion of takeoff depends on two requisites. In the first place, growth-sensitive groups must gradually pervade society, either eliminating others or winning them over. Thus, consensus on growth as a dominant goal is achieved. In the second place, the groups must learn that the sum of their immediate goals exceeds the nation's

[5] This point is debatable, since sometimes inflation may be a conscious policy to redistribute income and power in specific ways. Far more often, however, it results from the inability of power groups to decide how to allocate limited resources. Often they hope to please more of their constituents than they can, and they either do not know the consequences or want to postpone them until the next administration.

capacity to accommodate them, but that no group's goals will be achieved until all groups' goals are partially met. *It is preferable to sacrifice one's immediate goals rather than permit continued conflict to violate the dominant goal of growth.* Thus groups must agree on priorities. At this point, society turns to the formation of a dominant set of conflict-resolving values on which to form consensus.

Post-takeoff norms and institutions have a different character from those of the pre-takeoff stage in that they depend *for their survival* on continued growth. Once the social system learns *how* to manage the conflicts of growth, it discovers that it can manage them *only* if there is continued growth. More and more, conflicts become positive-sum games. The question is not one of who will win and who will lose, but of how much each will win. More effective institutions lead to efficiency in conflict management, and more and more solutions become Paretian-optimal (the point at which all positive-sum moves are exhausted). "Exile for the loser" gives way to "loyal opposition."

Summary of the Theory

We are now prepared to summarize a theory of the institutions of growth. The summary is intended to ease the path of the reader as he copes with concepts described in more detail in subsequent chapters. It is not an easy summary to write, since necessary limitations and qualifications (not to speak of illustrations) have had to be postponed.

CONFLICT AND THE DEFINITION OF INSTITUTIONS

Economic growth requires increasing social differentiation and the division of labor. Adam Smith proposed that the division of labor is limited by the size of the market. Indeed, this was the one limitation that Smith observed, for he lived in a society (western Europe) of relatively fluid institutions, capable of adapting themselves to handle the emerging conflicts of growth. In other societies, however, the scarce potential for collaboration and exchange may be a more serious limitation to the division of labor than the size of the market. Employers and laborers may be overly suspicious of each other; family firms may not expand because their management cannot be entrusted to "strangers"; citizens may refuse to pay taxes because of government graft, while politicians resort to graft because citizens refuse to finance them with taxes; all these, and many more, are cases where the division of labor is limited because of mistrust.

Exchange implies the collaboration of groups among whom labor is divided. These groups have many interests in common, including not only the opportunity for increased wealth but also the potential for personal and national development that accompanies it. But they also have conflicts over how to divide the wealth and allocate new positions of power. Continued growth depends on their vision and patience in emphasizing common goals and hammering out rules of compromise. But if the conflicts expand so as to submerge the goals, then growth will end.

We define an institution as any set of relationships between individuals that is designed to resolve their conflicts. If successful, the institution reveals each to the other as a reasoning individual capable of compromising in order to achieve mutual goals, with responses that are predictable. If this description is too generous to the individual, the institution may help him develop these characteristics. Any conflict is resolved either *ad hoc* or through an institution. If the same kind of conflict is resolved over and over in the same way, then the manner of resolution becomes the institution. At first the contestants acquire confidence in the institution, and only later in each other. Once mutual confidence is achieved, the original institution may be modified or abandoned if a more efficient form emerges.

This liberal definition of "institution" must now be accompanied by an equally liberal definition of "conflict." Whenever a decision is reached, it must be a decision between conflicting choices; therefore, every decision is a conflict resolved. We define every conflict as having a resolution, which may be its termination, its containment as it simmers over time, or its explosion into more serious form. Sometimes a conflict is internal to an individual, but all conflicts pertinent to this book are between individuals or organizations.

Recently, administrative theory has come to look upon institutions more and more as decision-making entities. But this interpretation is not the traditional one. Traditionally, institutions have been conceived as media through which tasks are accomplished. If two or more persons perceive a mutual goal, or each has a separate goal that can be achieved only if they work jointly, they need a framework of relationships (an institution) within which to cooperate. They establish either a formal organization or a normal pattern of behavior or some combination of the two.

Our approach to institutions is consistent with the traditional one, but its emphasis is different. We adopt the hypothesis of psychologists that whenever two individuals interact (as in friendship, family, etc.), each seeks to satisfy his own need. Any interaction therefore contains conflict potential, however great the goodwill may be.

Especially in the encounters of economic development, individuals often sense the conflict before they perceive the mutuality. Their goals appear different, and there is only a dim awareness that A's achievement of his goal depends on B's partial or complete achievement of his also. Ultimately, capital and labor must cooperate if gross national product is to be maximized, but their first perception of each other is likely to be in the conflict over how it is divided.

INSTITUTIONAL EFFECTIVENESS

According to the traditional definition, it is customary to define an institution's efficiency in terms of its capacity to perform tasks. As a new institution is formed during takeoff, however, there is often disagreement over precisely what its tasks are; usually, it is shaped intuitively and quasi-rationally. If we are not agreed on what the institution must do, we cannot say whether it is doing it efficiently. It may nevertheless be a valuable institution, if only because enough people see some benefit in it to have formed it.

It is, however, appropriate to our revised definition to consider an institution's value in terms of its conflict-resolving capacity. Let us therefore invent a new term, *institutional effectiveness*, to measure just that. The more capable an institution is of resolving the conflicts assigned to it in ways acceptable to the contestants, the more effective it is in inspiring mutual confidence. "Acceptable" does not mean that the contestants get what they want, but that they find justice and satisfaction in the institutional procedure.

In Chapter 3 we elaborate three measures of an institution's effectiveness. The first ("identification criterion") is its ability to define conflicts so that contestants understand precisely what the differences between them are. The second ("rules criterion") is its capacity to stipulate rules of resolution in ways understood by all contestants, as well as to enforce them. The third ("consensus criterion") is the agreement by all persons with an interest in the conflict that the institution is superior (or more "just") than any feasible alternative. All three criteria are measured in degrees.

To make these measurements, we draw on psychologist Kenneth Hammond's experiments in decision-making under conditions of quasi-rational thought. The contestant is not called on to state explicitly the points of conflict or the rules of resolution, for he may understand them without being able to express them. Instead, his capacity is tested to react consistently in similar conflicts and to predict the reactions of his opponent. Different abilities of contestants will depend both on their individual personalities and on the effectiveness of the institution. But we presume that if many contestants are tested their personality differences will fall randomly, and their remaining capacities will be attributable to the effectiveness of the institution. Of course, if all contestants who might be expected to use a given institution have high or low personal capacities as a group, then these will be attributed to the institution. This potential situation cannot be avoided, but it does little harm to a comparison with an alternative institution which presumably would service the same group.

Institutional *effectiveness* and *efficiency* are similar but not identical. Efficiency is the capacity to achieve high output with a given input. Obviously, the output of institutions must be definable or efficiency cannot be measured. But effectiveness can be measured even where participants in an institution have not defined its output or disagree on its objectives. We theorize that any institution (such as a business firm) must satisfy the three criteria of effectiveness if it is also to be efficient. This is so even in cases of apparent contradiction. Because of its coercion, slavery may *seem* never to rate high by the consensus criterion. But slaves may be duped into being contented with their lot. The more *dis*contented they are, the less effective the institution is by the consensus criterion (and probably the other two as well), but also the less efficient it is likely to be in terms of input–output relationships. Thus effectiveness is a measurable proxy for efficiency where the latter cannot be defined.

Development theories have long suggested that efficiency in government and in business are requisites of economic growth. If this is acceptable, it is but a short step to suggest that effectiveness in all institutions correlates with economic growth. But the assertion does not apply universally for either efficiency or effectiveness. In societies where growth is not a dominant goal, institutions can be very effective by the three criteria; yet effectiveness does not lead to growth. We must therefore limit the proposition to the following: that successful completion of takeoff requires an increase in institutional effectiveness. Institutions may or may not be effective before takeoff. With the emergence during takeoff of new conflicts with which the institutions were not designed to cope, effectiveness might be expected to decline (perhaps drastically, unless it was low to begin with); thereafter successful growth must be accompanied by an upward pull.

But we do not suggest that institutional effectiveness is a monotonically increasing function of growth, or vice versa. There is evidence that it may reach a plateau, beyond which growth may continue while effectiveness does not (or might decline). It may also be speculated (but it is only speculation) that such tapering off or decline in effectiveness may be a precursor to a declining rate of growth. It would not be surprising for future history to reveal that the United States is in precisely that stage now.

Our theory of institutions is therefore limited to a very narrow domain in the history of a nation's growth. It suggests that at some point in its life a growing nation must be characterized by increasing institutional effectiveness but that the increase need not be permanent. Mexico and Venezuela may be examples of countries whose institutional effectiveness increased along with takeoff: Mexico from the 1890s to 1910 and again from 1920 on, and Venezuela from 1958 onward. Argentina may be an example of takeoff in the early twentieth century which was aborted because the increase in institutional effectiveness did not continue after 1928. But the relationship between takeoff and effectiveness cannot be scientifically demonstrated. Not only are we unable to measure institutional effectiveness in any period but the present, but we also have no independent measure of when takeoff occurs.

THE CHANGING CHARACTER OF CONFLICT

Conflict is not only inevitable to growth but a requisite of it. Provided that institutions operate effectively, the continuing conflict between buyer and seller (over quality, performance, and price) leads the seller to seek ever less costly ways of production. If the political system operates well, conflict between candidates can lead to greater output by the government.

Furthermore, the character of conflict changes with growth. Before takeoff, most conflict resolutions involve victory by one party and defeat by another. But the very fact of increasing product converts many conflicts into positive-sum games. It is not a question of who takes from whom but of how the bigger pie is divided. Often these conflicts can be resolved *only* with increased output. Labor seeks higher wages, which management can pay only if productivity goes up. Thus conflict, properly contained and managed, actually propels growth.

COERCION VERSUS CONSENSUS

We have equated economic growth with the division of labor, observing (as classical economists did) that specialization leads to increased output. But specialization must also lead to exchange, and exchange requires institutions. We now question what are the principles by which "coercive" or "consensus" institutions are selected. The former are those by which one party compels another to behave contrary to his wishes; the latter are those in which both parties act with mutual consent. Obviously, coercive institutions will not rate high by the consensus criterion. But—at least at the beginning of growth—they may rate very high by the identification and rules criteria (e.g., *some* military governments in Latin America), and for that reason they may be selected.

Let us start with a simple model, including only two factors of production, A and B (both may be laborers in a primitive society where land is free), who have heretofore not cooperated with each other. For some reason which our theory does not explain, A perceives one day that his output (income) will be increased by cooperation with B in certain specific ways which he understands; he also comes to desire the increment. He may bring about the cooperation in one of two ways: by force (if he has the power), or by deceit or persuasion. The former makes for the "coercive society" and the latter for the "consensus society." Of course, an action by A upon B, and hence a society, may be partly coercive and partly consensus.

Either type of society will be costly to A: the coercive because he must devote time to subduing B and to supervising him thereafter, the consensus because he must spend resources convincing *B* of their mutual benefits. *A* will opt for economic growth only if the value to him of his expected increase in income and of the noneconomic attributes of his position, such as power, are at least as high as the cost of coercion or consensus, whichever is lower. Let us assume that he does opt for growth. He will then select whichever institution, coercion or consensus, is less costly for the rate of growth desired. There are no moral implications in this choice, except that if *A* has a cultural abhorrence of force, then overcoming his reluctance must be counted as a cost. *Any* sacrifice on the part of *A* is a cost to him, and it is not necessary to count those sacrifices in any common value measure. The comparison of the sum of costs with gains is totally subjective (in the mind of *A*).

If *A* initially chooses coercion, it is likely that over time he will either relinquish his goal of economic growth or will change to consensus. As the product of the two men working in combination increases, *A* will either share the increments with *B* or he will not. If he shares, then *B* is likely to become acculturated to the idea of increasing income and persuaded of the benefits of collaboration, and the consensus society will be formed. *A*'s reason for sharing will be to decrease the cost of coercion. If *A* does not share, then *B*, observing *A*'s increment in product, will become increasingly jealous and discontented over time. He will consider himself exploited and will be more and more reluctant to collaborate.

During this process, which follows the initial selection of coercion, both the cost of coercion and the cost of consensus rise. *B*'s increasing disaffection raises the cost of coercion. He may work less hard, go on strike, rebel, or in other ways hinder the productive process. The cost of consensus rises because *A*, once he has adopted coercion, finds that it becomes a way of life that is difficult to change. Besides the increased economic product, he has acquired prestige or other emoluments of office that he does not give up easily.

Nevertheless, it is likely that as growth proceeds the cost of coercion will rise relative to that of consensus, and at some point they will be equal. If *A* continues to be growth-sensitive, and particularly if he notices the relative trends, he will then shift to consensus. The shift will be gradual if *A* shares at first only to the extent necessary to offset

B's marginal discontent, and then increases the sharing until both are satisfied with their portions because no better distribution appears feasible to either. Or the shift may be precipitous, as in a partial revolution in which *B* wrests just enough power from *A* to conduce to mutual agreement on the division of product. Finally, the shift may be oscillatory, as in a full revolution in which *B* grabs power from *A*, becoming himself the dominant force in a reverse-coercion society. If so, further shifts will be necessary before the consensus pattern is established.

In all cases, however, economic growth will ultimately lead to the consensus society or it cannot continue. This society is defined as one in which *A* and *B* agree that the rules for dividing product and settling other disputes are just. It may be a market society, or it may be one in which *B* always does the bidding of *A*, but in either case both will be content with the arrangement. *A* may have so indoctrinated *B* that he voluntarily relinquishes certain freedoms (e.g., speech, religion, travel). It matters not whether society is totalitarian or democratic in the Western sense; the important element is the consensus.

How quickly growth will be achieved depends on how early in the process the consensus society is selected. This depends on the relative costs of coercion and consensus to the power groups (*A*), which in turn depend on the cultural characteristics of all groups (*A* and *B*), including their levels of education, the degree of communication among them, and the confidence they express in each other.

The consensus and coercive societies are, of course, polar constructs. Any society will fall somewhere in between, and its relative position may vary even within short periods. It might be argued, for example, that because of minority and student discontent the United States is less of a consensus society today than it was thirty years ago. Radical students would say that the United States has always been a coercive society but that only now are minorities waking up to their grievances. But our definition of the coercive society requires awareness. Slavery *may* be a consensus society; no one is coerced unless he is both aware and discontented.

The concept of the consensus society is not new; indeed, it plays a central role in modern political science. Furthermore, sociologists have long distinguished among societies according to their degrees of coercion and consensus. Comte's famous classification into militaristic, juristic, and industrial societies was perhaps the prototype.[6] Spencer divided them into military and industrial,[7] while Durkheim thought of them as segmental and integrated,[8] the former being those whose strata were structurally similar and the latter those in which different strata performed specialized functions and traded with each other. To all three, an essential difference between the military or segmental society on the one hand and the industrial or integrated on the other lay in the freedom of contract enjoyed by the latter. But modern development theory must account for another kind of society, the one which is centrally planned and directed and whose members have been indoctrinated to agree that its institutions are the most appropriate for economic growth. By our definition, such a society is founded on consensus as much as, and sometimes more than, those where contracts are freely and individually made.

BASIC PRINCIPLE

The basic principle in the selection of an institution is one of benefits and costs. An institution is chosen if its benefits exceed its costs, both being subjectively judged (and not necessarily measured) by members of the power groups capable of forming it. These groups (corresponding to A) may be politicians or appointed officials in a position to establish new government agencies; or they may be labor leaders who organize unions; or they may be heads of families who influence the design of the family system; or revolutionaries able to seize power; or other.

If these groups are growth-sensitive, any potential institution will, consciously or not, be judged by its capacity to achieve growth. We theorize that effectiveness measured by the three criteria (identification, rules, and consensus) then constitutes effectiveness in achieving growth, though the relationship need not be linear or continuous. If other benefits than effectiveness are perceived, we will treat these as

[6] Auguste Comte, *System of Positive Polity* (London: Longmans, Green and Co., 1877).

[7] Herbert Spencer, *The Principles of Sociology* (London: Williams and Norgate, 1897).

[8] Emile Durkheim, *The Division of Labor in Society* (New York: Free Press, 1933).

negative costs, which make it "easier" (less costly) to accept one institution than another.

The cost of an institution consists of the pain felt by the power group in forming it. This may include sacrifice of resources, prestige, values, or even life (in a revolution). Cost also includes the effort to overcome the resistance of others, by either coercion or persuasion. Such cost may include the attempt to increase the cost to others of maintaining archaic institutions that conflict with the ones the power groups wish to establish.

Our theory is therefore an economic one, for institutions have demand schedules, consisting of the sacrifices of the power groups, and supply schedules, consisting of the sacrifice of all other groups whose interests are adversely affected. We elaborate on these principles in Chapter 4.

INSTITUTIONAL DIMENSIONS

We turn next to the types of institutions from which a society may choose. "Coercive" and "consensus" are insufficient, for they are matters of opinion. Sociologists have customarily categorized institutions by their functions—family, education, government, and so on. But we seek characteristics common to all categories. What, if any, are the similarities in the family, education, government, and other institutions as they are developed in one growing country, and as they may differ from corresponding characteristics in another?

For these common characteristics, we select five institutional dimensions, as follows:

1. Centralized versus decentralized
2. Authoritarian versus nonauthoritarian
3. Formal versus informal
4. Employs incentives versus employs penalties
5. Neutral versus biased toward specific solutions

We presume that *any* institution (coercive or consensus) will occupy a measurable point on the five-dimensional surface, each dimension being spanned by one of these characteristics. Any dimension can have a range of zero to one hundred (or any other range that we choose). We do not determine in this book the precise way in which measurement will be done, though we do outline the general principles. The measurements might be based on objective criteria, or on subjective judgments determined through thematic apperception tests or the Hammond tests on quasi-rational thought. The manner of testing would be determined when empirical studies are done in different countries. We have discussed earlier why this has not yet happened.

The five dimensions are not necessarily exhaustive; it is hoped that others, to be developed in the future, will enhance precision. Nor are the dimensions necessarily independent of each other; for example, centralized institutions may tend upon investigation also to be authoritarian, employ penalties more than incentives, and the like. But the functional relationships, if any, may be different in different countries.

We have theorized that growth-sensitive power groups select institutions according to benefits and costs. The question is now whether their choices tend to cluster around one set of dimensional points in one society and another set in another, and if so, why. At first blush, the answer might appear to be a resounding "yes" with respect to the first dimension. Government and business institutions are more centrally organized in the Soviet Union than in Mexico, more so in Mexico than in the United States; and so on.

But the hypothesis goes beyond business institutions. It suggests that the set of dimensional points occupied by *any* institution depends on two forces: (1) the functions of the institution, and (2) the "institutional ideology" accepted in the country.

Based on the first force alone, institutions performing the same functions would tend toward the same dimensional points the world over. But based on the second, *all* institutions *in a given country*, regardless of function, would tend toward the same dimensional points, so long as the nation had achieved a high degree of consensus on "institutional ideology." The exact points occupied by a given institution would depend on the relative pulls of these two forces.

VALUES AND INSTITUTIONS

Before we elaborate on "institutional ideology," which is a value, let us refer to values in general. Values (objects or modes of behavior deemed desirable at all times and places) limit conflicts. Often a conflict does not explode because the contestants share a higher value (e.g., they refuse to kill each other). Specifically, a conflict is resolved successfully (1) if the contestants are united in accepting one or more values in common, (2) if these values would be violated if the conflict were not resolved satisfactorily to both, and (3) if the preservation of the values is more desirable to each contestant than victory in the conflict. Values may include such things as the sanctity of life, free elections, conservation of forests, or an annual 5 percent increase in the gross national product.

The role of values in limiting conflict is well established in sociological theory. Sociologists have argued that conflicts within the consensus strengthen the value, for it is tested and found true. We call such conflicts "constructive" because of this positive effect. Conflicts that threaten the consensus, on the other hand, are "destructive," or potentially explosive. We theorize that economic development includes a shift in the composition of conflicts, away from the destructive and toward the constructive.

It is also generally accepted that institutions conform to values; that is, that certain values lead to certain kinds of institutions. At first thought, this concept appears a valuable clue to formulating a theory of institutions. In fact, however, it leads down many a dead-end street. Values are very difficult to define, and most of them are impossible to measure. Sociologists and anthropologists have frequently catalogued values for particular societies and have presented compelling reasons for their selection. But their judgments are usually subjective and not measurable.

But it is possible to say something about values. First, the values in a pre-takeoff society were not designed to cope with the new conflicts emerging from takeoff. Consequently, existing institutions are also not adapted to those conflicts. Secondly, the first institutions of takeoff must conform to existing values or they will not be formed at all. We define an *optimal institution* as the most effective that can be established in the current value framework. At takeoff, however, the optimal institution must embody costly measures to protect one contestant against another whom he does not trust. For example, routine audits are not acceptable as a value (one is insulted to be audited), so elaborate detective work must be done on the sly. This kind of control would be considered foolish and onerous in a society where high performance standards, routinely audited, were expected. Thus the optimal institution in a takeoff society might be rated as very ineffective if transplanted into a highly industrialized country. Conversely, institutions of more developed countries often do not work in the less developed because the checks and balances required violate accepted ethics. Thirdly, the less the consensus on values or agreement on institutional functions, the less effective the optimal institution is likely to be. The concepts introduced in this paragraph are developed in the *micro*-theory, in Chapter 4.

Nevertheless, an institution in takeoff need not conform exactly to existing values. Since the conflict to which it is addressed is new, the institution is bound to strain values in order to encompass it at all. There are, however, psychological limitations on the amount of strain a society can accept. Even after a violent revolution the forms of new institutions are influenced by the previous value framework. However, after the institution has lived for awhile and come to be accepted in the community, then values have changed, and a new institution similar to it (according to the institutional dimensions) can be created. Indeed, the new institution can strain values further, and ultimately even the pace of strain may be accelerated. When a society becomes accustomed to having its values strained—that is, becomes change-oriented—then the strain involved in change may itself become a value. (Some people *like* to shock "the system.")

From this it follows that the institutions established early in takeoff have a profound effect on the kinds selected later. Values and institutions interact: an institution changes values, then a new institution is formed dependent on the changed values; it changes them further, and so on. Suppose there is more than one institution-value path that a nation might have selected in early takeoff. Once the crucial choice is made, it is *on* the path, and—like Frost's "roads in a yellow wood"—the return to try another may be difficult or impossible. The path itself becomes the nation's "institutional ideology."

The hypotheses suggested here cannot be tested because of the inability to define and measure values. But they appear reasonable and merit a place in the *macro*-theory developed in Chapter 5. This theory relates to the creation of the institutional framework, or ideology, which both facilitates the process of forming institutions and limits the choice to those that conform to the value path selected.

24

IDEOLOGY AND INSTITUTION SELECTION

Economic and political ideologies are values that are measurable, both intensively—the degree to which each ideology is held by one individual—and extensively—how widely each is held throughout the country. Consensus on economic and political ideology is essential to institutional effectiveness. *Total* ideology is one's vision of society, or one's belief about how social processes operate. Though ideology is many dimensional, *economic* ideology focuses on a single dimension: one's view of wealth and poverty. We distinguish between two polar extremes, also recognizing a continuum between them: (1) the "productionist" ideology, held by those who believe that fundamentally wealth is earned through production, while poverty is the result of personal failure to produce; and (2) the "appropriationist" ideology, held by those who believe that in the absence of social constraints, fundamentally wealth is acquired through conquest and exploitation, while poverty is the result of being exploited.

Political ideology also relates to a single dimension: one's view of how representative or how selfish are those with political power. Again there are two polar extremes, with a continuum between them: (1) the "popularist" ideology, held by those who believe that the political elite generally act on behalf of their constituents; and (2) the "selfist" ideology, held by those who believe that the elite represent only themselves and not their constituents.

In any research program relating ideology to institution selection, it would be necessary to investigate political and economic ideology separately. We presume, however, that in non-socialist societies, most holders of the productionist ideology will also be popularists, while most appropriationists will also be selfists. For simplicity, therefore, we always refer to the economic continuum alone, it being understood that political ideology is included.

The ideology function is continuous because it can be measured as "more" or "less." Most people recognize that some wealth is earned in one way and some in the other, or that some methods combine productiveness and exploitation. The same is true, *mutatis mutandis*, for poverty.

To substantiate measurability, we refer in Chapter 5 to a previous study in which I investigated the degree to which economic ideology was held by a wide range of subjects in both the United States and Latin America. This study showed the probability of a high degree of consensus on the productionist ideology as held by subjects in the United States, but considerable dispersion between the two among Latin American subjects.

Now, every more developed country has surrounded its institutions with an aura of ideology: primarily appropriationist in the Soviet Union and primarily productionist in the United States, for example. By contrast, less developed countries are characterized by severe ideological conflict. Furthermore, successfully developing countries (e.g., Mexico) often spend large sums fostering ideological consensus. From these observations we hypothesize that national consensus on economic and political ideology is a *sine qua non* of institutional effectiveness. Probably it does not matter which ideology is selected or where it is along the continuum; it is the *consensus* that counts. Where there is no consensus, it is difficult to form *any* institutions.

We should not suppose, however, that *maximum* ideological consensus leads to *maximum* institutional effectiveness. Some internal dissension, or the existence of those who do not accept the dominant ideology—like radicals in the United States—may impart institutional vigor and flexibility, provided these groups are not strong enough to destroy the institutions. There is probably an optimum degree of consensus, though to date no one has determined what it is.

It now follows that the set of institutional dimensions to which a nation tends is related to its economic and political ideology (among other values). Possibly centralized institutions are preferred by appropriationists, to protect the weak against exploitation, while decentralized are preferred by productionists, to give greater vent to individual initiative. These are, however, only *beliefs*. It cannot be objectively demonstrated that centralized institutions universally protect the weak more than decentralized, or that the latter universally promote initiative. Quite likely, one does both in the Soviet Union while the other does both in the United States (within a tolerable range), but neither would be successful in the "wrong" country.

THE TWO APPROACHES TO INSTITUTION FORMATION

Growth-sensitive power groups thus seek consensus on ideology. They have two approaches, and they usually follow both. One is to form institutions *ad hoc,* each one based on benefit-cost principles. If the first institution is successful, then another of the same dimensions will be easier (less costly) to form. This successive formation leads to consensus on economic and political (and institutional) ideology, for people will invent reasons why the institutions selected are superior to alternatives discarded. The other approach is to promote the ideology directly, through schools, political campaigns, books, movies, television, and other media.

Each approach has its costs. Those of successive selection are likened to direct costs in a business enterprise: you apply labor and materials and you get a product. The costs of ideology, however, are analogous to overhead. They do not pertain directly to any one institution (output), but they serve to decrease the direct costs of all of them. The mix that power groups select will depend (unconsciously no doubt) on their ability to perceive and minimize *total* costs (direct plus overhead).

If successive selection alone were followed, we might infer that power groups had no idea of which ideology was superior, but simply stumbled on one. This may describe how the "Protestant ethic" became acceptable in Britain, Western Europe, and the United States. If so, however, the ideology was recognized early, and overhead methods (such as Benjamin Franklin's sayings and Horatio Alger stories) were quickly employed. If the power groups follow both approaches from the beginning, then they must have some idea of which ideology will be more successful. The emphasis on government influence and ownership of business in todays' emerging nations doubtless reflects the belief of power groups that a "third ideology"—a mixture of productionist and appropriationist but neither of them in pure form—is most likely to be successful in commanding consensus in their countries. In Chapter 5 we describe the growth of this third ideology in Latin America.

What factors influence the power groups in favor of the third ideology? We do not know, but we can guess that they include the following:

1. Deep ideological divisions and polarization in their countries, which rule out the possibility that consensus can be found anywhere except in the middle.

27

2. Elements of the appropriationist ideology, which are bound to flourish because nations that have failed to achieve growth do not like to explain that failure as their own fault; they prefer to believe they have been exploited by others.

3. Elements of the productionist ideology, which has been strongly held by the traditional power groups and will likely survive even if these groups are overthrown by revolution—as they did in Mexico and Bolivia, though less so in Cuba.

Nevertheless, ideological consensus is expensive in nations that are not accustomed to achieve national consensus on anything. A common ideology is more economically formed in a country where groups are already united in some other common goal which gives them experience in achieving consensus. Nationalism is a likely choice for this other goal. It is cheap (easily obtained) because of the psychological need for identity. Though its "total cost" may be high (e.g., French nationalism was promoted through a bloody revolution), nevertheless much of this cost will be paid for other reasons than growth. We consider only the "marginal cost," or the increment that power groups must pay to promote that marginal amount of nationalism deemed necessary for ideological consensus.

The Landing

Most of this book is about institution-building in countries that have taken off, having selected economic growth as a dominant goal. In Chapter 8, however, we turn briefly to what will happen to countries that have been in sustained flight for a number of years. Will growth continue forever, and is the age of mass consumption really an ultimate? Classical economists foresaw the end of growth because of the law of diminishing returns; there would be a limit to the earth's capacity to produce. More recently, others have marveled that technology has been able to expand that capacity, and some would venture that it is unlimited. I take no sides on this issue. Rather, I believe indications already exist that economic growth will end, not because the earth is incapable of sustaining it, but because people no longer want it.

There is, however, a subtle relationship between ultimate supply limitations and the decline in demand. Once the supply limitation becomes foreseeable and the pollution-consequences of growth predictable, a change in values may set in. All values essential to growth are called into question: competition, product standardization, advanced technology, nuclear families, business friendships, corporate loyalty, and so on. Long before production reaches its physical limits, members of the social system may question the cultural structure they have erected to sustain growth. Those to whom the structure appears false or undesirable will try to escape it. They become growth-*de*-sensitized; to them, economic growth is no longer a dominant goal, and they seek something else.

Takeoff is the period in which growth-sensitive groups form and move into positions of power. Landing is the period in which power is sought by groups becoming desensitized to growth. The two periods are symmetrical. In each there is great confusion, as institutions of the previous period are unable to cope with new conflicts arising out of growth (in takeoff) or out of un-growth (in landing). Like takeoff countries, landing countries will find themselves in a severe ideological split. Institutions will weaken through lack of consensus on goals, and effective institutions will not be formed until a new consensus on ideology and goals emerges.

I dare not go beyond these ventures, for I cannot predict what will be the ultimate goals of landing countries. But economic growth cannot be an everlasting condition. Rather, it may be a brief flight, of about two centuries, in the span of man's existence.

Policy Implications

We have now completed our survey of the theory, but I would like to add a word about policy implications, which will be expanded in an Appendix. The most important of these follow obviously. Power groups aware of how institutions are formed will be more likely to weigh benefits and costs intelligently and to make judicious choices. But I want to emphasize a different point. The U.S. foreign-aid program, like all our policy toward less-developed countries, has two goals. One is to promote the economic growth of these countries, both for humanitarian reasons and because growing countries are deemed congenial neighbors. The other is to persuade them to adopt an ideology and institutions that, even if not exactly like ours, are at least "compatible" with ours (in a pejorative sense). *But the two goals are in direct conflict.* If "our" ideology (primarily productionist) is not the one on which consensus will be achieved at least cost in less developed countries, then the effect of our policy is to deepen and prolong their ideological conflict and to *postpone* effective growth institutions. Many less developed countries have *already* selected their path, and our effort to revert them to a different path is seriously retarding their growth. If this book does no more than make this point clear, it will have been worth the writing.

CHAPTER 2

Conflict

On the Limitations to the Division of Labor

> As it is the power of exchanging that gives occasion to the division of labour, so the extent of this division must always be limited by the extent of that power, or, in other words, by the extent of the market. When the market is very small, no person can have any encouragement to dedicate himself entirely to one employment, for want of the power to exchange all that surplus part of the produce of his own labour, which is over and above his own consumption, for such parts of the produce of other men's labour as he has occasion for.   Adam Smith, *The Wealth of Nations*

ADAM SMITH's famous dictum, that the division of labor is limited by the size of the market, tells only half the story. The division of labor is also limited by the capacity of people to cooperate. Though Smith was surely aware of this second limitation, he did not stress it. The two constraints do not exert equal force, and one may arrest while the other is in excess capacity. In the England of the industrial revolution, the size of the market no doubt *was* the limiting force. In the less-developed world of today, it is not.

Had Smith recognized the second limitation instead of the first, he would have written as follows:

> As it is the power of cooperation that gives occasion to the division of labour, so the extent of this division must be limited by the extent of that power. If the labourer and the purveyor of capital so dislike each other that they do not speak, there is little likelihood that they will form a fruitful union irrespective of the opportunities of sale that lie before them. Though potential purchasers be many, no person will have encouragement to dedicate himself entirely to one employment, for he lacks confidence that others will keep their bargains, or he so excessively fears he will be cheated in exchanging, that he will have no part of it.

One might argue, of course, that Smith's "size of the market" encompasses both limitations. Those who fail to cooperate condemn themselves to small markets. But this is not what Smith had in mind as he attributed the first appearance of civilization in the Mediterranean to the wide markets that the sea provided. Modern development theorists also—in an intuitive application of Say's law[1]—argue that the limitations to economic growth lie in the shortage of physical factors of production, such as capital and technology, whose provision would automatically expand the markets that make the division of labor attractive. A significant body believes that smallness in the size of countries is a major constraint to growth, to be overcome by economic integration of two or more nations.

There is, of course, nothing wrong with the idea that investment, technology, and markets must expand with economic development. What is wrong is the belief that a directed expansion of these factors will bring about development in and of itself. Growth theory has paid too little attention to the *reasons* for limitations in their expansion potential. These constraints lie principally (I believe) in the lack of trust that people in less-developed countries show for each other, which often prevents cooperation among owners of factors of production (land, labor, and capital) entirely. Where it does not, production becomes the more costly because owners of factors deceive each other or fail to keep their promises, or else cumbersome safeguards must be erected to require one to keep faith with the other.

Most development theories were proferred by economists from more developed countries. In Europe and the United States, the values, institutions, and behavioral norms have both reflected and reinforced the confidence of owners of factors of production in each other, which has enabled them to cooperate in production. I do not mean that limited capacity to cooperate has *never* been a restraining force in the more developed world. Indeed, western history is replete with labor violence, race riots, and civil wars. In less dramatic terms, the plant that automates *solely* to avoid strikes is not deploying the factors of production in the most economic fashion if unemployment results. By and large, however, the more developed countries have

---

[1] Jean Baptiste Say, 1767-1832. Say's *law of markets* included the tenet that "supply creates its own demand"; that is, suppliers, by earning incomes from the sales of goods they have produced, have the collective capacity to buy back all those goods for their own consumption and investment. Saving is presumed to be spent on investment goods, and if excessive saving (greater than the supply of investment goods) threatens a deficit in aggregate demand, the prices of consumption goods relative to investment goods will be lowered until people are encouraged to consume more and save less; thus equilibrium is restored.

exhibited cultural flexibility of such a kind that their capacity for collaboration has been amply increased along with productivity. To them, therefore, the size of the market has been the principal constraint.

But the assumption found in modern growth theory that this constraint is universal is a gross case of culture bias. The division of less developed countries into well-defined groups—such as the military, politicians, landowners, businessmen, laborers, farmers, tribes, and students—that not only do not communicate with each other but actively dislike and distrust each other and seek to do each other harm prevents the rational allocation of factors of production even where a high level of technology and capital investment (hence ample markets) would otherwise be available. The closest that modern growth theory has come to recognizing this fact has been to adopt the term "capital absorptive capacity"[2] which, however, has never been integrated into any of the equilibrium models of growth.

We turn now to a way of analyzing conflicts among groups such as these and to the effects of conflict on growth.

Definitions of "Conflict" and "Institution"

Economic growth generates conflict. A continuously growing national product brings with it disagreement over how increments will be divided. Growth spawns political and economic opportunities for power and influence over others. Not only are prestigious positions vied for, but relationships between persons in power and their subordinates must be articulated.

Indeed, economic growth depends on tensions. If they can be resolved or managed only through further growth of income and generation of new tensions, and if the means of resolution or management are available, then the economy has taken off. Most societies even laud certain types of conflict with adjectives such as "clean" and "sportsmanlike."

Nevertheless, conflict also impedes growth. Economic growth requires an increasing division of labor. Skills become more specialized, society more differentiated. The more rapid the rate of growth and the greater the speed of differentiation, the more difficult the generation of integrative forces. If those among whom labor is to be divided

---

[2] John Adler, *Capital Absorptive Capacity* (Washington, D.C.: The Brookings Institution, 1970).

become so alienated that they neither communicate with nor understand each other, cooperation becomes increasingly strained and may ultimately stop.

We have defined conflict as the joint action of two or more parties seeking inconsistent goals. We also define conflict as necessarily having a resolution. Some authors (e.g., Boulding) have preferred to distinguish between conflict resolution and conflict management. We find it easier to combine both under one term. Resolution is thus either the manner in which the conflict is settled once for all or the *modus vivendi* under which it continues. The rivalry of two schools is a continuous conflict, with a continuous resolution effected through repeated games of football and other sports. Conflict may be short, long, or eternal, and its resolution may involve eliminating the conflict, dissolving or transforming one or more of the contesting parties, or evolving containment mechanisms to limit its destructive effects while conflicting systems survive.

We define an institution as the means by which a society resolves a recurrent conflict. A conflict that occurs only once need not have an institution, but presumably this case is rare. If a recurrent conflict is resolved by a different means each time, we do not say that it has no institution but that its institution is ineffective (ineffectiveness being rated by the three criteria mentioned in Chapter 1). If a conflict cannot be easily defined, the institution is also ineffective.

Thus an institution is not necessarily an organization; more likely, it is a mode of behavior. Furthermore, a formal organization will encompass as many institutions as it has conflicts. Every conflict resolved by a corporate board of directors may be deemed to have a different institution, in that the board may behave differently every time. However, when similar conflicts possess similar institutions, it is practical to lump them together. Thus we might refer to the board of directors as being itself an institution, provided its behavior does not change drastically from one conflict to another.

In the theory of institutions, the conflict rather than the institution is the principal unit of demarcation. We now seek a technique to represent conflict graphically. In this, we need not start from scratch. Economics has already developed the production possibility curve, a graphic portrayal of conflict over alternative goods and services that limited resources can produce. We plan to generalize this

34

curve, making it applicable to a wider variety of social conflicts than the economic ones for which it was intended. In so doing, we will alter some of its fundamentals.

For those who are not economists, we now digress to explain the production possibility curve. Economists are invited to skip the next section and proceed with the following one.

The Production Possibility Curve

Suppose two producers, X and Y, whose products are x and y respectively, bid against each other for resources (land, labor, and capital) that exist in limited quantities. They are in conflict over resources, and the market is the institution through which that conflict will be resolved. The production possibility curve is a means of specifying that conflict by stating all possible alternative solutions.

Suppose all existing resources are supplied to X and none to Y. Then X, we shall presume, can produce OA quantity of x, in Figure 2-1. The horizontal axis measures units of x, such as gallons, gross, etc., and the vertical axis units of y. Since Y would produce nothing, A is the production point, or the conflict solution. Now suppose, conversely, that all available resources are allocated to Y and that with them he would

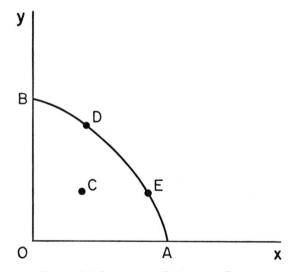

FIGURE 2-1. PRODUCTION POSSIBILITY CURVE.

produce *OB* amount of *y*. Since *X* would then produce zero, the conflict would be resolved at production point *B*.

Let us now presume (more realistically) that the resources are divided between *X* and *Y*. The curve *BA* is the locus of all efficient solutions, or maximum combinations of *x* and *y* that could be produced with all resources allocated. It is drawn concave to the origin because of the law of diminishing marginal productivity.[3] Given the present state of the arts, the society is not capable of producing combinations of *x* and *y* that fall northeast of the curve. Hence the curve is also known as the "production frontier." The solution might occur at an interior point, say *C*, but this would require that some resources be deployed inefficiently. Inefficiency, which includes unemployment, occurs if it is possible, with the same availability of inputs, to increase the output of one product without decreasing that of the other, or to increase both. Because the curve represents all the alternative opportunities at full efficiency—if more of *x*, then less of *y*—it is also known as the "transformation curve."

Thus all possible solutions to the conflict lie at points within and including the boundaries of the two axes and the production possibility curve. Solutions upon the curve are labeled efficient and those in the interior inefficient.

The production possibility curve is here outlined in terms of two products only because we are limited by convenience to a two-dimensional graph. The reader is asked to understand, intuitively, that the concepts of the frontier and of transformation could be extended mathematically to the many-product model of the real world.

Plus-plus and Plus-minus Moves

We continue our digression, but we invite the economists to rejoin us. We will later be concerned with moves from one solution point to another. We label as "plus-plus," hereafter +,+, any move to the northeast in conflict space (Table 2-1), since such a move benefits both parties (both *X* and *Y* receive more), and as "plus-minus," or +,−, any move to the northwest or southeast. For simplicity rather than accuracy, we consider +,0 moves (due north or due east) as if they were +,+, which therefore includes all moves that harm no one. We

---

[3] For an explanation of this, look up "production possibility curve" or "transformation curve" in any textbook on micro-economics.

are not concerned with —,— moves, since we assume that rational contestants do not seek such solutions. If one contestant wants so much to hurt another that he will do so at some sacrifice to himself, his move is still deemed +,—, since his satisfaction in harming the other is, from his point of view, a plus that outweighs his minus.

Obviously, any +,+ move must originate at a point below the production possibility curve and gravitate toward the curve. Any move from one point upon the curve to another upon the curve must be +,—. But +,+ moves may start from a position on the curve if the curve itself moves outward, as through improved technology or increased resource availability.

We do not use the terms "zero sum" and "positive sum." "Zero sum" implies a +,— move in which the plus is quantitatively equal to the minus. In the theory of institutions, we will be concerned with whether one contestant harms another, but we need not measure how much.

Any point where no further +,+ move is possible is called *Paretianoptimal*, after the Italian sociologist-economist Vilfredo Pareto. Provided x and y are both desirable commodities, all Paretian-optimal points must fall on the curve. With an interior point, it would always be possible to increase the holdings of one without reducing those of another. But not every point on the curve is Paretian-optimal. For example, X might not want as many resources as he has; he might prefer to trade some of them for Y's product. Hence X and Y might agree that *both* preferred, say, D over E, in which case E would not be Paretian-optimal. (Note that Paretian-optimality refers to a point and not to a move.)

The Solution Line

The production possibility curve and the two axes are the boundaries of a set of points representing alternative solutions of the resource conflict. We now expand this concept to cover *any* conflict in the social system. Many such conflicts involve quantities measurable on coordinate axes, such as seats in Parliament, hectares to be expropriated in agrarian reform, expenditures of a government budget in alternative ways, and value of foreign investment to be nationalized. Others can be quantified only in relative terms; the contestant sees one position as superior to another but cannot say by how much. Even these contests can be quantified by the use of arbitrary values, which are admittedly crude but often better than nothing.

Let us now refer to our generalized production possibility curve as a *solution line*, depicting all efficient solutions for any social conflict we choose. (Boulding uses a similar vehicle. His conflict matrix corresponds to our conflict space, and conflict line to our solution line.)[4]

The similarity between economic conflict and other conflicts extends even further. Economic theory holds that in perfect competition—when all markets are perfect—the equilibrium allocation of resources will be efficient; that is, the conflict will be resolved at some point on the production possibility curve. In our more generalized version of conflict, we will presume that where institutions are perfectly effective, the solution will occur on the solution line. A perfectly effective institution is one that receives perfect ratings by all three of the effectiveness criteria introduced in Chapter 1. (The method of rating will be explained in Chapter 3.)

It might seem from this that we deem the perfect market to be a special case of perfect institutional effectiveness. But this is not so. In economics, there is an elaborate theory (of general equilibrium)[5] explaining why the resource conflict solution must fall upon the production possibility curve if full employment is assumed. But we have no generalized general equilibrium theory. We simply *define* the solution line to any conflict as representing that set of solutions possible under perfect institutional effectiveness. It follows that the solution line is not the exact analogue of the production possibility curve.

---

[4] Kenneth E. Boulding, *Conflict and Defense* (New York: Harper & Row, 1962), pp. 11ff.

[5] Attributed principally to Leon Walras, but containing contributions from many others as well. This theory held that perfect competition would automatically lead to a set of prices for all goods and services that were proportionate to the marginal rates of transformation of those goods and services (i.e., the derivative of the production possibility curve). Before 1936, it was generally believed that this proportionality would require that all solutions be upon that curve. In the *General Theory of Employment, Interest, and Money* (New York: Harcourt, Brace, 1936), Keynes observed that perfect competition did not lead automatically to the full employment of resources. This element of Keynesian theory is now generally accepted by economists. The modern theory of perfect competition would hold that all price-quantity solutions would fall on the production possibility curve *provided* resources are fully employed. Full employment might be assured, for example, by appropriate monetary and fiscal or other policies.

Contrasts between Perfect Market and Perfect Institutional Effectiveness

PERFECT MARKET

Economists often use the term "perfect competition" and "perfect market" interchangeably. A perfect market has two attributes. First, the buyers and sellers of a homogenous product are so numerous that no one of them can affect the market price. Second, the buyer knows precisely what he wants, can find all available sellers, and understands their asking prices; sellers are equally astute about potential buyers. The second of these attributes approaches our identification criterion of institutional effectiveness.

In the real world there is no perfect market, though some economists aver that certain ones, such as markets for agricultural goods, textiles, and stocks and bonds, come fairly close. Like institutional effectiveness, market perfection is a point of reference, or zero milestone, from which we measure (or guess) how far away we really are.

INSTITUTIONAL EFFECTIVENESS

Let us now expand on the three criteria of institutional effectiveness as follows.

1. *Identification criterion.* This criterion considers the institution's capacity to identify conflicts within its domain in such a way that each contestant understands the elements of conflict and the precise consequences to him of every possible solution. In economics, the market identifies the buyer–seller conflict over product characteristics and price.

2. *Rules criterion.* This criterion considers the capacity of the institution to establish and enforce rules of wide or universal applicability, so that similar conflicts are resolved in predictable ways whether or not they involve different persons or occur in different places. An institution would be high-rated where categories of persons are clear and known (e.g., staff member, boss, senator, constituent, childhood friend) and where all relationships of a given type and within a given category or between categories, are based on universal principles.

3. *Consensus criterion.* This criterion considers the acceptability of the institution to all persons or groups that use it, poten-

tially use it, or have a stake in the resolution of conflicts by it. A high-rated institution is one in which each related person or group believes his individual goals or values would be threatened if the institution were destroyed. The government of Nazi Germany would have been high-rated on the identification and rules criteria, but it perished, partly because millions of Jews did not join in the consensus. "Law and order" as proposed in the 1968 United States presidential campaign was scoffed at by minorities who considered themselves disadvantaged by the laws of the social system; hence they did not participate in the consensus.

A DISTINCTION BETWEEN COMPETITION THEORY
AND INSTITUTION THEORY

In the theory of perfect competition, a solution on the production possibility curve is *objectively* defined as a point where it is technologically impossible to increase the output of one good without decreasing that of another. It is not necessarily the solution that any contestant has desired, nor one that all would consciously strive for. The perfect market operates in an impersonal way; buyers and sellers are usually unaware of total production possibilities. In the theory of institutions, on the other hand, we are concerned with the *subjective* feelings of contestants. Suppose we were to rate the market for cotton by the three criteria of effectiveness. This market would be perfectly effective if there were no misunderstandings between buyer and seller as to availability and quality—hence full awareness, just as in perfect competition. In addition, buyers and sellers would recognize precisely the same rules of trading. Finally, buyers and sellers, *and the general public*, would be content with institutional procedures. But the market might be monopolized and still be perfectly effective. If so, then the solution, according to economic theory, would not fall on the production possibility curve. But it would fall on our solution line. In the resource conflict, therefore, our solution line (or some parts of it) might fall to the southwest of the production possibility curve.

From this it would seem that a solution *can* occur outside our solution line. If so, however, we aver that not all the elements of the conflict have been taken into account. A monopoly market may be perfectly effective and lead to production of fewer goods and services than the limit of which society is capable. But why would a society with capability for perfectly effective institutions opt for monopoly rather than competition? It must be that there are other objectives than the static maximization of output. If so, these should be measured on the axes of our now many-dimensional orthant.

We might now become embroiled in the never-ending controversy of monoploy versus competition. While all agree that in a static sense competitive output is greater than that of monopoly, nevertheless there is wide disagreement over whether monopolies generate the technology that pushes the possibility curve outward. Many believe that over the long run output is greater, rather than less, with monopolies. Because general equilibrium theory applies only to perfect competition and economists have no such theory with respect to monopolies, there is no rigorous theoretical answer.

It does appear reasonable, however, that given perfect institutions the many-dimensional Paretian optimality will be achieved. Perfect institutions imply the awareness to know all $+,+$ moves as well as the faith and will to take them. If a society with perfect institutional capability opts for monopolies, it must be presumed that the conflict has other dimensions than the static division of resources. These might include political and economic power and expansion of production possibilities. Taking all these factors into account, the multi-dimensional analogue of the solution line would contain all Paretian-optimal solutions.

With the assumption of perfect institutional effectiveness, furthermore, the solution line (or surface) would contain *only* points both technologically possible and subjectively desired by contestants. Unlike the production possibility curve, therefore, every point upon it would be (by definition) Paretian-optimal.

LEGITIMATE COSTS VERSUS INEFFICIENCIES

As we contemplate the comparison between market perfection and institutional effectiveness, some doubts arise about the economist's concept of the perfect market. Since our aim is not to improve the theory of perfect competition, we do not follow these doubts as far as we might. But we express them because they help reveal the concept of institutional effectiveness.

The principal doubt lies in the distinction between a firm's "legitimate" costs of production and those deemed to be inefficiencies. A legitimate cost helps determine the location of the production possibility curve; for example, certain combinations of factors of production *must* be used to achieve certain levels of output. An inefficiency is a cost that might have been avoided; for example, an engineer is assigned to menial duties for which an unskilled worker might have been employed at lower cost.

Now, what costs are avoidable often depends on the cultural characteristics of a people. In Hamburg, tickets are not collected on the municipal transit system. There are occasional spot checks and fines for offenders, but infractions are rare. In New York, however, there are subway turnstiles, which operate at some cost. Is the New York system inefficient, in that Hamburg has proved that it is possible to operate a transit system without turnstiles? Or are Hamburgers more honest than New Yorkers, so that turnstiles are a legitimate cost in New York but would be an inefficiency if they were installed in Hamburg?

The question is directly related to that of a perfect market. Market perfection assumes not only awareness of product, cost, and the like, but also a certain amount of trust between buyer and seller. Marshall noted that arms-length transactors take precautions that would not be necessary with trusted family members or friends.[6] Buyers must assure themselves they are receiving the quality contracted for, and "obviously" a market would be imperfect if they so mistrusted most sellers that they would buy only from a limited few. But no one (to my knowledge) has shown how to measure trust or has stipulated how much mistrust is permissible in a perfect market.

The cost of mistrust consists of all expenditures, both private and public, that are undertaken because people are, or are believed to be, unwilling to keep promises and to obey rules. It covers not only the cost of maintaining a police force and institutions for trying and penalizing offenders, but also that of internal control systems in business, auditing to detect fraud, cash registers, subway turnstiles, time clocks, night watchmen, private detectives, and theft insurance. But it is even more subtle; it includes the increment of cost caused by selecting a more expensive production method when one's collaborators can-

---

[6] Alfred Marshall, *Principles of Economics*, 8th ed. (New York: Macmillan, 1920), p. 6.

not be trusted to implement a less expensive one. For example, more costly machines replace less costly workers not because the workers lack training but because they do not arrive and leave at agreed hours. It also includes the cost of racial discrimination, which causes the employment of certain people rather than others who might have done the job equally well or better.

It is here that the culture bias of economic theory is revealed. Only the cost of mistrust regularly paid in "our" society is deemed legitimate; that paid in "other" societies constitutes inefficiency. Economists from the United States would surely argue that expenditures for auditing and theft insurance are legitimate costs, but that nepotism is an inefficiency. But wherein lies the difference, other than in one's culture bias toward what is acceptable behavior? A society "ought" to have embezzlers and thieves, but employers "ought not" to hire their nephews. Yet employers in other societies argue that they must employ their nephews because they can trust no one else.

The question of legitimacy makes cross-cultural comparisons of market perfection impossible. Presumably a market is perfect if the degree of awareness and trust corresponds to the highest of which the culture is capable. But this becomes a matter of judgment by the observer. Indeed, the "perfect market" is not an objective concept at all.

We do not concern ourselves with how to improve the economic theory of competition, but we must overcome this objection as it applies to institution theory. We do so by drawing two solution lines. The outer one (Figure 2-2) is the *physical solution line*, based on the assumption of perfect trust. It is the standard—or zero milestone—being the locus of all solution points if the institution were perfect. All policemen might be discharged, criminal courts dismantled, and auditors and theft-insurance salesmen employed elsewhere. The inner curve, known as the *apparent solution line*, measures the limit of attainable solutions given the level of trust, honesty, and obedience to rules currently found in the culture. The difference between the two curves represents the cost of mistrust.

We will refer to Paretian optimality with respect to either curve, for there is both apparent optimality and physical optimality. For example, suppose country X could devise a tax-collection system which, if properly implemented, would bring about greater spending for economic development. This in turn would yield individual *A* a higher income (after tax, of course) than he is now earning. But *A* refuses to pay his taxes. Does he fail to grasp that the social goal will benefit him?

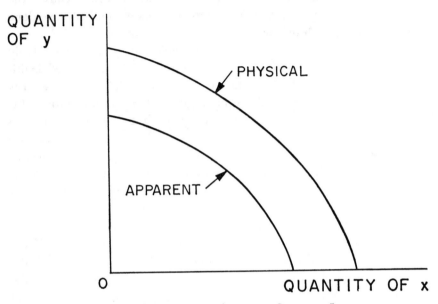

FIGURE 2-2. PHYSICAL AND APPARENT SOLUTION LINES.

Or has he correctly assessed the proposal, concluding that he will not benefit by paying taxes unless others do, and they will not? Or that the economic planners are in fact incapable of spending the revenues for the public good, and his money will fatten the pockets of superannuated politicians?

Suppose we take the case to the other taxpayers, who will not pay, and we find their answers similar to those of *A*. We then approach the planners and politicians. We explain that if they spent the government revenues wisely and well, they would be so loved by their constituents that they would be reappointed or reelected. Their legitimate incomes would be greater than what they now gain through graft, since *A* and the others would pay their taxes and national product would increase. The politicians smile and say that *A* would not pay his taxes under any circumstances.

It is not the technological possibility of the politicians, planners, and taxpayers to act in the common interest that is lacking. Rather, each optimizes his welfare subject to his own constraints as he sees them. Hence there is *apparent* Paretian optimality. But *physical* optimality has not been achieved, for collectively they suboptimize in a situation of mutual mistrust, even hatred.

The Institution as Determinant of the Solution Line

Still another point disturbs us about the concept of the perfect market. Economic theory is concerned with market *structure*, but its *function* is deemed peripheral. The market is not thought of on the same plane as the production unit, as an institution capable of affecting cost and output or of operating more or less efficiently. Of course, an individual market such as the New York Stock Exchange or Safeway Supermarkets is so conceived, but the broader market, consisting of all the functions of buying and selling, say, cotton, is not. The market in this broader sense is not deemed to have "technology."

As a result, economists tend to think of the production possibility curve as independent of the market (broader sense). It is determined solely by the level of production technology and the quantity of available resources. *If* the market is perfect, *then* the solution lies on the possibility curve. But this dichotomy blinds us to an essential role of the market (broader sense). Together with production technology and resources, the operational efficiency of the market may also determine the location of the production possibility curve and the rate at which it is expanding.

In many cases, the act of bargaining itself propels the solution line outward. The effective market demonstrates needs of which buyers and sellers were previously unaware; it causes inventions. Indeed, it is surprising how many conflicts are more easily resolved if more material goods are available. Conflicts on zoning are more quickly settled if a city's physical boundaries are expanding than if they are fixed; the very act of negotiation may cause those boundaries to expand. Conflicts over school curricula are less explosive if a larger budget is available; the explication of that conflict before the legislature may, one might hope, expand the budget. But more importantly, the greater the number of +,+ moves, the more a society becomes oriented toward them, and the more it tends to seek them. People who find +,— moves to be unacceptable tend to fashion institutions that work well only when the moves are +,+. The proper functioning of the institution thus propels the solution line outward.

Takeoff versus Post-takeoff Societies

We now distinguish between takeoff and post-takeoff societies. Again we recognize the vagueness of the demarcation, and we polarize for simplicity. Takeoff societies have been stimulated by the desire for growth but have not agreed on institutionalized ways of dividing its limited increments. Many individuals do not accept the decisions of existing institutions or would upset them if they could; they consider their share of the national dividend to be unjust.

The ease by which a conflict is resolved depends on the degree of consensus on the institution. (This is a tautology.) Over time, consensus is more easily formed on institutions that lead to +,+ rather than those that lead to +,— solutions. (If everyone gains, the institution is good.) Thus, growth itself biases a society toward acceptable institutions. If X and Y together want more resources than there are, the conflict is more readily resolved if the volume of resources is increasing. We therefore theorize that growth leads post-takeoff societies to understand that satisfactory solutions must be, by and large, +,+. In the remainder of this chapter, we will introduce illustrations of what is now presented as a general principle: that *solutions tend to be +,— in takeoff and +,+ in post-takeoff societies.*

Furthermore, certain kinds of conflicts are not only resolved solely by economic growth with +,+ solutions, but inevitably spawn repetitions of the same conflicts, or new ones, which in turn require growth. Thus conflict is both resolved by, and becomes an engine of, growth.

TAKEOFF SOCIETIES

Takeoff societies are in the turmoil of selecting economic growth as a dominant goal. Desire for product inevitably exceeds the means of satisfaction, for neither the physical nor the culture capital (including technology) is abundant enough to permit large numbers of +,+ moves. The have-nots often believe their problems are to be solved by taking from the haves, not by sharing greater output with them.

Groups whose interrelationships were well defined before takeoff, such as politicians, soldiers, businessmen, laborers, peasants, landowners, and students, now find a new divergence. They disagree on the nature of growth, what causes it and what suppresses it, and on the rules by which its increments should be divided. Except for ephemeral coalitions designed to meet specific circumstances, the groups tend to cooperate but little with each other. Often each believes that what is good for the others is bad for it, and vice versa. Landlords and feudal peons have no vision beyond that of who owns the land. Ownership alternatives, such as small family farms, haciendas, plantations, cooperatives, government or corporate farming, are not conceived as value-free choices whose only constraint is the desire to maximize production; they become ends in themselves. Unaccustomed to thinking of wage increases as both cause and effect of increased productivity, employers picture laborers as their enemies. Laborers, for their part, view employers as an economic aristocracy bent on keeping its workers at the minimum level of subsistence. Businessmen and consumers do not understand that high-volume output at low-unit profit would benefit both. In contrast to post-takeoff societies, the belief is widespread that profit-seeking does *not* maximize human welfare.

Proposed conflict resolution includes confiscatory agrarian reform, military coups, wage settlements with no reference to productivity, inflation, monopoly pricing, taxation without reference to benefits, the milking of corporations or the public exchequer, refusal to admit nonfamily members to family firms, and business inefficiencies designed to promote personal gain, all of which are +,— moves. Conversely, when +,+ moves are proposed, such as regional development of a river basin or economic integration of neighboring countries, the inability of all but a few visionaries to see beyond immediate conflicts poses enormous obstacles to implementation.

POST-TAKEOFF SOCIETIES

It is always easier to defeat an opponent if he wins too. Such is the nature of wage disputes in the United States. Union pressure, Kendrick has found,[7] has caused wages in the twentieth century to increase more rapidly than the physical productivity of labor. Since this

[7] John W. Kendrick, *Productivity Trends in the United States* (Princeton, N.J.: Princeton University Press for the National Bureau of Economic Research), pp. 124-30.

47

fact implies lower profits, why do employers agree to it? Only because the early application of technology now on the drawing boards will enable them to substitute less expensive capital for labor, thus recouping their losses. But this solution implies unemployment. Why does labor tolerate it? Only because the growing economy is expected to provide jobs for workers displaced. Some firms (like New York newspapers) may go out of business, but even this resolution is all the easier in a society of mobile factors of production. The fact that the only solution acceptable to both parties lies northeast of the old, now obsolete, solution line means that an unchanging national product would have been incapable of meeting their needs.

Examples of $+,+$ moves are so numerous as to dwarf the $+,-$.[8] Unable to decide which of two men to promote, management creates a new position so that both are accommodated. Professors not selected for tenure in their preferred universities find good positions elsewhere. Rotten ghettos will never be scraped clean if suburbanites must give up their material comforts in favor of the center city. No, only *increments* in the pie will be carved in a different way. Contrary to much popular belief, private consumption in the United States increased in both World War II and the Vietnam war. Any belt-tightening in the guns-versus-butter conflict has been relative to the appetites of people with growing waistlines.

The $+,+$ move has been beatified in a whole array of social and economic theories, doctrines, and clichés emanating from the more developed world. By the "law" of comparative advantage, post-takeoff economists "proved" that trade freely entered into *always* benefits both parties. While the United States government may spend money derived from tax increases to promote the general welfare, it may not tax one group for the specific benefit of another. Seekers of private gain are believed to promote the general well-being. In a corrected (accurate) version of Charles Wilson's famous remark, "What's good for the nation is good for General Motors."

---

[8] It might be argued that the punishment of an offender is a $+,-$ solution. There are, however, alternative ways of viewing punishment in a $+,+$ sense. First, if the penal code is designed to rehabilitate the offender, then it is $+,+$, *based on socially accepted definitions.* Secondly, punishment may be deemed a social sanction against an offender for a previous violation of laws based in general on $+,+$ moves. That is, he has committed a $+,-$ move in the past and must now be punished if the $+,+$ system is to be preserved.

The $+,+$ move takes on a different sheen in socialist societies, where the state rather than the individual determines which positions are "better" and which are "worse." In the Soviet Union, the promotion of socialist values and defeat of capitalist ideology are dominant goals, perhaps even surpassing the maximization of national product, which becomes a means. Consensus on goals is reached through political control of education and news media, as well as restriction upon foreign travel. Government-determined budgetary allocations between consumer goods and military and space expenditures, the particular division selected between agricultural and industrial output and incomes, and even the suppression of literary freedom, all are deemed $+,+$ moves, for they promote the ultimate goals on which there is presumably consensus.

It was not always so in the Soviet Union. Takeoff, which comprised roughly the period from the Revolution through Stalinist times, was replete with executions and purges $(+,-)$. Though it is too early for positive pronouncements, nevertheless the decreasing frequency and increasing humaneness of purges may indicate a move toward the $+,+$ game. Even the invasion of Hungary (1956) and Czechoslovakia (1968) were "justified" in terms of "mutual benefits," a point that was hardly made when the Czar and his family were shot.

THE ENCOUNTER BETWEEN TAKEOFF AND POST-TAKEOFF SOCIETIES

What happens in an encounter between societies with differing appreciations of $+,+$ and $+,-$ moves? These confrontations are unique to our time, for never before have such large numbers of post-takeoff and takeoff societies had to deal with each other. The conflicts relate to trade, aid, investment, mutual versus individual defense, and similar issues of a political-socioeconomic nature.

In virtually all cases, the governments of post-takeoff societies insist that solutions are "easy" and to mutual advantage. Often they cannot understand why governments of less developed countries refuse to collaborate when moves are "clearly" beneficial to both. The latter governments, however, see no mutuality. To them, proposed solutions ought to involve unilateral concessions by post-takeoff societies, the admittedly $+,-$ nature of which is justified as indemnity for $+,-$ wrongs committed upon them in the past through colonialism and unfair monopoly pricing.

49

Politicians from more developed countries regard foreign aid as being of mutual advantage. Recipients benefit through the transfer of resources. Donors benefit from the strengthened political relationships which contribute to the solidarity of the "free world" or the "socialist bloc," as the case may be. Officials of less developed countries see no such advantage. They justify their acceptance of foreign aid as compensation for unfair prices paid for their exports or charged for their imports. Some, who oppose accepting it at all, regard foreign aid as a sinister means by which imperialist countries compete unfairly with industry in the recipient country and even suppress its growth.[9]

Foreign investment has the reputation in lending countries of yielding returns to investors while bestowing technology, products, and higher incomes upon recipients. The latter, however, often view it as infringement of their sovereignty, creating a second-class citizenry and unfair competition for local industry. Many believe they did not welcome it of their own free will, that it was foisted upon them by powerful "imperialists." Victor Urquidi, a prominent Mexican economist, has argued that Latin American opinion is in general rather negative toward foreign investment.[10] Leff has observed that in Brazil, "giving considerable prominence to the theme of imperialism, nationalist intellectuals have considered foreign capital both central to all Brazilian political and economic issues, and enormously prejudicial to the country's development."[11] Hirschman refers to the "displacement of local factors and the stunting of local abilities which can occur in the wake of international investment."[12]

Economists from less developed countries do not view the law of comparative advantage as one that yields mutual gains. To them, it has *static* validity only: given the factor endowments *of the moment*, less developed countries can maximize incomes by specializing in primary products. This in turn prevents them from ever developing compara-

[9] John P. Powelson, *Latin America: Today's Economic and Social Revolution* (New York: McGraw-Hill, 1964), p. 222.

[10] Victor Urquidi, *Viabilidad Económica de América Latina* (Mexico City: Fondo de Cultura Económica, 1962), p. 103.

[11] Nathaniel H. Leff, *Economic Policy-Making and Development in Brazil* (New York: John Wiley & Sons, 1968), pp. 66-67.

[12] Albert O. Hirschman, *How to Divest in Latin America, and Why*, Essays in International Finance, No. 76 (Princeton, N.J.: International Finance Section, Princeton University, 1969), p. 6.

tive advantage in manufactures. The illiterate boy who becomes a bootblack may benefit as income dribbles upon him from well-shod clients. But if he spends all his time being a bootblack, he will never learn anything else. Furthermore, the "law" assumes that all societies are of the consensus type. In the coercive society, the disaffected slave is not better off serving his master than he would be if he were free.

The differing legitimacy of $+,+$ and $+,-$ moves hovers over confiscation of private property, which is immoral in the $+,+$ society (e.g., United States) but quite moral in the $+,-$ (e.g., Latin America). The United States gives financial aid to Latin American agrarian reform through colonization ($+,+$), but many Latin Americans believe the only meaningful reform is through confiscation ($+,-$). The General Agreement on Tariffs and Trade is dominated by $+,+$ societies, who prefer reciprocity in tariff concessions. The $+,-$ societies cannot understand why. When delegates of less developed ($+,-$) countries seek nonrefundable financial compensation for low prices of their primary exports, those of the more developed ($+,+$) societies suppose they are seeking some illegitimate, undeserved gain. If delegates to the United Nations Congress on Trade and Development and meetings of the International Monetary Fund would recognize that conflicting opinions stem from deep and differing ideological concepts of conflict resolution far more than from the surface arguments they enunciate concerning terms of trade or mutual benefits, it is conceivable that greater understanding of complex situations would emerge. Whether this would lead to better solutions, however, is debatable.

Constructive and Destructive Conflict

Why do groups have more faith in each other to fulfil obligations in some countries than in others? Why can the taxpayers, government planners, and politicians in some countries coordinate their efforts to collect taxes and spend proceeds wisely, while in others they cannot? Why is the cost of mistrust so much greater in some countries than in others?

In searching for an answer, we distinguish between two basic types of conflict, which Ortega y Gasset, the Spanish philosopher, has characterized as follows:

51

Internecine strife, Cicero had read in Aristotle, arises when members of a society disagree about political matters—a somewhat hackneyed statement. However, have we not just seen that discord may also give the impulse for further development and perfection of the state? On the other hand, a society obviously relies for its existence upon common consent in certain ultimate matters. Such unanimity Cicero called *concordia,* and he defines it as "the best bond of permanent union in any commonwealth." How does the one tally with the other? Quite easily, if we picture the body of opinion from which the life of a nation draws its sustenance as made up of various layers. Divergencies in surface layers produce beneficent conflict because the ensuing struggles move upon the firm ground of deeper concord. Questioning certain things, but not questioning all, minor divergencies serve but to confirm and consolidate underlying unanimity of the collective existence. But if dissent affects the basic layers of common belief on which the solidarity of the social body lastly rests, then the state becomes a house divided, society dissociates, splitting up into two societies—that is two groups with fundamentally divergent beliefs.[13]

Coser summarizes the distinction in the following words: "The distinction between conflicts over the basis of consensus and those taking place within consensus, comprises part of the common ground of political science from Aristotle to modern political theory."[14]

Following Oregeta y Gassett, Coser, and others, we distinguish among a hierarchy of goals, from immediate to ultimate. To win a piece of territory is an army's immediate goal, to win a war is less immediate, and to combat Communism (or capitalism) is an ultimate goal. Likewise, to collect taxes is an immediate goal of the minister of finance. His ultimate goal may be to protect his job. If this protection depends on pleasing the taxpayers, which he does through promoting the stability and growth of the nation, then he and they have ultimate goals in common. If on the other hand his job is protected through pleasing powerful politicians with payoffs, then he and the taxpayers

[13] José Ortega y Gasset, *Concord and Liberty* (New York: W. W. Norton Co., 1946), p. 15; quoted in Lewis A. Coser, *The Functions of Social Conflict,* (New York: Free Press, 1956), p. 74.

[14] Coser, *Social Conflict,* p. 75.

52

share no goals in common. A common goal is not necessarily the *same* goal for two parties. More accurately, we would refer to joint goals, in the sense that one is achieved only if the other is also.

Adequate communication, understanding, and confidence are essential to parties who share common goals. Mere interest in achieving joint outcomes does not constitute common goals if the parties do not communicate with each other.

Examples abound where two contestants agree on ultimate goals but conflict over immediate ones. Buyer and seller disagree on price but concur on maintaining an orderly exchange process through which both satisfy their needs. Professor and student may disagree on grades, but they (usually) concur on enough ultimate goals to keep the university running. Naturally, some ultimate goals, such as the purchaser's use of product or the student's choice of profession, are not relevant to the conflict. A relevant goal is one in which *both* parties have an interest, either concurring or conflicting.

Both Simmel and Coser have proposed that conflict is a binding force. It brings together contestants who might otherwise have had no transactions with each other, thus setting the stage for building institutions to resolve or manage their conflicts.[15] But it can bind only if contestants have ultimate goals in common. If *over the long run* taxpayers, politicians, and government planners cannot find ways to cooperate in contributing to economic growth through fiscal actions in which all concur, then we must conclude that they do not hold economic growth as an ultimate goal in common. Other goals not compatible with economic growth are separately more important to each. If on the other hand they do hold growth as a mutual goal, and if this goal dominates their lower-order conflicting goals, then at least one will sacrifice the lower goal, or there will be a compromise and *some* satisfactory resolution will be reached. If conflicts are repeated, an institutionalized way of resolving them will be found.

In analyzing takeoff countries, however, we are more interested in the *short run*. Groups in these societies have recently discovered economic growth to be a dominant, mutual goal, or are in the process of discovering it. They are only beginning to communicate with each other, and mutual confidence is yet to come. They have conflicting

[15] Georg Simmel, *Conflict*, trans. Kurt H. Wolff (New York: Free Press, 1955), pp. 26, 35; Coser, *Social Conflict* p. 121.

ideas on the form of institutions needed to resolve such conflicts as tax-paying (what is A's share, what is B's, etc.) and government spending. Within an appropriate period they will either resolve these conflicts and set up the institutions, or they will abandon the goal. In some countries abandonment has occurred because groups have been unable to acquire the values and institutions essential to communication and confidence. It is the process of selecting and building institutions that we will examine in subsequent chapters.

So long as contestants have no ultimate goals in common, we label their conflicts *destructive*. Taxpayers and politicians who fight over enforcing collections or eliminating graft are each seeking individual ends, the achievement of one being the destruction of the other. Solutions can only be +,—.

Constructive conflict occurs when the contestants hold ultimate goals in common which they value more highly than immediate ones, and when the satisfactory resolution of immediate conflict is an indispensable step in achievement of those ultimate goals. The earlier example (page 47) of wage disputes in the United States is a case in point. Maximization of productivity, an ultimate goal of *both* labor and management, would not occur if there were no wage disputes between them. *The process of economic growth demonstrates time and again that ultimate goals cannot be achieved unless conflicts occur over immediate goals.*

Simmel and Coser have attributed positive value to "conflicts within the consensus" simply because they strengthen the consensus. A marriage is threatened if the quarrel is about the consensus itself (such as over one partner's infidelity). However, if the consensus is strong to begin with, it will be further strengthened by quarrels over (say) whether to have a picnic or not, for these bring with them the institutionalized means of resolution which is then applicable to other disagreements.

We go one step further. Not only are constructive conflicts necessary to strengthen system *structure*, as Simmel, Coser, and others have argued, but they are an essential element in system *functioning*. The intersection of supply- and demand-curves is the resolution of continuing constructive conflict that serves the ultimate goals of both buyer and seller. For example, the appropriate amount of investment in an economy is determined through a conflict, over interest rates, between saver and borrower.

Let us now define constructive conflict in such a way that the solution is always +,+. This requires a broader view than the single encounter. Take, for example, two candidates for the presidency of the United States. In the short-run, the election appears to be a +,— move. The winner is obviously better off. The loser is worse off, for presumably before the election he had some hope of winning, however slim. Instead of treating the conflict in the frame of this one encounter, however, we consider the series of steps through which it was formed and waged. A candidate nominated and not elected is probably better off than if he had not been nominated at all. He holds the prestige of the nomination and probably has better employment opportunities than if the conflict had not occurred. Not only would he feel personally threatened if the *system* of elections were destroyed, but society *expects* him to accept defeat gracefully. Similar observations may be made about wage-rate conflicts in which the union loses an encounter, conflicts over positions in business, conflicts over the price of a product, and many more.

We now propose that destructive conflicts with +,— solutions are characteristic of early takeoff societies, while constructive conflicts with +,+ solutions are characteristic of post-takeoff. The takeoff process is one of forming consensus on goals and of selecting and agreeing upon the institutions to resolve those conflicts. This proposition cannot be proved, but abundant illustrations from the western hemisphere will be cited in succeeding chapters.

The difference between constructive and destructive conflict bears on our selection of the criteria of institutional effectiveness. Some might challenge the appropriateness of equating institutional effectiveness with high ratings by the identification and rules criteria, especially the former. It might be argued that conflicts are *more* readily resolved if products and rules are not clear. Proponents of this position would argue that clarification frightens and polarizes contestants. Hirschman has suggested that many development projects would not be undertaken if the investors were initially aware of all the problems they would encounter.[16] It is classic theory that economic development

[16] Albert O. Hirschman, *Development Projects Observed* (Washington, D.C.: The Brookings Institution, 1967), ch. 1.

requires a transfer of resources from agriculture to industry, a transfer to which farmers might submit only if duped into it. How then do I suggest that full knowledge of the consequences of any action should be taken as a measure of institutional effectiveness?

The answer is that all the polarized positions cited above constitute *unclear* rather than clear comprehension of the *ultimate* consequences of action. Hirschman argues that project-undertakers are *also* unaware of their own capabilities of solving problems. Likewise, the farmers are unaware of the ultimate advantages to them of economic growth.

Suppose in the United States the president's Council of Economic Advisers, fearful of depression, should encourage moves to increase sales by retailers. Suppose they argued that if the customer had less knowledge of merchandise quality and potential performance, he would be more susceptible to the guile of salesmen and more likely to buy. The Council would therefore propose that department stores be forbidden to display their wares publicly and catalogue stores to print pictures of products. All fair labeling laws would be repealed, and the buyer would depend on the salesman's verbal description. It is conceivable that once the public became adjusted to the new situation sales would increase. It is hard to believe, however, that satisfaction would be maximized or long-run economic growth promoted.

The identification and rules criteria must be viewed in an environment of economic development in which contestants have, or are seeking, ultimate goals in common and in which conflicts are being converted from destructive into constructive. Under these circumstances, institutions that assist in understanding the anatomy of mutual interests are more effective than those that do not. As blacks move into previously white neighborhoods in the United States, present residents are often gripped with panic, supposing that their real-estate values will decline (despite studies that have shown this is generally not so[17]), crime will increase, the standards of public schooling decline, and peace and quiet be disturbed. If there were some institution through which they could be shown what kinds of activities are necessary to avoid these results (e.g., how to improve schools), what would be their costs, and how the anatomy of the neighborhood would appear ten years later if these were undertaken, it is likely that many of the

[17] Luigi Laurenti, *Property Values and Race* (Berkeley, Calif.: University of California Press, 1960); see esp. the general conclusions in chs. 4 and 5.

fears would be allayed. Indeed, polarization is *more* likely to occur when product and rules are not known, for it is then that fears are exaggerated out of proportion.

We do not consider in this book whether destructive conflicts are a *necessary* condition of takeoff. It is often argued, for example, that the consensus society could not have been achieved in Mexico or the Soviet Union except through their respective revolutions, which were clearly destructive conflicts according to our definition. These two cases bear striking similarities. In each, the gross national product was, by all available evidence, growing at the rate of approximately six to seven percent in the first decade of the twentieth century. Each country was embroiled in a series of wars and revolution in the second decade. In each case, approximately one quarter-century elapsed before the prerevolution GNP, both level and rate of growth, had again been achieved. Those who argue that the revolutions were "necessary" to economic growth must demonstrate that growth would probably have stopped had they not occurred. Those who pass ethical judgments in favor of the revolutions must demonstrate that the same consensus and the same growth, after the quarter-century hiatus, could not have been achieved in less costly fashion. We avoid this discussion by concerning ourselves only with the postrevolutionary period. Our task is to outline the principles by which the institutions of consensus are selected. What are the alternative institutions of consensus? Why are some chosen and others turned down?

CHAPTER 3

The Consensus Society: Definitions and Problems
of Measurement

IN CHAPTER 1 we proposed that all more developed countries, whether socialist, capitalist, or mixed, display two characteristics in common: consensus on economic growth as a dominant goal, and consensus on a set of dominant values whose object is to resolve conflicts arising out of growth. We argued that coercive societies have historically been unable to maintain growth over long periods; only a consensus society can sustain it. In Chapter 2 we set forth the necessity for conflict-resolving institutions, and we distinguished among goals (immediate and ultimate), conflicts (constructive and destructive), moves (+,+ and +,—), and solutions (physical and apparent). These distinctions are all conceived as continua, although it is frequently more practical to refer to their poles as dichotomies. We argued that while institutions must conform to values, no one set of values and institutions will maximize growth at all times and in all places, though there is probably a unique set that will maximize it at any one time in any one place. In subsequent chapters, we will approach the principles by which that unique set is selected. In the present chapter, we pause for some definitions important to the consensus society.

In Chapter 2 we postulated that consensus both on economic growth as a dominant goal and on a set of dominant values to resolve conflicts arising under growth are requisites for a post-takeoff society. We consider these points separately below.

Economic Growth as a Dominant Goal

When is economic growth a dominant goal? Above all, we must not impute goals to persons or groups on their word alone. They may possess goals of which they are unconscious, or they may proclaim goals that are false. But at least we must have an objective definition: *economic growth is a dominant goal only if the essential features of a person's or group's way of life* (system structure) *would be destroyed if growth did not occur.*

Economic growth is a dominant goal for experimental scientists whose contributions would not be in demand if they could not be put to use in producing an increased GNP. It is a dominant goal for politicians in societies where unemployment and distress would occur among residents if growth should stop. It is a dominant goal for competitive businessmen aware that others will drive them bankrupt if they do not constantly seek innovations in product and technology. It is also a dominant goal for the laborers they employ. Indeed, it is very difficult to find *any* groups of substantial size in post-takeoff economies that do not have economic growth as a dominant goal.

Whether economic growth is a dominant goal for any individual or group is probably something that social psychologists can determine. Tests would involve both identification and ordering. Since most individuals probably cannot state their goals explicitly, the psychologists might either ask questions or apply such tests as thematic apperception (in the manner of McClelland on entrepreneurship),[1] and record whatever goals are mentioned or inferred. It is not necessary to quantify goals (they either exist or do not), but it is necessary to order them. Enough questions should be asked or other tests applied, involving a large enough sample of cases, to determine a high probability that, in case of conflict, goal A would be sacrificed for goal B. The psychologist would then determine which goals (e.g., survival) outrank economic growth. Some standard must be set up to assess the frequency with which such outranking goals might come into conflict with growth and whether that frequency is great enough to call any one of them, rather than growth, a dominant goal for the purposes of the study.

Economic growth may well be an unconscious and even unintended goal, as in Great Britain during the eighteenth century and Japan during the Tokugawa regime. Consensus upon it may likewise be unconscious in the sense that some may not be aware of the injury that growth might inflict upon them. England in the eighteenth century may be an example of a high, unintended consensus.

Values

We now amplify the proposition on values, as follows.

To sustain a maximum rate of economic growth, a society must generate among its members consensus on a set of dominant values, covering all areas of social intercourse, whose purpose is to legitimate

[1] David McClelland, *The Achieving Society* (New York: Van Nostrand, 1961).

and support institutions that resolve the conflicts of growth. The stronger the consensus, the greater the potential for growth, subject only to the maximum set by technology and available resources.

Values are the most elusive elements in the model, and we have no suggestion on how to specify or measure them. Rather, we propose that institutions serve as their surrogates. The conformity of institutions to values is well established in sociological theory. We believe that it will be possible, using the three criteria mentioned earlier, to measure the effectiveness of institutions. We will return to that later.

The less the value consensus, the lower will be the apparent solution line compared to the physical; for economic growth, this would be a production possibility curve well below what is physically possible. As value consensus is generated, the apparent line moves closer to the physical. The production possibility curve appears to move outward at greater velocity than might be explained by increased technology or added factors of production. Social scientists usually explain that this results from better organization or administrative capacities. Economists call it an increase in the absorptive capacity for capital.

For the definition of value, as well as norm, we turn to Parsons:

> In social structure the element of "patterned relation" is clearly in part "normative." This is to say that from the point of view of the unit it includes a set of "expectations" as to his or its behavior on the axis of what is or is not proper, appropriate, or right. From the point of view of other units with which the unit of reference is in interaction, this is a set of standards according to which positive or negative sanctions can be legitimated. Corresponding to the distinction between role and collectivity for the case of units is that between norm and value for that of relational pattern. A value is a normative pattern which defines desirable behavior for a system in relation to its environment, without differentiation of the functions of units or of their particular situations. A norm, on the other hand, is a pattern defining desirable behavior of a unit or class of units in respects specific to it, and differentiated from the obligations of other classes.[2]

[2] Talcott Parsons, "Some Considerations on the Theory of Social Change," *Rural Sociology*, xxvi, no. 3 (1961), reprinted in A. Etzioni and E. Etzioni, *Social Change* (New York: Basic Books, 1964), pp. 85-86.

A value thus not only governs one's own behavior but also the expectations of the behavior of others, and social restraints are legitimate for its enforcement. Furthermore, values are held by systems. "It is an essential proposition of the conceptual scheme used here that every social system has a system of values as the highest-order component of its structure."[3] The values of the social system become institutionalized as they are internalized in the individual.

We accept it as axiomatic that the values of an individual are ordered; that is, some are superior to others, in that inferior ones are violated or sacrificed in the event of value conflict. It follows that for each individual there is a set of dominant values, containing at least one value, and consisting of all those values of the highest order that do not conflict with each other.

KUNKEL ON VALUES

Sociologist John Kunkel has argued that "the major problem of economic development is not the alteration of character, values, or attitudes, but the change of those selected aspects of man's social environment which are relevant to the learning of new behavior patterns."[4] Since there is an apparent conflict over the role of values between Kunkel's approach and my own, it is well to digress on this point.

Kunkel does not provide his own definition of values, though he cites a variety of definitions by other sociologists, and he concludes—as we do also—that values are so difficult to specify that they are not operationally useful in a growth model. Kunkel believes that economic development is promoted or hindered by rewards and punishments designed to influence the behavior of individuals in certain ways—toward saving and entrepreneurship, for example. "It all depends on *which* behavior patterns are reinforced and on *what* types of chains are slowly established over the years. Little is gained by postulating an intervening variable, such as value orientation, which explains nothing and only clutters up the analysis."[5]

Kunkel's appreciation of the role of values differs from my own on two points, one semantic and one substantive. The first (semantic) is

[3] *Ibid.*, p. 96.
[4] John H. Kunkel, *Society and Economic Growth* (New York: Oxford University Press, 1970), p. 76.
[5] *Ibid.*, p. 81.

that Kunkel appears to believe values stem from an individual's internal state, from subconscious forces such as the need for achievement (McClelland) and the concept of self-worth (Hagen). He contrasts these forces with observable behavioral stimuli, which he believes are the real motivations for individual action. I do not limit values in the same way. They may also be derived from one's concept of how society functions, or, in Kunkel's terms, from "contingent stimuli" (persistent rewards or punishment following specific behavior), and they need have no subconscious content.

The other point (substantive) is that Kunkel emphasizes those behavior patterns (e.g., saving) that are compatible with economic growth and others (e.g., nonsaving) that are not, and he devises a system to explain how the former may be promoted. My own argument develops on a different plane. Growth-inducing behavior—*whatever* it may be—is impossible without effective institutions for decision-making, and in discussing the selection of these, I find values to be a useful concept. If I have any criticism of Kunkel, it is of his *categoric* statement that value alteration is not "the major problem" of economic development. Had he written instead that values are not of great import to the limited subset of development variables that he intended to explore, he would have been on safer ground.

Consensus on Dominant Values

Both "consensus" and "dominant" require further clarification.

Consensus.[6] "Consensus" is distinguished from "unanimity" in two ways. The more obvious lies in the number of people. Unanimity requires the inclusion of all. But there may be national consensus on, say, the supremacy of law even though it is not shared by criminals (to whom it is not a dominant value), mentally incompetents (unable to hold dominant values), or easily controllable fringe elements (such as a few Communists in a capitalist society or vice versa).

Consensus on a dominant set also breeds consensus on values of lower order, and herein we encounter a second difference between "consensus" and "unanimity." Suppose that individual A rejects proposition *w* on its intrinsic merits, while an overwhelming majority of his

[6] The meaning of consensus in labor relations, and its relationship with the process of industrialization, is discussed by James O. Morris in "Consensus, Ideology, and Labor Relations," *Journal of Inter-American Studies*, VII, no. 3 (July 1965).

society accepts it. Nevertheless, he agrees to *favor* it (not simply to tolerate or obey it) because, *given the decision of the others*, he agrees that society is better off with his concurrence. The good of society is a dominant value whose impairment would personally threaten A. He joins the consensus on proposition *w*, though there is no unanimity.

Operation of this principle is frequently seen in wartime, when those opposed to a war on its intrinsic merits nevertheless join it with a fervor equal to those in favor. (We refer, of course, to World War II and not to Vietnam.) It is found in political parties that close ranks behind the selected candidate, each politician acting after the primary as if the candidate selected had been his personal choice before.

Dominant. "Dominant" implies that when a value within the set conflicts with any value outside, the latter yields to the former. For a value to be dominant to an individual, he must feel personally threatened if it is impaired. Thus he does not "uphold the law" because of some vague moral responsibility to society, but because it is to his own personal interest that the *system* of law be maintained.

Shortly after the passage of the Civil Rights law of 1964, a group of newspaper reporters toured the South to determine the extent of compliance. In one case an owner had closed his hotel rather than serve blacks, and in some instances there was violence (burning of churches), but in most cases the reporters found establishments open and hotel- and restaurant-keepers complying with the law. Though segregation was to them a value, nevertheless the supremacy of law was a dominant value.

The supremacy of law and segregation were both dominant values to the owner who closed his hotel peacefully. He found a means to avoid the conflict that would have required him to select which value was dominant and which not. For those who burned churches, however, segregation was the dominant value and supremacy of the law a value of second order.

There remains the in-between case of the person who will permit a nondominant value to outrank a dominant one in his own behavior, believing he can get away with the violation without destroying the value's dominance for the social system as a whole. Such is the case of the traffic violator who believes his violation will not destroy the system. Whether or not the law is really a value to him depends on his other behavior, such as whether he proclaims it unjust, condoning and encouraging violation by others, or whether he is shamefully silent about his offense and would vote for the law if he were a legislator.

The payment of taxes is a much-debated case in point. In 1951, Richard Goode listed six points which he considered to be conditions for the successful use of income taxation. Among these was "a voluntary compliance on the part of taxpayers."[7] Vito Tanzi has criticized this point, arguing that tax payment is not a dominant value in any country. "The idea that the people of some countries have a greater propensity than those of others to evade taxes," he writes, "is one of the myths still generally accepted."[8] He quotes an official of the U.S. Internal Revenue Service who wrote that "the North American is not motivated in his compliant behavior by any love of taxes but, on the contrary, . . . he has a well-developed capacity for tax resistance."[9]

Unfortunately, Tanzi has missed the point. The question is not whether the U.S. taxpayer likes to pay taxes, or even whether he would cheat. Rather, it is whether, when all factors are considered, there is consensus on tax-paying as a dominant value. The other factors are implied in the answers to such questions as the following. Does the individual argue that tax payment is unjust because the proceeds go into the pockets of corrupt politicians? Does he boast to his friends of his prowess in evasion? Will he support instruments, such as electronic computers, which restrain him and his fellow citizens from tax evasion? Does he elect representatives who will pass an income-tax law?

Values in the dominant set may not conflict with each other. A conscientious objector may hold both respect for the law and "thou shalt not kill" as dominant values. He continues to hold them both if he presents himself voluntarily for punishment when he violates the draft law, according to the civil-disobedience principles espoused by Thoreau, Ghandi, and others. If he goes underground or flees the country, then respect for the law is not a dominant value.

To have a set of dominant values implies decision-making capability.

[7] Richard Goode, "Reconstruction of Foreign Tax Systems," *Proceedings of the Forty-Fourth Annual Conference on Taxation* (New York: National Tax Foundation, 1951).

[8] Vito Tanzi, "Personal Income Taxation in Latin America: Obstacles and Possibilities," *National Tax Journal*, xix, no. 2 (June 1966), 158.

[9] Joseph P. Crockett, "Common Obstacles to Effective Tax Administration in Latin America," *Joint Tax Program*, OAS/IDB/ECLA (Baltimore: The Johns Hopkins Press), p. 1.

Had the conscientious objector been unable to make up his mind, but merely waited for history to take its course, he would have lacked decisiveness. The decisiveness of individuals is another variable worthy of measure and correlation with the rate of economic growth. Pye has made a similar observation concerning individual security and the political development of Burma.[10]

Finally, we come to the violation of dominant values in the face of severe stress. Here we are tempted to argue that stress should be treated as an unusual circumstance and therefore an exception to our general tenet. Nevertheless, since all conflicts involve stress, and since there are degrees of tension, we find it more fruitful to suggest that dominance is measurable by degrees. Support for law and order may be a dominant value under ordinary circumstances. But small groups "take the law into their own hands" in *any* society when they consider that their own interests have been unjustly threatened beyond a certain limit and the law either does not agree with their interpretation or is powerless to do anything about it.

In 1964 a mass of Peruvian football fans, unhappy over the defeat of their team by Argentina, rioted against an umpire's decision, with a resulting stampede that led to many deaths. A similar circumstance occurred in a match between two local teams in Turkey in 1967. Do we at once conclude that these occurrences were symptoms of underdevelopment in Peru and Turkey, in that no value consensus restrained the spectators from rioting? Or is respect for an umpire's decision *normally* a dominant value in the subculture of Peruvian and Turkish football fans, governing their behavior in other games day in and day out, and set aside only under the stressful circumstance of the loss of an important game by what they considered to be an umpire's unfair decision?

The answer, I believe, is neither. Rather, the dominance of the value is an inverse function of the amount of tension. Even before the value is set aside, it is weakened as tension rises. The breaking point is but one position on the range of the function.

The United States is generally believed to be a society with respect for law and order. Nevertheless, in recent years large segments of it have engaged in violence. Even in the thirties, there was rioting during

[10] Lucian W. Pye, *Politics, Personality, and Nation-Building: Burma's Search for Identity* (New Haven: Yale University Press, 1963), p. 44.

severe unemployment, and throughout our history there have been outbreaks of violence in labor disputes. More recently, racial conflicts have erupted, ghettos have been burned, university buildings have been occupied. One leader of the black-power movement overstated the case by declaring that "violence is as American as apple pie."

Clearly, the shift from coercion to consensus is only gradual and is not complete even in the most developed countries. It must be studied institution by institution, as surrogate for value by value, and social sector by social sector. Much is yet to be learned about the social relations of economic development.

The Effectiveness of Institutions

The core problem of the model lies in the measurement of institutional effectiveness. We ignore the identification and measure of values because institutions serve as their surrogates. But we cannot escape measuring the capacity of institutions to resolve the conflicts of growth.

In Chapter 1 we suggested three criteria of institutional effectiveness: identification, rules, and consensus. High ratings on all three would, we proposed in Chapter 2, testify to an institution's capacity to identify the physical as opposed to the apparent solution line and to instil confidence that contractual obligations would be met. We proposed the "perfect market" as an example from economics, and we suggested that the concept of market perfection might be extended (with some revisions) to other types of conflict arising out of growth.

We therefore become committed to a "conflict" approach to decision-making. We hypothesize that if there is consensus on economic growth as a dominant goal, then institutions with high ratings on the three criteria will lead to more effective decisions, or conflict resolutions, for the achievement of growth.

Our three criteria depart from the definition of efficiency, which is the capacity to maximize output with a given set of inputs. This definition does not fit the case of takeoff countries where consensus on growth is only now forming. Unless the goal (output) of an institution is well defined, it is impossible to tell whether it is using its inputs wisely to maximize it. Businesses might produce economic output inefficiently but be very efficient in producing nepotism. We need a concept of ineffectiveness, as opposed to inefficiency, that includes *both* vagueness on goals and poor allocation of resources to achieve them. Since vagueness on goals cannot be measured, we assume that it is reflected in the surrogate criteria: the inability of participants in an institution to define their conflicts or the rules by which they should be resolved and lack of consensus on institutional structure.

To illustrate how vagueness in goals may affect our concept of institutional effectiveness let us take two hypothetical development banks, in the same or different countries. Both issue bonds on the private money market and lend the proceeds for development projects. Bank A, we will suppose, sets minimum standards of project quality, estimates the volume of projects that meet those standards, and issues the necessary bonds at the going interest rate. Bank B, on the other hand, issues as many bonds as it can at the going rate, then lends the entire proceeds for whatever projects it can find, employing the highest standards of evaluation consistent with the money available. The greater the amount, the lower the quality of the marginal project selected. Under most circumstances, bank B will have a greater volume of lending, while bank A will have a higher average quality of projects.

Only bank A's ordering of its goals, however, is legitimate in the private bond market, since bondholders insist on minimum project standards for their own security. For bank B to enter that market, it must insist that its goals are ordered in the same way as A; it cannot state its priorities overtly. As a result, the staff of bank B receives conflicting instructions. Written orders emphasize project quality, but pressures from management conduce to greater quantity.

As a result, the staff of bank B is likely to be confused and to make inconsistent decisions. For example, while bank A might always reject a loan to an industrial applicant lacking a cost-accounting system of minimum specifications, bank B might sometimes reject it and sometimes approve it. New members of B's technical staff might at first base recommendations on the written policy-guides and not know why management reverses them. Some may suspect more quickly than others. Then they may adapt their own standards to the reality of management decisions in varying degrees according to individual personalities.

How can the differences between bank *A* and bank *B*, or between *any* two institutions, be uncovered through a quantification of institutional effectiveness? The identification and the rules criteria can be measured through tests developed by psychologist Kenneth Hammond in his studies of quasi-rational thought.[11] The consensus criterion requires a different technique, which will be explained later in this chapter. To demonstrate how the criteria are measured, we have simulated an exercise based on a hypothetical development bank in a hypothetical less developed country, whose staff must reach a decision on whether to award a loan or not. We will estimate a rating, from zero to 1.000, of the institutional effectiveness of the bank's loan committee, which is charged with making the decision.

Normally, such a loan committee would consist, besides the loan officer (chairman), of those technicians—such as an engineer, an economist, a financial analyst, and an administration specialist—who have studied the technical criteria of the proposed loan project. Any pair of these may have different perceptions of the project; consequently there is a potential conflict between each pair. To simplify, we will assume there to be only two members of the committee: an engineer and an economist, whom we hereafter refer to as "the contestants."

THE IDENTIFICATION CRITERION

Let us presume the contestants are in conflict on whether to award a loan, and we wish to identify the conflict. The statement that "the engineer says 'yes' and the economist says 'no'" tells us little. Only if we list and quantify the reasons for each one's opinion can we determine in what respects they differ, whether it is by much or by little, and what might be required for each one to bring the other round to his point of view.

Each, no doubt, will state the cues prompting his decision. The economist may say the project is not profitable enough, while the engineer may counter that it would introduce needed skills into an underdeveloped region. From this we infer that the economist stresses

[11] Kenneth R. Hammond and Berndt Brehman, "Quasi-Rationality and Distrust: Implications for International Conflict," in L. Rappoport and D. Simmons, eds., *Human Judgment and Social Interaction* (New York, N.Y.: Holt, Rinehart, & Winston Press).

profitability and the engineer the introduction of skills. We have identified part of the conflict. But as yet we have no measure of how
profitable the economist thinks a project must be to merit approval or
how many skills and what kinds the engineer believes should be introduced. Nor do we know how each evaluates the influencing cues of
the other. Would a reshaping of the project to make it more profitable
by sacrificing the introduction of some skill render it acceptable to
both? If so, what are their trade-off functions?

Not only can we not readily answer all these questions, but—Hammond argues—the contestants may themselves not be aware of all their
cues. Like most people, they are *quasi*-rational. The engineer may be
awed by the political power of the loan applicant, while the economist
may be influenced by a chance comment that the bank's president does
not "like the looks" of the loan.

Somehow, the conflict investigator must select all possible cues that
might influence the decision of each of the contestants. There is no
unimpeachable method of doing this, but probably the most comprehensive is to begin by asking them directly; then to query others
familiar with the institution; and thirdly, to add to the list any that the
investigator himself may deem possible. There is no limit to the number of cues that might be listed in this manner.

To simplify our simulation, we have assumed that there are only five
such cues. We have given them brief names to enable the computer to
understand them.

	Cue	*Computer name*
1.	The administrative capacity of the loan applicant	ADMIN
2.	The profitability of the proposed loan project	PROFIT
3.	The employment effect of the proposed loan project	EMPLOY
4.	The conformity of the proposed project to the national development plan	PLAN
5.	The degree of modernity of technology in the proposed loan project	MODERN

We assume that each cue can be measured on a common scale.
ADMIN might be based on the existence or nonexistence of specific
administrative procedures, such as cost accounting and budgeting, or

on the education and experience of the loan applicant's management. Points would be awarded for specific factors strengthening (and negative points for factors weakening) ADMIN. PROFIT would depend on the projected rate of profit for the loan project over time. EMPLOY would be based on the number of persons that the project would employ, perhaps expressed as a percentage of need in the region. PLAN presupposes the existence of a national plan with priorities and depends on how high a priority would be filled by the proposed project. MODERN would depend on whether the technology were the latest (i.e., that in current use in the most developed countries) or whether it corresponded to what was current in some bygone year (the earlier the year, the lower the rating). All ratings would then be cast on a scale of zero to twenty.

Our objective now shifts. Instead of examining a particular conflict over a particular loan proposal, we examine many hypothetical loan proposals with different combinations of ratings for the different cues. Instead of asking the contestants whether they would approve or disapprove each of these loans, we ask them to rate the loans on their probability of success (success being subjectively defined by the contestant). We want to know how *close* to approval a contestant would come, and we presume that "probability of success" is a good indicator.

The economist and the engineer, each in the absence of the other, inspect a number of trial charts. For simplicity (and to save computer time), we limited ourselves to ten such trials in the present simulation, though a real test would probably require more (say, twenty-five or fifty) in order to have an adequate sample. Each chart is similar to the one shown on Table 3-1.

The ten charts used in the present simulation are recapitulated on Table 3-2. Each contestant was asked to state his estimate of the probability of success of *any* loan with characteristics shown on each chart, on a scale from zero to ten. After each entered his own judgment, he took the test again, this time predicting the judgment of the other on each of the ten loans projected. All these judgments, as simulated in the present exercise, are entered in Table 3-3.

In this exercise it was assumed that the economist and the engineer were agreed on the values of the cues: in Trial 1, for example, each was agreed that cue no. 1 (ADMIN) measured 12, cue no. 2 (PROFIT) measured 19, and so on. If they were not agreed on these, then there

TABLE 3-1

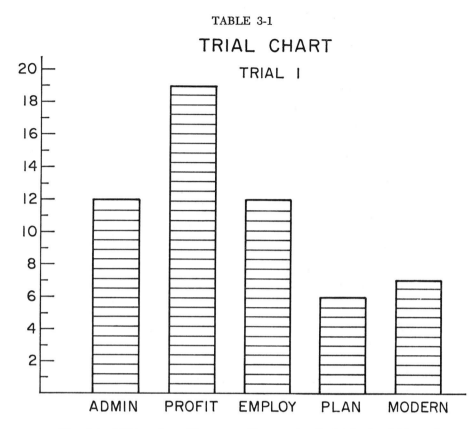

TRIAL CHART
TRIAL I

would exist additional conflicts, on a "lower tier," which should be subject to similar testing. For example, what are the cues by which each determines his rating of ADMIN, of PROFIT, and the others? For simplicity, we have ignored these "lower-tier" conflicts.

Four sets of judgments are shown in Table 3-3, and our next task is to determine the dependence of each judgment on the various cues. The relationships may be linear or nonlinear. For example, the economist will depend linearly on PROFIT if he believes that the probability of success of a loan increases in exact proportion to the increase in profitability. If, on the other hand, he believes the probability of success increases with employment up to a certain point and declines thereafter, his dependence on EMPLOY would be nonlinear. In the present simulation, we have assumed linear relationships throughout. With a little more complicated mathematics, it would be possible to

71

TABLE 3-2

TRIAL CHARTS

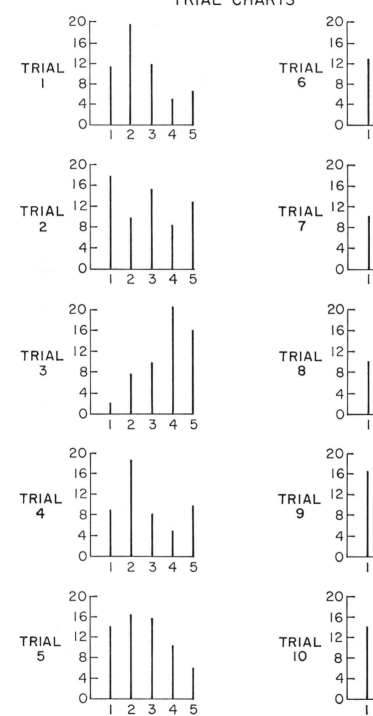

TABLE 3-3

RATINGS GIVEN FOR EACH TRIAL:
PROBABILITY LOAN WILL SUCCEED

Trial No.	1	2	3	4	5	6	7	8	9	10
Economist's judgment	8	7	4	6	8	3	9	4	6	5
Engineer's prediction of economist	7	7	2	6	8	3	7	4	7	4
Engineer's judgment	5	4	7	6	6	3	10	6	7	2
Economist's prediction of engineer	3	7	8	5	3	10	9	6	3	2

determine a nonlinear relationship in any case where it should turn out to have a better fit.

The four sets of relationships between the values of the cues and the probability of success are shown in Table 3-4: one each for economist and engineer and one for each one's prediction of the judgment of the other. The direct judgments of economist and engineer are then recast into Table 3-5, where the length of the solid line for each cue represents the degree to which each contestant relied on that cue for his judgment.

The *degree of conflict* is now measured at 0.465, which is the coefficient of correlation between the values for the ten trials as judged by the economist and those as judged by the engineer. This coefficient depends both on the consistency (R^2) of each contestant's choices (i.e., his ability to rate similar cards similarly though he sees them at different times) and on the coincidence of judgments by economist and engineer. If both contestants were fully consistent in their judgments ($R^2 = 100$) and the width of the bars on Table 3-5 were the same for each contestant, the correlation would be 1.000. It seems reasonable to combine consistency and ability to predict the other into a single measure, since deficiencies in either would aggravate the conflict.

The intensity of feeling of each contestant might be of additional interest. For example, the economist might give up easily because he did not care, whereas the engineer would not (or vice versa). The degree of conflict intensity would then depend on both the degree of the conflict (0.465) and the intensities of feelings of the contestants. Such a measure of conflict intensity might be important to further

TABLE 3-4

RATINGS AND COEFFICIENTS OF DETERMINATION (r AND R²)

PROBABILITY LOAN WILL SUCCEED

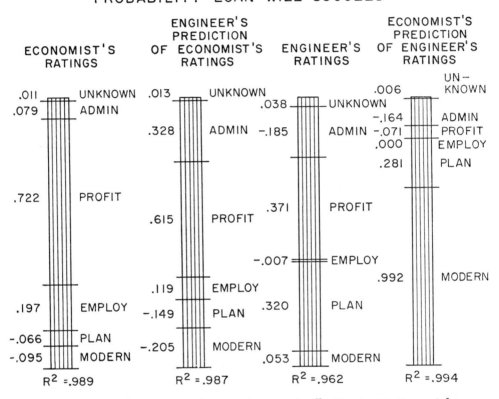

ECONOMIST'S RATINGS	ENGINEER'S PREDICTION OF ECONOMIST'S RATINGS	ENGINEER'S RATINGS	ECONOMIST'S PREDICTION OF ENGINEER'S RATINGS

applications of institution theory, since an ineffective institution might handle a low-intensity conflict tolerably well but be inadequate if the intensity increased. At present, however, we are concerned only with how effective an institution is and not with the degree of effectiveness required for conflicts of different intensities.

Now, the index of institutional effectiveness depends not on how well *we* identify the conflict, but on how well the contestants do. To solve this, we might ask each contestant separately to estimate the values that he would expect for his own ratings in Table 3-4. This would not be very useful, however, because most contestants would not know what a correlation coefficient was. (Of course, the techni-

TABLE 3-5

STATEMENT OF CONFLICT
PROBABILITY LOAN WILL SUCCEED

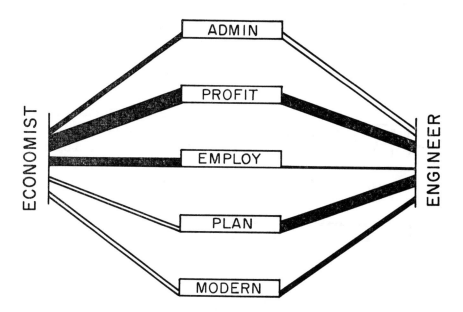

cians of a development bank might know.) Furthermore, the capacity of each contestant to know his own weights does not seem to be a useful index of effectiveness; many people operate very effectively in a quasi-rational way. What is important is the ability of each contestant to predict the other's reactions. We would say that if each can do this well, then the institution has identified the conflict well.

We observe (Table 3-4) that the economist's coefficient of correlation with respect to PROFIT is 0.722, and this is the only cue where the correlation is significant. He paid some attention to employment (0.197) but this could have occurred randomly. The other cues show no significant correlation.

Now, what is the engineer's capacity to predict the economist's decision? He need not state explicitly the cues he believes the economist depends on, because he may not know. But we know (Table 3-4) that the engineer believed the economist weighted profitability heavily (0.615), though not quite so heavily as he actually did (0.722). The engineer also believed the economist paid some attention to the loan applicant's administrative capacities (0.328).

The engineer has predicted the economist's responses quite well indeed, but the economist was a poor predictor of the engineer. He believed that the engineer based his judgment entirely on how modern was the technology to be employed by the borrower (0.992). (This may be his stereotype of all engineers.) But the engineer in fact did no such thing. He divided his weights almost evenly between the profitability of the project (0.371) and its conformity to the national plan (0.320). He showed a negative correspondence to administration (the poorer the administration, the better the loan prospects); this not only does not make sense but it is statistically insignificant (−0.185).

The perception of the conflict is demonstrated on Table 3-6. Here the engineer's superior capacity to predict the economist is shown in the correspondence of bars in the diagram and in his high coefficient of correlation (0.886), while the economist's poor capacity to predict the engineer comes out in the disparity of the bars as well as in the low coefficient (0.248). Once again, the correlation coefficient depends not only on the correspondence of the bars in Table 3-6, but on the consistency of judgments by the two contestants.

A sample of one conflict between two persons is not a good measure of institutional effectiveness. The economist's low ability to predict the engineer might be associated with his own personality and not the effectiveness of the institution. Likewise, the engineer's high ability might be a personal idiosyncrasy not attributable to the institution. If many samples are taken involving many contestants, however, then it may be supposed that the effects of personality will balance out randomly, and the remaining achievement will be due to institutional effectiveness.

The present exercise is only a demonstration of how the estimate of institutional effectiveness is calculated, so we ignore the smallness of the sample. The rating of the loan committee is 0.567 by the identification criterion, out of a possible 1.000, or the mean of the correlation coefficients of the contestants in predicting each other's responses.

THE RULES CRITERION

We now turn to the contestants' perception of the rules by which the conflict will be resolved. These are not necessarily formal rules

TABLE 3-6

PERCEPTION OF CONFLICT
PROBABILITY LOAN WILL SUCCEED

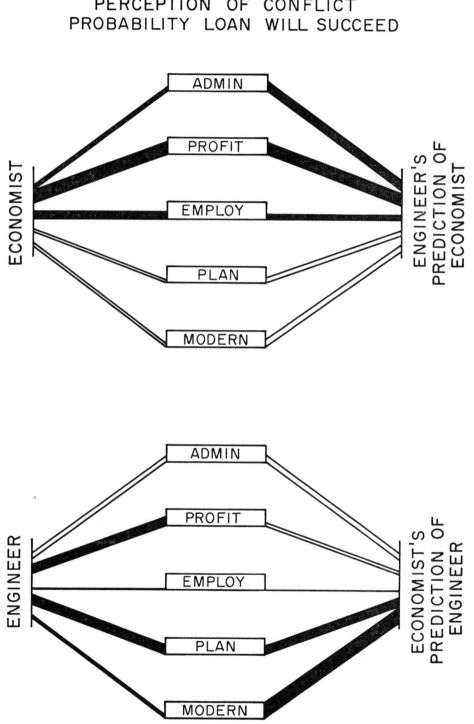

(though they might include such); they cover also the informal procedures and pressures that "everybody knows" occur. In fact, however, there may be wide differences of opinion about what "everybody knows."

In the present simulation exercise, we used five cues, as follows:

	Cue	*Computer name*
1.	The technical characteristics of the project	TECH
2.	The political power of the loan applicant	POLIT
3.	The prestige of the protagonists on the loan committee	PREST
4.	The desire of the bank president to see the loan approved	BANPR
5.	The conformity of the loan to the bank's lending strategy	STRAT

Once again, the cues are selected by questioning the contestants and other knowledgeable persons and adding any cues that the investigator may believe the contestants rely on latently.

TECH consists of application of the five cues that were used in the identification criterion, however they may be weighted. Thus, to what extent does the loan committee *really* pay attention to the technical merits of the project? Do they really base their decision on the strength of these qualities (if you think so, rate this cue high), or is the technical debate just a farce (if you think so, rate this cue low)? POLIT is a measure of the loan applicant's political power, which might be based on the number of political positions he holds or some subjective judgment (on which the contestants would agree) of his influence upon the national power groups. PREST refers to the prestige of those members of the loan committee who favor the loan. Are they able to persuade the other members on the basis of their prestige alone? Of course, there may be some correlation between PREST and TECH if committee members gain their prestige through high technical competence. But there may also be correlation between PREST and BANPR if they gain it through their close affiliation with high personalities in the bank.

BANPR depends on some subjective estimate of how intensely the bank president (or other high official, if you prefer) wants to see the loan approved. If you think the president has much voice, rate this one high, and vice versa. STRAT presumes that the bank has previously adopted some lending strategy; for example, this year it will stress agriculture because that is the nation's most backward sector. Contestants whose evaluations correlate high with STRAT would believe the bank takes its strategy seriously; conversely, a low correlation would mean the bank ignores its strategy and decisions are made on other grounds.

The cues for the rules criterion might be the same or different from those for the identification criterion. For example, the five technical cues used for conflict identification might be adopted in the investigation on rules and new ones added if necessary. In the identification test each contestant votes on how he *wants* the decision to be made, and in the rules test he votes on how he thinks it *will* be made, willy-nilly.

To save computer time, in the present test the same trial charts (Table 3-2) were used for the rules as for the identification test; the new cues were simply substituted for the old. Results are shown on Table 3-7.

TABLE 3-7

RATINGS GIVEN FOR EACH TRIAL;
PROBABILITY LOAN WILL BE APPROVED

Trial No.	1	2	3	4	5	6	7	8	9	10
Economist's judgment	6	8	5	3	8	6	8	5	7	9
Engineer's judgment	6	4	7	6	5	2	10	6	8	4

Table 3-8 states the rules disagreement. The black bars on this table demonstrate that the economist and the engineer demonstrated totally different ideas about how their original conflict would be resolved. Their correlation coefficient was practically zero (-0.054). The economist believed the decision would be based mainly on the prestige of the protagonist on the committee (0.911 on Table 3-9), though he gave some credibility to the technical characteristics (0.380). The engineer believed the decision would be made by outside pressure, relying mainly on POLIT (0.357) and BANPR (0.231).

In the rules criterion, it is not necessary to ask for the engineer's prediction of the economist's ratings, and vice versa. We are interested

TABLE 3-8

STATEMENT OF CONFLICT
PROBABILITY LOAN WILL BE APPROVED

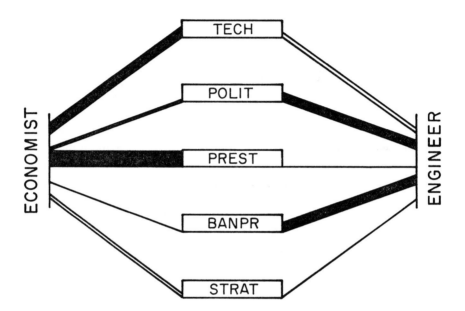

only in the *conflict* over the rules, not in the ability of each contestant to predict the other's perception. In the present case, the coefficient of correlation between the engineer's judgment of the rules and the economist's judgment (Table 3-8) turned out to be —0.054. Since a negative correlation is absurd, it must be attributed to error. Any quantity below zero will be counted as zero. In the present simulation, the economist and engineer had been instructed in advance to rely on different cues, and, as expected, the institution received a low rating by the rules criterion.

THE CONSENSUS CRITERION

The consensus criterion measures the degree of agreement *among all persons with an interest in the resolution of the conflict* that the institution is the appropriate one to handle it, compared with other hypothetical institutions (including modifications) perceived as possi-

TABLE 3-9

RATINGS AND COEFFICIENTS OF DETERMINATION (r AND R²)

PROBABILITY LOAN WILL BE APPROVED

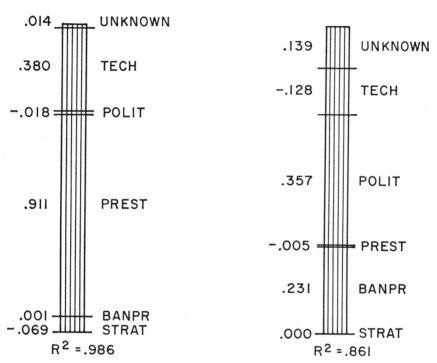

ble. All interested parties are included in the test because the contestants are often really waging the conflict on behalf of others. Sometimes interested groups are denied access to institutions, and this denial may decrease the consensus rating. Witness the race conflict in the United States!

In the present case, the interested parties would include not only the contestants (economist and engineer) but also the bank management, other technicians contributing information, the loan applicant, his employees, potential customers of the loan applicant, and so on.

At once we question how the investigator would set his bounds. It would seem that interested groups could be identified in the case of most conflicts, but that their degree of interest would vary. For example, potential customers of the loan applicant might find it to their advantage that the loan be granted, but they could always buy the product elsewhere if it were not. They are only mildly interested. The loan applicant, on the other hand, might have a great interest; indeed, the loan might be necessary for his economic survival. The contestants themselves would consider their interest high, since their bread and butter depends on effective resolution of these conflicts and their professional prestige is involved.

For want of a better means, it would appear reasonable for the investigator to draw up samples of interested groups and to ask the following two questions, which would be rewritten according to the circumstances of the particular conflict.

1. Do you believe that the institution [in this case, the loan committee] as it is currently constituted is a desirable means of resolving the conflict, as compared with other possible institutional organizations that you can think of? Check one.

(a) It is highly desirable. (rating 1.000)

(b) It is generally desirable, though there are ways in which it could be improved. (rating 0.750)

(c) I am indifferent whether it or another kind of institution is selected. (rating 0.500)

(d) It is not a desirable institution and ought to be greatly improved or replaced. (rating 0.250)

(e) It is definitely not desirable and ought to be abolished; any other institution would be better. (rating 0.000)

2. How strongly do you feel about the way you have answered question no. 1? Check one.

(a) Very strongly; one of my highest values (my life, my family, my (rating 1.000)

income, my job, etc.) depends
on it.

(b) Strongly. I would personally   (rating 0.750)
suffer if the institution is
not retained, modified, or
replaced as I have indicated.

(c) Moderately. No personal suffering   (rating 0.500)
is involved, but I do have an
intellectual opinion.

(d) Weakly. It doesn't make a great   (rating 0.250)
deal of difference.

(e) Not at all. I just answered the   (rating 0.000)
question because it was asked.

The consensus rating by each individual would be his answer to question no. 1 only. The consensus rating for the institution would be the mean of the ratings of individuals sampled, each one weighted according to his answer to question no. 2. Thus a respondent who checked (a) for question no. 2 would have his answer to question no. 1 entered at full weight. But a respondent's answer to question no. 1 would not be considered at all if he checked (e) for question no. 2.

Let us assume—arbitrarily—that the consensus rating for the loan committee in our hypothetical bank turns out to be 0.712.

AN OVERALL RATING FOR EFFECTIVENESS

Is it reasonable to arrive at an overall rating of effectiveness for any institution? Possibly not. It might be that three separate ratings would serve better in all analyses of institutional effectiveness. In Chapter 7, where we develop the concept of aggregate institutional effectiveness on a national scale and suggest that AIE may correlate with gross national product under certain conditions, it may be that three separate measures of AIE are called for. Only empirical investigations will tell us whether the preference is for a single measure or multiple measures.

There is, however, a statistical simplicity in one measure that is not present in three. If it can be demonstrated that, say, the mean of the three effectiveness ratings is just as reliable an indicator of the institutional contribution to economic growth as the three are separately, it would be useful to adopt it. In Chapters 4 and 5 we will develop the concept of demand for and supply of institutional effectiveness. If the capacity of an institution to identify and resolve a conflict appears upon investigation to be a single quantity in the minds of demanders and suppliers, then a single measure should be developed.

At the moment, we leave the question moot. We also leave moot the question of whether an arithmetic mean or a geometric mean would be superior. If the effectiveness of an institution is deemed nil when *any one* of the three criteria rates zero, then the geometric mean would be the better measure. Probably, however, a high rating in each of two criteria would somehow offset a low rating in a third, and in this case the arithmetic mean would be preferred.

If the arithmetic mean is adopted, then the loan committee we have been investigating would have an overall effectivensss rating of 0.426 out of a possible 1.000, based on the following individual ratings:

Identification criterion	0.567
Rules criterion	0.000
Consensus criterion	0.712

The purpose of this exercise has been to demonstrate that the concept of institutional effectiveness exists and is quantifiable. Much refining needs yet to be done in order to answer such questions as the following. Should all conflicts of a given institution be weighted equally, or should higher-tier and lower-tier conflicts be treated separately? Do lower-tier conflicts always reduce themselves, after several tiers, to elements on which contestants are agreed (because the facts stand out), or do they lead to ever-widening pyramids of disagreement? Should there be one measure or three of institutional effectiveness, or even more? Such questions will best be answered after empirical studies have been made.

In later chapters we develop a theory of institutions and consider what kinds of institutions a newly developing country is likely to select to resolve the conflicts of economic growth. This theory depends on the existence of a concept of institutional effectiveness. For all the refining yet to be done, I nevertheless believe that the concept as it is developed here is adequate for the construction of this theory.

In a study of consensus and ideology in American politics, Mc-Closky concluded that consensus on the "fundamentals," which de Tocqueville believed was the foundation of American democracy, in fact exists only among the political elite and is not shared by the bulk of the people.[12] He divided his subjects into political influentials ($n = 3020$) and general electorate ($n = 1484$) and asked them such questions as the following (with percentage of affirmative answers shown):

	Political influentials	*General electorate*
A man ought not to be allowed to speak if he does not know what he is talking about.	17.3	36.7
In dealing with dangerous enemies like the Communists, we cannot afford to depend on the courts, the laws, and their slow and unreliable methods.	7.4	25.5

As in the two instances shown, the results indicated that political influentials paid more heed to the traditional axioms of American democracy than did the general electorate.

I have, however, two criticisms of the McClosky method. The first is that he has surmised behavior in particular circumstances from the answers to general questions. People—especially politicians—do not always behave according to the values that they mouth. It would be more Freudian to subject them to Hammond policy tests or thematic apperception tests and to deduce their beliefs from their decisions or their fantasies. The second, which involves a disagreement on concept, is that McClosky weighted all respondents equally. In the measurement of consensus I would not count a respondent who felt little personal interest in the subject-matter investigated. This is the object of my question no. 2, which determines weights. McClosky himself ex-

---

[12] Herbert McClosky, "Consensus and Ideology in American Politics," *American Political Science Review* (June 1964), pp. 361-82.

plained the differences in opinion between political influentials and the general electorate as stemming from differences in their "political activity, *involvement*, and articulateness."[13] Of course, a person may have vicarious involvement in that a situation *might* happen to him. In that case, however, the respondent and not the investigator must stipulate the degree to which this is felt. Had McClosky agreed with these two points, he might have achieved different results.

Institutional Effectiveness in Business Administration

We have characterized an institution as a conflict-resolving system whose effectiveness is measured by its capacity to identify conflicts, enunciate and enforce rules, and command consensus on the part of all potential users. An institution is more likely to be effective if the communality of goals of those users leads to constructive conflicts among them. In this section we consider systems of administration in these terms, making some comparisons between takeoff and post-takeoff societies.

BACKGROUND ON ADMINISTRATION THEORY

Since we are invading the ground of administration theory, which is already well traveled by sociologists and political scientists, it is well to summarize the state of the field. For this summary we draw on Beuchner, who has distinguished four approaches to administration: the traditional, the behavioral, the decision-making, and the ecological.[14] Though sequential in their evolution, he argues that all four have been blended into modern concepts of the polymorphic character of administration. Though Beuchner's analysis is in terms of public administration, nevertheless the concepts are equally applicable to business, public or private.

The traditional approach emphasizes organizational form and scientific management. The form is read in the organization chart. Ordinarily, this will be a pyramid, with executives at the top and those at different levels of responsibility below. Information flows upward from the base toward the apex, while instructions flow downward. At each level the appropriate officer must decide whether the information

---

[13] *Ibid.,* p. 374. Italics added.

[14] John C. Beuchner, *Public Administration* (Belmont, Calif., Dickenson Publishing Co., 1968), pp. 4-20.

he has received constitutes a mandate for action or whether he should pass it up to the next layer for decision, perhaps with a recommendation. He maintains his own staff, specialists who analyze the data for reasonability, check that the proper information is in fact forthcoming, and assist in decision-making. Thus there are line and staff functions. Only crucial information reaches the top, where only crucial decisions are made. All along the way, less crucial information is stopped and analyzed and decisions are made. Of course, the executive must remain in charge of everything. He may have legitimate "spies" on his staff, whose purpose is to communicate with lower levels to see that all is well. They consist of the controller, efficiency experts, management consultants, and the like. In socialist states, there will be officers from the central plan to visit participating enterprises. Some (controllers) operate continuously, others (management consultants and plan officials) only from time to time.

The scientific-management approach has been concerned with the question of whether there is one way of organizing an enterprise and performing the functions within it that is universally optimum, so that efficiency is automatically maximized when that form is adopted. Frederick Taylor's comparative measurements of the activity of factory workers in the early 1900s were aimed at finding that "one best way." Critics of the traditional emphasis and the scientific-management approach have argued that, despite intersystem similarities the behavioral and environmental elements affecting different administration systems are nevertheless so diverse that every system is unique; hence universal optima cannot be found.

The behavioral emphasis focuses on the effect of these diverse characteristics on human behavior. To behavioralists, "administration is conceived as a study embracing many disciplines, including psychology, social psychology, anthropology, and other sciences."[15]

The behavioralists did not themselves emphasize efficiency. Nevertheless, their view of administrative organization as a social system helps us to recognize efficiency (or lack of it) as an element interacting with others within the system, such as definable cultural attributes of employees. If these differ, as for example between two countries or between two areas within a country (e.g., ghetto and suburb), then

[15] *Ibid.*, p. 12.

differing organizational forms may be called forth to maximize institutional efficiency in each case.

The decision-making emphasis "views the organization as a unit consisting of many decisional situations in which the administrator is the decision-maker."[16] Now, one test of efficiency in any enterprise is that of whether the right decisions are made at the right places. Here we must know whether the officer in charge of each level has the right number of staff with the proper amount of training and perception. If the goal of the enterprise is stated in specific economic terms (e.g., maximum profit, maximum output subject to certain constraints, etc.), then ordinarily maximum efficiency will require that each employee be loyal to the office of his superior, not to his superior as an individual.

The ecological approach to administration stresses the role of the environment in determining organizational form and process. The differing pressures of government, businessmen, laborers, landowners, the military, and other groups upon administration systems, both public and private, and their differing expectations of their purposes and functions, will lead to quite different organizational structures and operational procedures to maximize efficiency in takeoff as compared to post-takeoff countries.

Efficiency experts from post-takeoff countries have often criticized the organization charts and operational policies in takeoff countries for not being designed or implemented to bring about maximum output (revenue) at minimum cost. Such criticisms should distinguish among three potential causes. First, the ecological pressures upon the administrative systems in take-off countries may be such that the same combinations of inputs that the efficiency experts are accustomed to at home would not lead to the same outputs. Secondly, the dominant goal of the enterprise may be something other than maximum output at minimum cost. Thirdly, there may be no consensus on the dominant goal at all. The last case, which is not conducive to administrative reform until goals are clarified, is generally the characteristic of underdevelopment.

Our own concept of institutional effectiveness, as opposed to efficiency, comes closer to Buechner's decision-making approach than to the other three. It differs from the traditional approach to efficiency

16 *Ibid.*, p. 15.

in that it abstracts from goals. Only when a goal is defined is it possible to measure efficiency in the traditional way. But our concept is intended to synthesize the behavioral and ecological with the decision-making approach. With respect to behavior, we recognize that a multiplicity of goals (e.g., pleasant working conditions and traditional efficiency) may conflict. The conflict will be resolved more profitably for each contestant if they possess a higher consensus ("constructive conflict"). With respect to ecology, we recognize ways in which extra-system pressures obscure both conflict identification and rules, especially when such pressures have only varying degrees of social legitimacy.

In the subsections immediately following, certain observations are made of business administration systems in the United States, in the socialist countries, and in Latin America. At the conclusion of these subsections, the contrasts will be discussed in terms of the three criteria of institutional effectiveness.

BUSINESS ENTERPRISE IN THE UNITED STATES

A corporation is a legal person. It has a name in which to do business, and the right to own and convey property, contract debts, sue and be sued. What has only recently come to be recognized in the United States is that the corporation is far more than a legal person. It is a social person as well, with the capacity to love and be loved, to give and receive loyalty, to have ideas independent of its stockholders and management, to communicate with other persons, both flesh-and-blood and corporate, to propose and influence legislation and all manner of less formal, interpersonal relationships. It makes decisions that would be different from those made (to resolve the same conflicts) by any of the natural persons who participate in the process. It is governed by and contributes to society's behavioral code, and it has—shall we admit it?—a set of values. Many of these facts have been brought out in Whyte's *The Organization Man*.[17] Galbraith has gone so far as to state that the goals of American society are not really to produce the goods and services that consumers want, but to preserve and foster the industrial corporation.[18]

[17] William Hollingsworth Whyte, *The Organization Man* (Garden City, N.Y., Doubleday & Co., 1956).

[18] J. K. Galbraith, *The Industrial Society* (Boston, Mass., Houghton Mifflin Co., 1967).

It is characteristic of the insights of both Whyte and Galbraith that they discern the excesses of America's most sacred cows; it is characteristic of their temperament that they enjoy attacking them. Nongovernmental decision-making and supremacy of the private sector are dominant values in the United States. Whatever their excesses now that our economy has taken off, they nevertheless have served well in institutionalizing a set of rules for conflict resolution.

The personality of the American corporation is epitomized by the loyalty it demands and evokes. The loyal employee works for the good of the corporation. He will not divulge its secrets (though he may be employed to spy on another corporation), and he will not give comfort or aid to a competitor. Even if the competitor is a relative or close friend since childhood who demands and receives loyalty in other ways, nevertheless the two types of loyalty are clearly distinguished. There is one kind of loyalty to the corporation, another to the friend.

The loyal employee also does not use corporate secrets or "inside" knowledge to his own personal gain. Our society recognizes that this value, like taxpaying, does not always evoke voluntary, individual compliance, and it is therefore enforced through legal restraints on which there is social consensus. If the employee is a researcher, the results of his investigation belong to the corporation. At the same time, the corporation owes him appropriate facilities. If the employee knows of a professional colleague needed by the corporation, it is his duty to inform the officials and to assist in the recruitment.

The corporation often influences and restricts the employee's personal life: the kinds of friends he has, the type of entertaining he does, the neighborhood he lives in, how much he spends for his home, what kind of car he drives, and the like. The employee, especially if he is an executive, carries the corporation's "image," and he must do so according to carefully designed standards.

But corporate loyalty is not identical to personal loyalty. The employee may resign and move to another corporation. If he does, the set of mutual obligations with the first continues until the moment of his departure; then it is instantly transferred to the second. Such clean-cut surgery must be surprising to persons in other social systems where the same rules have not evolved. For corporate loyalty bears so many similarities to personal that it may appear "shocking" that it should be switched so readily and so "properly" from one object to another.

Indeed, our standards of loyalty will appear peculiar to many outside our culture. How, then, did such a strange system evolve? The answer is reached by asking what would happen if corporate loyalty were not instantly transferable. Corporate loyalty is essential for the most effective use of factors of production; its shift from one institution to another is essential to factor mobility.

CONTRASTS WITH SOCIALIST SOCIETIES

While transferable corporate loyalty is appropriate to American society, it is not readily inducible in others. The prospect of valuing the corporation as a person may demean the dignity of real persons. Since transferable corporate loyalty is in a sense "unnatural," it requires years to be internalized, and latecomers to industrialization are impatient.

The tendency of newly developing countries toward socialism may be partly explained by this fact. Loyalty to the state is recognized as a desired value in any new country and is easily taught. If it is extended to include social ownership of the means of production, it can serve those two purposes which in the United States are served separately by national loyalty and by corporate loyalty.

Socialist states realizing such a set of values then fulfill the necessary conditions of economic growth. Loyalty to the state is the dominant value, providing the rules for both effective use of factors of production (as defined in the plan) and their mobility from enterprise to enterprise. Loyalty to the enterprise is not so necessary (although it has developed in Yugoslavia). Socialist states that have been less successful in economic growth, such as Albania and China (at least in the rural areas), have had difficulty in achieving consensus on the dominant-value set and consequently in defining a widely accepted set of conflict-resolving rules.

BUSINESS ENTERPRISE IN LATIN AMERICA[19]

Certain characteristics of business enterprise in Latin America, outlined below, tend to limit its institutional effectiveness.

[19] These observations on Latin America, and the implicit contrasts with business enterprise in more developed countries (socialist or capitalist) are drawn from my own visits in 1963-1964 to all Latin American countries (except Cuba), where I had extensive conversations with business men and government officials. They are also based on a study in 1960 of the industrial credit program of the

In the first place, the goals of productive enterprises are vague. In the United States, a strong mutuality is recognized between profit maximization and service to society. In Latin America, these are often felt to be in conflict, and it is unclear whether the enterprise should primarily serve the one or the other. According to some sanctions and values, it should do whatever is necessary to maximize profits. According to others, it should provide maximum employment, housing, commissaries, and other services to labor, as well as improve the distribution of national income. The rules vary from time to time and from place to place, and their enforcement may depend on the personalities of government and corporate executives.

In the second place, while organization charts exist in abundance on paper, their implementation is deficient. Lines of communication are sketchy, as are channels for transmitting instructions. Information received from friends is often more trusted than that received through formal organization channels.

With the depreciation of formal, depersonalized information, cost accounting is unacceptable to some of the largest corporations, especially those of the government. There is (to foreigners) a striking inconsistency between the advanced stage of accounting instruction in the area's universities and the failure to utilize learned procedures in business. Lack of knowledge of costs leads to the inability of local businesses to compete with foreign.

In the third place, except for family businesses, the producing enterprise usually has no personality. As an organization it does not evoke loyalty from its employees. There is little compunction about revealing the secrets of large, impersonal companies or about milking them to the point of bankruptcy. Government corporations are called on to solve social problems, overburdening themselves with excess employees. In family businesses, on the other hand, there is employee loyalty not to the enterprise but to the person of its owner. The infusion of this fact with the closeness of family ties conduces to strong

---

U.S. foreign-aid program in Bolivia, in connection with which I visited several businesses; on informal interchanges with over one hundred U.S. foreign-aid officers from 1958 to 1963; on visits to several private and government corporations in Mexico in 1963-1964; and a one-year study in 1967-1968 of loans undertaken by the Inter-American Development Bank. None of the above experiences constituted a carefully structured review of business practices, but I believe my sample is large enough for the observations to have some meaning.

reluctance on the part of owners to incorporate. The most obvious reason is the unwillingness to admit "strangers" (from outside the family) to the decision-making councils. But just as real is the unwillingness to surrender the enterprise to the indignities suffered by the impersonal, large corporation. The result, of course, is a sacrifice of the economies of scale.

In the fourth place, there is a *patrón* system of protector-dependent, conflicting with the orderly flow of information and instructions in the business enterprise. Often an employee's chief is his *patrón*, to whom he owes personal loyalty. If the *patrón* should move to another employment, either the employee also moves or he remains with unclear and divided loyalty. By contrast, the employee's loyalty in more developed countries will tend to be to the *office* of his chief, regardless of who the incumbent may be.

In the fifth place, there is a reluctance to accept clearly defined rules and regulations. The dichotomy between written work orders, policy guides, and administration-flow charts on the one hand, and procedures actually followed on the other, appears far greater than in the United States or Europe. Associated with this is the mañana philosophy, that tasks may be legitimately undertaken without one's knowing precisely how or when they will be completed. The inexactitude of timing, of course, interferes with the close scheduling of work programs.

The result is a stoppage in the flow of upward communication in business organizations. Chiefs do not take their staff into their confidence. Decisions based on hierarchical authority, to be accepted without question by inferiors (implementers), need not require the approval of technical, evaluating personnel. They may thus not be the decisions most apt to achieve the productive goals of the enterprises. Pye observed the same phenomenon in the Burmese government:[20]

> The urge to withhold confidence in subordinates permeates almost all hierarchical relationships within the present-day Burmese bureaucracy. Thus barriers are established to casual, relaxed, and informal relationships, creating a situation especially disturbing to men who initially learned that government service could and should offer warm, close, and exciting personal associa-

[20] Lucien W. Pye, *Nation-Building, op. cit.,* p. 228.

tions. Now all relationships seem to be cold and indifferent. There is an increased need to emphasize status considerations in order to insure one's security in the hierarchy.

The problem is not that the Latin American cultural characteristics have led to a different set of rules and regulations from the North American. Any rules must serve their environment, and it may be supposed prima facie that the Latin American and North American rules will differ. What is important is the unclarity of the rules and their propensity to shift from time to time and place to place within the same country.

For example, in many countries the payment of debt is in some circumstances a matter of shifting political power. The Ministry of Finance may not be able to demand tax payments from powerful domestic corporations, especially those owned by the government. Management presumably answerable to the president of the Republic may simply be too powerful to have to yield to the president's bidding. Sometimes guile, rather than power, is the key. An investment program may be undertaken for no other reason than to use up cash the government would otherwise discover and grab. On the other hand, the government may refuse to pay its bills to businesses, possibly because it does not have the money and possibly as leverage for concessions demanded in exchange. Another example is that of labor laws set aside, and illegal strikes suddenly declared legal if the union is momentarily powerful. A third example is the government that declares "illegal" the agreements made by a preceding government now in opposition or exile. Any twistings of laws or revision of contracts to accommodate special circumstances or to yield to those in positions of power render the rules of the game unclear. The sanctity of contract and supremacy of law, both relatively dominant values in the more developed countries, command a much narrower area of respect in Latin America.

THE CONTRAST

The contrast outlined above between Latin American administration systems and those of more developed countries, both socialist and capitalist, can be cast in terms of the three criteria for institutional effectiveness. Take, for example, the question of tax-paying mentioned in the preceding paragraph.

First, take the identification criterion. In the United States, the conflict over whether and how much a corporation will pay in taxes is relatively well defined by a set of institutions including the Congress, which proposes and passes tax laws; the executive branch, which administers them through the Internal Revenue Service; and the courts, which try offenders. The reasons for tax-paying are widely understood, the rates well publicized, and penalties known. In Latin America the degree of identification varies widely by country. In a few, the tax laws are highly developed. In others, the schedule passed by the legislature is only a basis for bargaining. There is no consensus on the reasons for tax-paying. The penalties for noncompliance vary widely and are not universally enforced. All these factors add up, in some countries, to a low rating by the identification criterion.

Secondly, there is the rules criterion. Corporations that negotiate their taxes in the United States do so on the basis of established procedures. Though it is not humanly possible for all Internal Revenue officials to come to identical opinions, nevertheless there is some effort to base decisions on precedent so that a taxpayer will not get different treatment depending on the negotiating officer. Once again, the rating under the rules criterion in Latin America will vary widely by country. In some, the political power of the company over the government may cause severe bending of rules; personal relationships between corporate and government officials influence decisions; and legal penalties may be set aside in favor of solutions that are negotiated or bought.

Thirdly, there is the consensus criterion. We have already considered the consensus on tax laws in the United States. It is not measured by the willingness with which people pay their taxes or individually cheat, but by their agreement on the procedures by which tax laws are passed and enforced. In many Latin American countries, the existence of large segments of the population that do not participate in governmental processes or that consider the government to be their enemy or illegally constituted would indicate a lower rating on the consensus criterion.

Other Systems

As surrogates for values, institutions transcend the realm of business administration. The three criteria of institutional effectiveness are intended to apply not only to businesses, banks, and the like, but to all social institutions. But the number of institutions in a social system is legion, and we cannot rate them all. Even if we could, we would be hard put to decide which carry more influence on economic growth than others. But we can hypothesize that effectiveness is contagious. Therefore, if some institutions rate high, others probably will also. An empirical study of economic growth and institutional effectiveness would be required to examine which institutions become effective first and the routes by which their effectiveness spreads to others. Such a study is beyond the scope of this book. By way of brief illustration, however, let us make some observations concerning the effectiveness of two social subsystems: family and friendship.

THE FAMILY

Social scientists have long recognized that economic growth brings with it a transformation from the extended to the nuclear family. Growth demands that factors of production respond quickly to opportunities, and the nuclear family is more mobile than the extended. It is reasonable that the degree of "nuclearity" of family is a function of economic growth and that its emergence reflects the dominance of growth over other, conflicting, goals more consonant with extended families.

Conflicts within the family relate principally to the obligations of one member to another. Both the conflicts themselves and the means of resolution may be relatively clear in both the extended and nuclear systems. It is in the takeoff or transitional stage from one to the other that they become obscure. What obligation does a family that wishes to move to another city feel toward an aged grandmother who wants to continue living in the ancestral home? Who is expected to be the wage earner in a family, which others is he expected to support, and in what amounts? Any empirical study based on the three criteria of institutional effectiveness would judge the family system for its capacity to identify these conflicts (do the members really know what the conflicts are, and can they discuss them freely?), to set clear rules for resolving them (does the father decide, or are decisions made in family council?), and to command consensus (does the grandmother accept that the welfare of the family is best promoted by the move, while she remains alone in the ancestral home?).

FRIENDSHIP

Friendship is another social subsystem molded by dominant goals. In white, middle-class United States, friendship is a function of activity and not of family ties many generations old or of school connections. One's friends are found in business, in professional activities, and in political and social organizations. In contrast to other ages and other places, white middle-class Americans have little need for the kind of friendship where ideas and aspirations are valued for no other reason than that they belong to one's friend. Rather, friendship is only as deep as is necessary to maintain the activity that brought it about. Many white, middle-class Americans do not know the names of their best friends' brothers. We make no moral judgment of this system of friendship but only comment that it embodies the mobility and flexibility required for maximum economic growth. Somewhere in our history, the opportunity cost of maintaining another system of friendship became too high.

Social scientists are agreed that friendship is selfish in that it serves the separate psychological needs of each partner. Each friend therefore has certain expectations of the other. In the family-related or school-connected model, friends tend to be more intimate in sharing personal thoughts and experiences than in the activity-related type that predominates in the United States.

Let us assume that economic growth transforms friendship from one kind of value into another. Most likely, not all friends will be equally affected. Some will want to end the traditional obligations and assume new ones earlier than others. The latter may have difficulty identifying what has happened, and there are no rules to resolve the conflict of expectations. Only as growth-sensitive groups pervade society will consensus on a new kind of friendship evolve, with new rules for identifying and resolving the conflicts between friends.

A deeper probe of the action-reaction impact of friendship on development would be a fascinating study, but it is beyond the scope of this book. It might, for example, determine the effects of friendship on development in ascriptive- and achievement-oriented societies, which types of friendship favor development, which hinder it, and why. This may be a factor not only in the formation of associations that con-

97

tribute to innovation but also in the way the associations affect persons in the innovative process.

Recent Conflict in the United States

In the conflicts over black power and university reform, the United States in recent years has displayed characteristics that have been attributed, in this book, to underdevelopment. The commonly heard phrase, "what do these people want, anyway?" symbolizes the inability to identify the conflicts. The burning ghettos, looting, and occupation of university buildings reflect lack of agreement on the rules of resolution.

On Saturday, April 21, 1969, one hundred armed black militants occupied a Cornell University building, protesting a decision to discipline five leaders of demonstrations demanding a black college within the university. On Sunday, the students were persuaded to evacuate on the promise of a dean that he would intercede with the faculty to nullify the punishment. On Monday, the faculty refused, on the ground that terrorism should not cause established procedures to be set aside. By Wednesday, it was clear that several thousand students backed the black demands. Believing the campus would otherwise become an armed camp with probable loss of lives, the faculty reversed itself on Wednesday, acceding to the student demands.

To many, the "capitulation" emerged as a violation of a dominant American value, that disputes shall be resolved by appropriate legal and administrative procedures. So it had also seemed to the Cornell faculty on Monday. By Wednesday, however, the majority of that faculty had become convinced that the campus possessed no consensus either on this value or on the disciplinary process as a means of resolving the dispute. Institutions function properly only when contestants display confidence in them. In the situation at hand, the enforcement of institutional procedures would have *intensified* the distrust between the contestants, not mitigated it as is the usual role of institutions. Aware that values cannot be imposed by an elite, the faculty retreated to a higher value, that of saving lives.

This incident, together with the many similar ones that have occurred recently, raises two major questions about the application of institution theory to the United States. First, is the United States a consensus society? Second, is economic growth a dominant goal?

Is the United States a consensus society? Those who challenge the view that the United States is a consensus society often cite its many social conflicts. Some are with us perennially, some occur in waves. Each historical epoch brings conflicts not previously known. But it is not the number or even the intensity of conflicts that determines whether a society is consensus or not. Rather, it is the extent to which contestants agree on the legitimacy of the institutions that exist to resolve them. Whether or not the United States is a consensus society depends on the rating its principal institutions would receive according to the consensus criterion, discussed earlier in this chapter. I do now know of any convincing research on this. Our theory of institutions (to be elaborated in subsequent chapters) will lead us to believe that the United States is more of a consensus society than most less developed nations and that consensus increased during the latter part of the nineteenth and first half of the twentieth centuries. But the Cornell incident, and others like it, are evidence that consensus may be decreasing during the 1960s and 1970s.

Is economic growth a dominant goal? It is, by definition, if the reasonable expectations of members of the society can be fulfilled only if a certain percentage increase in gross national product occurs annually. We have cited evidence in Chapter 2 that growth is a dominant goal in the United States. (This is, nevertheless, also an area in which research to date is inadequate.)

We suspect, however, that this dominance is declining. The Cornell incident brought into question the legitimacy of the faculty's right to discipline. Other challenges have struck the most revered institutions in the United States. Do our courts supply impartial, just, trials in which the guilt of defendants is not presumed in advance? This question, which would have been answered by a resounding "yes" only fifteen years ago, now evokes a "no" from partisans of radical groups such as the Black Panthers.

University students increasingly question the institutions through which values are transmitted from generation to generation. Many deem the family system to be an instrument for inculcating materialism into the young. Choice of spouse, cost and location of house, type of entertainment and standard of life are all felt to be geared into a "business-profit" complex. The response of the young is to explore new relationships, such as living together, contract (or limited-time) marriage, and communes. The educational system is also challenged. Universities are considered a means of casting students into the social mold so that they become competitors for increased material output. Many students argue that instead universities should be vehicles for exploring every value, or potential value, critically and without prejudice. This would happen, they argue, only if course requirements were abolished and even the privileges of the professor. If courses were adequate to explore new values, these students would presumably select them. If the professor distinguished himself by his superior knowledge and analytical abilities, these students assert, they would respect him; if not, they should have the right to ignore him. The grading system, they say, is especially foul, for it squelches the "free" student. It judges him by how well he has assimilated the social imperatives, and it puts a premium on hypocrisy.

All these challenges to institutions—universities, the family, the courts—are symptomatic of a generation that doubts the dominant social goal. That this doubt is directed at economic growth is evidenced by the high percentage of college dropouts, by the number of graduates who have opted for "simple" professions requiring handicraft skills rather than professional education, and by the desire of students to live "simply" in mountain cabins. It is symbolized by a new style of dress, increasingly inexpensive and informal.

We do not now have the historical perspective to judge whether the present moves are a cyclical disturbance from a static equilibrium to which we will return, or whether they represent an irreversible tendency to change the social structure. Those who would guess the latter might argue that the United States, having taken off into self-sustaining growth a century and a half ago, is now in the landing pattern. Landing requires the desensitizing of growth-sensitive groups and their sensitization to some other dominant goal. It presents many of the characteristics of takeoff: accompanying the new social goals are disruption of consensus on institutions and a search for new values on which new institutions would be based.

But landing itself is still for the future, and we cannot discuss it properly yet. Our theory of institutions must, for the moment, be confined to problems of the takeoff and post-takeoff periods. To speculate on landing is a luxury in which we will indulge a little more in Chapter 8.

Conclusion

The need for a new concept of institutional effectiveness is two-stemmed. First, the old concept of efficiency—maximum output per unit of input—applies only to institutions whose goals are known. Secondly, traditional definitions of efficiency belong principally to administration systems, such as are found in business and government agencies. But measures common to other social subsystems as well may reveal similarities that will promote an understanding of the growth process.

Nevertheless, we have emphasized administration for two reasons. First, the tests of institutional effectiveness will be technically easier to apply to these systems than to others. Secondly, administration is probably more susceptible to change, planned or unplanned, than, say, friendship or the family. The Soviet Union, for example, found it impractical to interfere with the family system,[21] and Chinese experiments in collective living in communes have not generally been judged successful.[22] Nor is it practical for any society consciously to manipulate the friendship system. Though one system is more effective than another in promoting economic growth, nevertheless these are culture objects hard to change. It is better to take them as parameters.

In the next two chapters we develop the theory of institutions. We address ourselves to the question of which institutions, government or private, and which values are more susceptible of change with economic growth and which less. This will require a concept of cost, or the sacrifices necessary for the generation of institutional effectiveness. A related point will be contagion—how effectiveness is passed from one system to another. These theoretical guidelines may help us assess such phenomena as black power and university reform. When does the demand for such movements arise, and how does it spread to other institutions and values? It will also help in planning for economic growth in less developed countries.

[21] H. Kent Geiger, *The Family in Soviet Russia* (Cambridge, Mass.: Harvard University Press, 1968).

[22] Audrey Donnithorne, *China's Economic System* (New York: Frederick A. Praeger, 1967), pp. 62-63.

The Institutional Effectiveness of the Program of Rural Credit in Nicaragua

BY WILLIAM LOEHR*

IN ORDER to test the practicality of measuring institutional effectiveness in less developed countries, an examination was made of the Program of Rural Credit of the National Bank of Nicaragua. As in the simulation exercise in Chapter 3, the conflict selected was that of whether or not to award a loan.

Summary of Results

The National Bank of Nicaragua was most cooperative in making its facilities available to the investigator, and both central office and field staff participated willingly. While the most interesting conflict would have involved the borrowers as well, it was nevertheless the opinion of both the investigator and the bank staff that it would be useless to ask the farmers to fill out questionnaires. Virtually all of them were illiterate; they were ordinarily unable even to fill out their applications for credit, which had to be done instead by the field staff. It was therefore decided to limit investigation to potential conflict between the field staff and the central office.

Four identification cues were selected in cooperation between the investigator and both staffs. Each respondent was asked whether loans should be granted on the basis of the following: quantity and quality of farmer's land (and other natural resources); quantity and quality of farmer's labor; farmer's available capital (other than the loan); and farmer's receptivity to modern techniques. Both staffs relied heavily on the first two cues and the degree of conflict was 0.597 (with 1.000 being complete agreement and 0.000 complete disagreement).

The field staff was rated 0.571 in its capacity to predict the responses of the central office staff, while the latter was rated 0.573 in predicting the former. The rating of the institution by the identification criterion is the average of these two quantities, or 0.572, out of a range of 0.000 (low) to 1.000 (high).

* The author is indebted to the National Science Foundation for a grant which made this research possible.

The rules cues selected were quality of the technical factors (i.e., the four identification cues); farmer's credit rating and collateral; conformity of the farmer's project with the bank's investment plan; and the percentage of its programmed loans that a local office has achieved before receipt of the application. Both the central office and field staffs relied heavily on the first cue and less heavily on the second. There was therefore substantial agreement on rules, the rating for this criterion being 0.716 out of a range of 0.000 (low) to 1.000 (high).

After conversation with both staffs, the investigator concluded that use of the consensus questionnaire developed in Chapter 3 would be impractical. As loyal employees of the National Bank, any *general* statement that respondents would make about it would be highly favorable. There were, however, specific criticisms that came out in informal conversations after they had known the investigator long enough to achieve confidence. The investigator concluded that it would be possible to arrive at a *subjective* judgment on consensus, but only after investigating several institutions with a view to rating them ordinally.

Identification Criterion

We expand on the four cues as follows:

1. Quantity and quality of land, including fertility, location, rainfall, and other natural resources (LAND).

2. Quantity and quality of labor, including the training, age, capacities, and physical fitness of the farmer himself, his extended family (if available for work), and capacity for hiring temporary workers (LABOR).

3. Capital includes all financial resources that the farmer might have available from all sources other than the present loan (CAPITAL).

4. The receptivity of the farmer to modern techniques covers the field staff's estimate of his willingness to employ new methods suggested (MODERN).

None of the above cues was measured objectively, and no tests were made of the specific degree of fertility, the trade-off function between fertility and rainfall, etc. Rather, cues were rated on a scale of zero to ten, covering "worst possible" to "best possible" in the judgment of the respondent. Each respondent was asked to imagine that five was the average for his area, and that all variables not included in the cues were average for the area and the same for each loan proposal.

Each respondent was then asked to fill in the blanks for the following questions applied to each of forty hypothetical farms presumed to be applying for credit (each farm represented by a four-cue bar diagram, similar to those in Chapter 3).

1. I estimate the probability of success to be ——% [success being defined subjectively by the respondent].

2. I believe the central office staff, as a group, would estimate the probability of success to be ——%.

3. I believe field workers, as a group, would estimate the probability of success to be ——%.

The same questions were given to all staff, whether central office or field. Thus a central office staff member, in answering question no. 2, would be predicting the responses of his colleagues, the same being so for a field worker answering question no. 3. The group to which each respondent belonged was noted, so that he could later be placed in the hierarchy. There were seven respondents (out of a possible nine) from the central office and twenty-two (out of a possible hundred and two) from the field staff.

Table 3.10 shows the correlation coefficients (r) and multiple coefficients of determination (R^2) resulting from a regression of responses upon cue values.

From this table it is seen that individuals of both staffs predicted quite successfully the responses of their immediate colleagues. Central office staff, however, believed that the field staff placed greater emphasis on quality of labor than in fact they did. The field staff, for their part, underestimated the central office's reliance on available labor and on the farmer's receptivity to modern techniques. On line 3, the central office appears to be aware that the field staff places less emphasis on modernity than they do themselves.

It would appear that understanding might be improved by a closer examination of the role of labor in agriculture. Furthermore, the central office would do well to communicate to the field their reasons for strong reliance on receptivity to modern techniques. Possibly the central office has not done so because individuals in that office are un-

TABLE 3.10

IDENTIFICATION CRITERION

(r and R²)

	R²	Correlation coefficients (r) Cues			
		LAND	LABOR	CAPITAL	MODERN
Central office					
1. Grouped individual estimates	0.84	0.55*	0.39*	0.11	0.47*
2. Prediction of central office colleagues	0.78	0.53*	0.50*	0.17	0.35
3. Prediction of field staff	0.76	0.57*	0.45*	0.19	0.34
Field Staff					
4. Grouped individual estimates	0.74	0.52*	0.28	0.23	0.34
5. Prediction of field colleagues	0.72	0.54*	0.27	0.26	0.33
6. Prediction of central office	0.71	0.50*	0.29	0.23	0.35

* Significant at 90%.

aware that their immediate colleagues as a group stress this cue as much as they themselves do. On this point there appears to be lack of communication within the central office itself.

The Rules Criterion

The cues employed in the rules criterion are amplified below.

1. Technical factors include the probability of success of a loan based on the cues used in the identification criterion (TECH).

2. Security includes the amount of collateral the farmer is willing and able to supply as well as his general credit rating. Until two years ago, collateral consisted only of the crop or animals for which money was borrowed, but more recently crop and animals in excess of this amount have been required in some cases. Mortgages have been required only in loans for house construction or in refinancing old loans overdue (SECURITY).

3. The extent to which the farmer's investment plan conforms to the lending strategy of the National Bank (PLAN).

4. The percentage of total loans programmed for any given field office which have already been loaned, on the assumption

that the final month of an evaluation period has been reached. This cue was selected because conversations with the staff revealed the belief that there were pressures to make additional loans if necessary to meet goals (PROGRAM).

Respondents were asked to fill in the following statements for each of the forty hypothetical situations.

Under the circumstances a loan would be:
1. ——% acceptable to me.
2. ——% acceptable to the central office.
3. ——% acceptable to field workers.

The r and R^2 values resulting from the regression of percent acceptable in each case upon the cue values appear in Table 3.11.

TABLE 3.11

RULES CRITERION
(r and R^2)

	R^2	Correlation Coefficients (r) Cues			
		TECH	SECURITY	PLAN	PROGRAM
Central office					
1. Grouped individual estimates	0.81	0.72*	0.54*	0.26	−0.11
2. Prediction of central office colleagues	0.86	0.64*	0.74*	0.21	−0.15
3. Prediction of field staff	0.83	0.66*	0.61*	0.26	−0.20
Field staff					
4. Grouped individual estimates	0.82	0.74*	0.50*	0.22	−0.08
5. Prediction of field colleagues	0.78	0.61*	0.59*	0.23	−0.12
6. Prediction of central office	0.80	0.58*	0.60*	0.27	−0.21

* Significant at 90%.

Once again there is continuity in all the estimates. Both groups value first the technical factors and second the collateral. While this correlation alone determines the institution's rating by the rules criterion (and the corresponding correlation alone was calculated in the simulation exercises in Chapter 3), nevertheless the investigation was carried further, to determine each group's prediction of the responses of the other. Interestingly enough, each group thought its own colleagues relied more on collateral than they in fact did and less upon probability of success. Furthermore, while both the central office and field staff agreed in their emphasis on technical factors and collateral (lines 1 and 4), they were unaware of their agreement (lines 3 and 6).

The response to PROGRAM, while not significant, is nevertheless of interest. Here a negative correlation would be expected, since a high percentage of fulfillment of goal would be reason for *not* making a loan, and vice versa. While most respondents ignored this cue, nevertheless several would accuse others of wanting to lend so as to fulfill the programmed goal. For example, the individual response of one field staff member revealed that he both ignored the cue ($r = 0.09$, insignificant) and thought his field colleagues also ignored it ($r = -0.08$, also insignificant). But he accused the central office of having this as a primary motive ($r = 0.96$, significant at 99%). Though limited to a single field individual, this type of response—which could hardly be random—indicates a serious lack of understanding between that individual and the central office. Since, however, such responses are few, even though the correlation coefficients for the group tend to rise, these coefficients do not become significant in the aggregate.

Consensus Criterion

The consensus criterion was the most difficult to quantify. All persons concerned—central office staff, field staff, and farmer-borrowers, stated their confidence in the program when first asked. Field staff—but not central office—expressed less favorable opinions as their acquaintance with and confidence in the investigator increased. It shortly became apparent that any formal questionnaire on consensus would have little meaning, though an evaluation might be made on the basis of anecdotes.

After confidence in the investigator had increased, several field officials expressed the belief that other types of agricultural programs —such as price support and extension education—would be more valuable to the farmers than the current credit program.

The farmers themselves criticized the program even more strongly than the field staff. Many believed they had not been helped at all, ending up with greater debt but no higher income. Once again, the responses changed as confidence in the investigator increased; the farmers were more willing to express unfavorable opinions as time went on.

Discontent among the farmers is clearly justified. According to field-staff estimates, twenty-four out of thirty-seven farmers who received a total of 156 loans (1966-1970) had greater liabilities (ranging from $143 to $3,570 equivalent) than before, while only two had decreased their debts (by $75 and $45 equivalent). Nineteen of the same farmers had lower net worths at the end of the five-year period than at the beginning; only fourteen had higher, and four were undetermined. The net worth of five farmers had become negative.

These results are attributable in part to uncontrollable factors, such as weather and price fluctuations. But they are also due to poor evaluation of loan applications, inadequate technical assistance and super-vision, and most important of all, to the illiteracy of farmers who were unaware of the extent to which they were encumbering themselves. As a result, loan projects would be presented which either had little chance of being fulfilled from the start, or else failed because the farmer did not know how to make them succeed. The farmer would be saddled with an increase in debt but would enjoy little or no increase in income.

CHAPTER 4

A Micro-Theory of Institution-Building

WE TURN now to the theory of institutions. What institutions are selected in economic growth, what functions (conflicts) are assigned to each, and what are the principles by which the selection is made?

The problem has micro and macro aspects. The micro concerns the individual institution, with the framework of national values given. The macro concerns the formation of new values and institution-types to which the individual institution will conform. We treat the micro in the present chapter and leave the macro for Chapter 5.

We now take up the micro in the following way. First, we demonstrate by example that institutions transplanted from one country to another may adopt different functions in the latter. Transplanted institutions tend to be ineffective because their functions, caught between two cultures, are not clear. We might therefore suppose that different kinds of institutions would have grown in the second location had there been no transplants. Second, we construct some principles of supply and demand for institutions. Finally, we question what are the forces that would determine institutional structure and function in any country facing free choice (without transplants).

Transplanted Institutions

For our example of transplants, we select the system of market prices, which was evolved in Europe and was later transplanted to Latin America, partly by way of the United States. Conflicts relating to the allocation of resources and to the distribution of income were assigned in certain ways among pricing institutions in Europe and the United States. But these assignments did not fit Latin American cultural conditions. Though the Latins reassigned the functions, they failed to make all necessary adaptations. As a result, pricing institutions operate with an uncertain mix of instructions, and their effectiveness is probably lower in Latin America than in the countries of their origin.

INCOME DISTRIBUTION VERSUS INCOME MAXIMIZATION

We first consider whether income can be maximized and "appropriately" distributed at the same time. This dilemma is expressed by the ethical question (frequently heard in Latin America) of which ought to come first, economic growth or a "just" distribution of income. Whoever asks this question must believe that the two are not fully compatible.

Now, it is *physically* possible for a society to distribute its income in any way it wishes, paying it all to one person or spreading it evenly over the entire population. Any "inability" to do so stems from lack of agreement. Furthermore, lack of agreement implies that the institution through which the distribution would occur either does not exist or is ineffective.

We depict the conflict between income maximization and distribution in Figure 4-1. On the vertical axis we measure the real value of

FIGURE 4-1. POSSIBILITY CURVES: INCOME QUANTITY VERSUS INCOME DISTRIBUTION.

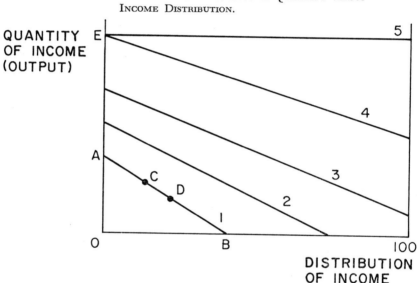

gross national income (or output), and on the horizontal axis the equality of distribution, based on some measure of skewness to which we agree.[1] Let us measure total inequality (one person has all the income) at zero and complete equality at one hundred.

Curve 5 is the physical solution line. *OE* is the maximum output the

[1] A measure generally accepted by economists is the Gini coefficient to the Lorenz curve.

society is capable of producing, given its technology and resources. The horizontal slope of this curve indicates that *OE* quantity can be produced regardless of how it is distributed. But the lower curves (1 to 4 inclusive) are apparent solution lines whose levels and shapes—they are not necessarily linear—depend on institutional effectiveness. Curve 1 might represent a highly stratified, ascriptive society unable to increase output beyond *OA* because of institutional limitations. Even this maximum is presumed achievable only if a small elite control the productive process and distribute the entire proceeds to themselves. The more income they are forced to yield to others, the less eager they are to organize production, and total output falls; hence the curve descends to the southeast, approaching a limit of *OB* distribution at zero output. Such a society might rationally opt for a more egalitarian income, say at *D*, than one where greater output would be possible, say at *C*. As institutional effectiveness is increased after take-off, the apparent solution lines might move successively to curves 2, 3, and 4, possibly even to 5. Most likely, however, the physical curve would simultaneously shift outward because of increases in technology and resources.

Under classical economic theory the free price system determines both the allocation of economic resources and the initial distribution of income. If society is not satisfied with that distribution, then—according to North American values—nonprice institutions (e.g., taxes, subsidies) ought to be employed for the redistribution, so as to minimize interference with the "proper" role of prices. In Latin America, however, these other institutions are not so well developed. Because the proportion of income paid in wages is considerably less there than in the United States, there is also greater dissatisfaction with the initial distribution under the price system.

Since adequate institutions for redistribution have not achieved political consensus, Latin American countries have tended to resort to the price system itself for the income redistributions they deem desirable. That system therefore acts with mixed instructions. Is its purpose principally to maximize output by allocating resources to their most efficient uses, as classical theory says it should? Or is its major function one of redistributing income? This lack of clarity stems in part from the fact that the price system is a transplant, but it also reflects a lack of consensus among the Latins themselves on how income ought to be distributed.

The case is of sufficient interest to the theory of institutions for us to consider it in some detail below.

COMPARATIVE FUNCTIONS OF THE PRICE SYSTEM:
LATIN AMERICA AND THE UNITED STATES

On the surface, there is little conceptual difference between the price systems of Latin American countries (except Cuba) and the United States. Private pricing (absence of government controls) predominates in all republics of the hemisphere. Yet further examination reveals a deep schism. Though the exceptions to private pricing are virtually the same in Latin America and the United States, the reasons they occur are vastly different in the two areas.

Exceptions apply to foodstuffs (agriculture), minimum wages, rates of interest, railroad and utility rates, and in emergencies to other products as well. But government interference with price in Latin America differs from its counterpart in the United States in justification, purposes, and individual duration.

All price controls in the United States are temporary, or designed to simulate the results of competition where monopoly alone is feasible, or intended to provide specially designated public services. We examine these three classes separately, comparing each with its Latin American counterpart.

Temporary price controls. Temporary departures from private pricing in the United States are of four types: (1) emergency price controls, (2) price supports for agricultural goods, (3) minimum wages, and (4) rate of interest. Only the first is also viewed as temporary in Latin America. The other three are deemed temporary in the United States either in that the type of control is ultimately expected to perish (agricultural supports) or in that individual prices will not long deviate from market conditions (minimum wages and rates of interest). In Latin America, all three types are widely viewed as of indefinite duration, both in their institutional aspects and in the deviation of individual prices from market conditions.

Emergency price controls. These include measures to meet a crisis whose end is foreseen, such as World War II and some inflations. Because of their nonroutine nature and converging motivations in Latin America and the United States, we do not dwell on them.

Agricultural price supports. Price supports for agriculture were initiated in the United States in the thirties as a temporary measure. Though their persistence for more than three decades will lead cynics to suppose they are now built-in, nevertheless there is much evidence that this is not so. They have only softened the otherwise brutal consequences of a technological revolution that suddenly diminished the numerical need for farmers. To prevent thousands from being pushed precipitously into industries not expanding rapidly enough to absorb them, the price supports eased the adjustment, allowing it to occur over a longer time. But at no point was the "market" effect reversed. Farm incomes have not risen proportionately to those in manufacturing and services, and migration to the city has not been stopped. Furthermore, controls are no longer uniformly wanted by farmers, and important farm organizations have declared themselves for freedom of acreage and pricing.

Both motivation and duration of price controls for foodstuffs appear to be different in Latin America. Rather than assist the farmer, they are designed primarily to protect the low-income consumer. In Mexico, the CONASUPO buys corn at controlled prices and sells it at a loss, so that most Mexican families (primarily urban consumers) will have *tortillas* even if they can afford little else. In Bolivia, a frequently heard argument for controlling gasoline prices is that they are an important element in the transport of food, which must be kept inexpensive for the benefit of the poor. Similarly in other countries, articles of prime necessity are often price-controlled in the interest of consumption by the poor. Such controls are generally considered to be of indefinite duration.

Minimum wages. Whenever a minimum-wage law is passed in the United States, wages are temporarily distorted from free-market levels. The economy, however, is so resilient that shifts in factor proportions and productivity soon restore equivalence. New technology, either hitherto known or now invented, raises marginal productivity to the new wage level. Though the institution of minimum wages is permanent, the rates themselves distort only temporarily.

The ostensible function of minimum wages is to improve the welfare of recipients. Their latent function, which assures support by the rest of society, is to force productivity increase. The result is a system by which congressional support of a minimum wage is possible only within the limits of readily achievable marginal productivity.

Such is not the case in Latin America. In country after country, minimum wages are sustained at levels above what the marginal productivity of labor would or shortly could justify under free market conditions. Such minima are designed to force a redistribution of income, not an increase in productivity. Once again we see the $+,-$ versus $+,+$ move. The institution of minimum wages in the United States depends on continuously increasing productivity and output for its very survival. In most Latin American countries it does not.

Rate of interest. According to Western economic theory, the rate of interest may be controlled by the monetary authorities in the short run, but in the long run it must conform to the supply of and demand for savings. We have discussed earlier (page 47) the relationship among productivity, wages, and interest in the United States. Over time, wages increase by more than the productivity of labor, thus encouraging labor-saving technological change. The investor's share in productivity increase is paid through capital gains, not by higher interest rates. The resulting constancy of the interest rate conforms to a system by which the money supply increases over time only *pari passu* with output. Greater increases cause inflation and lesser increases unemployment, neither of which is acceptable as long-run policy. Consequently, the rate of interest cannot long deviate from the marginal productivity of capital.

Though the surface mechanisms of monetary policy are similar in Latin America, the real role of the rate of interest is not only different from that of the United States, but it differs among countries, and within countries from time to time. In some countries at some times it is an effective instrument of monetary stability. At other times, however, it is a means of compensating investors (particularly if they are politically powerful) for having had to yield to higher wage rates. In exchange, they are permitted to borrow at artificially low real rates of interest. Under these conditions, the rate of interest does not become the principal allocator of credit, since greater reliance is placed on licenses and other non-price instruments. The result can be a long-term divergence between controlled and free rates of interest, made possible by the artificial insulation of one market from another.

Controls Designed to Simulate Competition. In both Latin America and the United States, public utility and transportation rates are government-controlled or -regulated, and once again we see a surface similarity. Utilities and railroads are by their nature monopolies. Regulation in the United States was designed to compel them only to charge rates that would yield a return equal to what a comparable investment would earn under competitive conditions. This is sanctified by the *Smyth* v. *Ames* decision, calling for "fair return on fair value."

The philosophy behind controlled rates is different in Latin America. Except for foreign firms (rapidly diminishing in number), the vast majority of utilities and transport companies are owned by governments. Such companies are often perennially in deficit, for there is no *Smyth* v. *Ames* rule. Rates are set by considerations of public policy: buses and trains are the transport of the poor, who should be charged no more than they can afford to pay. The same applies to electric power and in some countries to gasoline.

Public Services. The third area of price controls is well established in all civilized societies. It consists of goods and services made accessible to all members with limited or no regard to purchasing power. Goods fully subsidized, such as police and fire protection, are the extreme case. Less extreme are those partially subsidized, such as New York subway rides and state-supported education. The subject is well documented and need not detain us.

What does interest us, however, is the relative clarity in the United States and lack of clarity in Latin America between the preceding and the present case. In the United States, there is little dispute that controlled utility and transport rates are quite different from subsidized tuitions in state universities. In the former, fair return on fair value is constitutionally required; in the latter, it is not. In Latin America, however, there is often confusion as to whether utility and transport rates are being controlled to simulate competitive pricing or whether to provide public services regardless of ability to pay.

Comparison of Price Systems. Already we see that economic institutions that on their surface appear to be performing the same function in Latin America and the United States are in reality doing different things. In general, in the United States the system of private pricing is intended as a clear set of rules determining which goods and services will be produced and what factors will produce them, balancing demand and scarcity according to the laws of classical economics. Income redistribution is performed by another set of institutions (income tax, social security, unemployment insurance, and welfare). In Latin America, on the other hand, while the same functions are assigned to the pricing system as in the United States, it is additionally responsible for redistributing income according to rules that change from time to time and from place to place, one time favoring one group and one time another. It would appear that the Latin American pricing institutions are not so effective as those of the United States and Europe, according to the definitions proposed in Chapter 3.

What are the forces that determine the allocation of one set of functions to a certain set of institutions in one country and to another set in another? We turn to this question at the end of the chapter. Before that point, it is useful to define laws of supply and demand with respect to institutions.

Supply and Demand of Institutions

A nation's institutions are part of its culture capital. So long as culture has a reason for existing—and the science of anthropology is founded on the assumption that it has—there is a cost to change it. It would seem reasonable that the demand for and supply of new institutions, or improvements in the effectiveness of old, could be subject to benefit-cost analysis. If the benefits of an institution exceed its cost, and if the beneficiaries are either able to compensate those who pay the cost (i.e., are hurt by it) or force them to yield with inadequate or no compensation, then the new institution will be formed.

Like physical capital, culture capital is possessed by someone. If, for example, an administrative change is needed to promote efficiency in a given plant, there are those with vested interests in the old system whose culture capital must either be confiscated or compensated. So long as military officers consider a potential coup d'etat to be one of the perquisites of their office, they can be deprived of this capital only if it is bought or taken.

It is now possible to think of the demand, supply, and markets for institutions in much the same way as for economic output. We envisage economic development as the continuous acquisition by society of a set of objects, including (but not limited to) capital goods, consumption goods, values, attitudes, norms, and institutions. Each object is both demanded by some and supplied by the same or different persons. Supply and demand have been defined by economists for capital and consumption goods, but we modify these definitions as we apply them to economic and noneconomic objects alike. The *demander* (who becomes a buyer if he succeeds in the acquisition) both desires the object and is willing and able to make sacrifices to obtain it. The extent of his sacrifices is the demand (or buyer) price. The *supplier* consists of all those who, including the demander, incur sacrifices if the object is created, and their sacrifices, for which they may or may not be compensated, are the supply (or seller) price. The supplier is not necessarily the producer. For example, the "encrusted" managers whose inefficiencies would be exposed by the new administration system referred to above are by our definition the suppliers of that system. Either they must be "bought off" or their culture capital (vested interest in the old system) must be expropriated.

If we think of supply in the traditional economic sense, then the supplier is compensated for his sacrifices. This compensation constitutes the price, and supply is an increasing function of price. Since suppliers are often not compensated for the culture products we are thinking of, however, it is more convenient to think of supply price in terms of sacrifice. Thus, the greater the sacrifice, the less willing the supplier.

The demander, therefore, has two options. He must either compensate the supplier,[2] or he must increase the supplier's suffering from *not* supplying. The former is characteristic of consensus relationships and the latter of coercive. Ordinarily, a landlord willingly supplies agrarian reform if the penalty for not doing so is death. Any supplier will supply if the cost of not supplying (either relinquishment of the compensation offered or incurrence of threatened suffering) is equal, in his own mind, to the value of the sacrifice he must make by supplying.

Thus there are those who demand new institutions and those who supply them, though sometimes the exchange is a transfer payment, uncompensated. (The analogy to economic products is so far com-

---

[2] When the supplier is other than himself. To the extent that he is both demander and supplier, he is compensated by the benefits of the new institution supplied.

plete.) The demanders may be ministers of planning, presidents of republics, managers in progressive businesses, or university students who seek new liberties. The suppliers may be military officers with unsheathed sabers, civil servants with irregular channels of income, labor unions that resist automation, or university administrators who enjoy acting *in loco parentis*.

Economists are accustomed to think of demand and supply prices as identical once a bargain is struck. By the conventional definition, this is so (and Walrasian equilibrium depends on it). By our modified definition, however, the buyer may incur personal or psychological sacrifices unknown to the supplier, such as those of a student whose education is paid for not only by tuition but by the opportunity cost of his own time. Likewise, the supplier makes uncompensated sacrifices if he incurs a loss. To tip the scale the other way, a supplier may be compensated for what is not a sacrifice ("psychic benefits").

The asymmetry between demand and supply prices is the more clear in the market for institutions (or for improved institutional effectiveness). Here the buyer may pay part of his price in political agitation, riots, revolution, and death, which may benefit the supplier not one whit. For the supplier, the expropriation of an "obsolete" institution occurs when the opportunity cost of defending it becomes too high as revolutionary threats increase.

The problem is compounded by the fact that the formation of each institution requires another institution in which the "trading" takes place. Take, for example, the old fashioned administrator referred to above who, much against his will, "supplies" a new administration system in a business corporation. Not knowing in advance exactly how the system will function, he exaggerates its fearful consequences. Meanwhile, the demander overrates his claims for it. The "trading" institution consists of whatever way society has selected for buyer–seller communication to explicate the function of the product and to convince both of them to make the necessary sacrifices. The transaction will occur more smoothly if buyer and seller are united by a higher value, such as enhanced production of the firm, which would be threatened if agreement were not quickly reached according to institutional norms. The absence of these higher values and the inadequacy of "institutions to trade institutions" are the hallmarks of underdevelopment.

By the definitions proposed above, only part of the cost of supplying a new institution is measurable—for example, income lost or property expropriated from the supplier. The nonmeasurable costs are disutility or psychological suffering. Nevertheless, it may be possible to rank alternative institutions ordinally. Suppose two institutions are substitutable for each other (i.e., will perform the same functions). Without knowing exactly the cost of either, it may be possible to know, or guess, which costs more than the other. The demander will seek the institution that he believes is less costly. Indeed, politicians make such judgments all the time.

THE SOCIAL COST OF CHANGE

Finally, we must question what is the *social cost* of institution-forming. We have suggested two kinds of costs: sacrifices by the demander and sacrifices by the supplier. In the Mexican revolution, part of the cost paid by the revolutionary Francisco Madero was that of mustering an army to threaten the position (and possibly the life) of incumbent Porfirio Díaz. (Madero was the demander.) Díaz's cost (he was the supplier) consisted of losing his job as president. Now, if Madero's cost could be considered *income* to Díaz (as the demander's cost is the supplier's income in economics), then it would be canceled out in the social consolidation. But Díaz had no "income," only costs. The social cost of the Mexican revolution must therefore include the suffering of *both* Madero and Díaz, plus that of the many contestants that followed them in the ensuing decade.

Since the decision for change is made only by comparison of the demander's benefits and costs, without reference to those of the supplier, it might be argued that the social cost of reform frequently exceeds its social benefits. But the subjective nature of benefit and cost precludes this conclusion, which would be tantamount to saying that the excess benefit over cost to the demander is less than the excess cost over benefit (if any) to the supplier. Decisions for reform are usually made on the basis of some subjective welfare function, in which the costs to the supplier are weighted far less heavily than the benefits to the demander.

The Selection of Institutions

We assume that institutional change is demanded by growth-sensitive groups who have attained the political, economic, or other power to carry it out. They correspond to individual *A* of Chapter 1, whose task was to decide whether to impose instruments of consensus or coercion upon individual B. Such groups are not necessarily politicians; they may be heads of families, section chiefs in a business, or priests with a constituency whose way of life they are trying to change. But it will help if the political structure is in the hands of growth-sensitive groups. Indeed, at some time such groups must accede to power or growth will not continue.

The answer to our principal question is now implied. *The growth-sensitive groups will select those institutions whose effectiveness rating is high enough (in their belief) to increase the gross national product at an annual rate which, in their subjective judgment, has a value at least equal to the cost, to them, of acquiring the institutions.* The selection may be only quasi-rational, for the power group may not know it is motivated by economic growth. It may select the wrong institution, sense the error without knowing why, and change. Thus the final choice may be by successive approximations.

If an institution can be broken down into parts, in such a way that any one can be added independently of the others; if the expected marginal effectiveness contribution can be estimated for each part; and if (as would seem logical) there is a law of diminishing marginal effectiveness (i.e., the incremental effectiveness decreases as more parts are added)—then there may even be a demand schedule with marginal benefits. Subjective judgment is necessary, as was mentioned in Chapter 1, because the benefits (increments of GNP) and costs (which may be psychological, physical, monetary, or other) are not necessarily measured on a common scale.

Usually the cost to power groups consists of the expenditures of effort toward increasing the opportunity cost to other groups (the other "suppliers") of maintaining obsolete institutions that conflict with the ones demanded. Again, if the institution can be broken down into separable parts, a supply schedule may conceivably be constructed, based on marginal costs.

In the *macro*-theory of institution selection, which we take up in the next chapter, we assume the possibility of changing the nation's value structure, albeit at some cost. Since this change requires time, the macro-theory has a longer-run perspective than the micro-theory. In the *micro*-theory, we take national values as fixed, and we examine the

120

selection of those institutions that will achieve maximum effectiveness given that value constraint.

We now illustrate the micro-selection process by assuming two countries, C and S, each one in need of some institution for organizing the division of labor in a way most conducive to collaboration among factors of production. We assume that the two countries are identical in every way except one. They differ in the acceptance of a single, dominant value that cannot be changed in the short run. For country C, this is consensus on a "capitalist" ideology, or the belief that the self-seeking individual promotes the common welfare. In country S, the value is the "socialist" ideology, or the belief that the self-seeking individual who gains power deteriorates the welfare of the others. In real situations, norms and institutions consistent with these values would have grown up *pari passu*, with mutual reinforcement. For analytical purposes, however, we assume that no institutions have developed in either country. Rather, we investigate the means to achieve consensus upon them.

Assume that each country has the choice between two institutions, c and s, which, given the most favorable environment for each, are equally capable of promoting clear rules to govern the division of labor in either country. That is, each bears the same *physical* solution line. They are defined as follows:

$c =$ communication among factors of production such that consensus on the division of labor and its remuneration will evolve through the unfettered right to make contracts.

$s =$ socialist direction by an intelligent planning board, which will allocate factors of production and determine their remunerations centrally.

In country C, s is abhorred because of its infringement on human "rights." Central planning will be viewed with suspicion; the apparent solution line of s will be much lower than that of c. In country S, by contrast, the normal evolution of consensus by unfettered right to contract is feared because power groups would presumably emerge to threaten the rights of others. In it, c presents an apparent solution line lower than that of s.

Given the micro-constraint that no change in values is possible, the institution (c or s) with the greater effectiveness (higher apparent solution line) will be selected in each country.

We now propose that the objects mentioned are indeed to some degree substitutable, and to the extent that society opts for one it need not acquire the other. If this is so, then the selection of central control in the Soviet Union would imply less need for easy, lateral communication among suppliers of factors of production. Conversely, the United States economy would require institutions for cross-cultural communication so designed as to enhance understanding and cooperation among those who supply factors of production.

Cross-cultural communication is an area well trod by sociologists. Since this book is addressed to social scientists in all disciplines, however, it is well to digress briefly into it before we make our comparisons between the United States and the Soviet Union.

CROSS-CULTURAL COMMUNICATION

Each individual belongs to many subcultures. Each subculture is a group with sufficient internal consistency to take on the attributes of a culture, including behavior code, set of values, language, and symbols. There is a teen-age subculture, a secretaries' subculture, a Flatbush Avenue subculture, an Andean Indian subculture, an economists' subculture, and so on ad infinitum.

Members of a subculture possess shared experiences, possibly physical and possibly academic (from learning common subjects), which become points of reference for communication. Each idea passed from one member to another relates to something both have experienced. Members of the football-fan subculture will talk about goals, penalties, star players, and which team won last year. If they do not share many other subcultures, these may be the only subjects on which they can communicate. Subcultures may be international. An economist from Nigeria will understand one from Britain who speaks of the marginal propensity to consume. But their subculture is further subdivided, and he may feel that his British counterpart does not even understand him on problems of the terms of trade.

Now, the number of subcultures to which an individual belongs, possibly hundreds or thousands, depends on how specifically they are defined. The ability to communicate with another individual is a function of the weighted index of shared subcultures (weighted because some may supply more communication-possibility than others). Two professors of economics, both football fans, have two subjects on which they can communicate. If they are also fathers of teen-age children, they have a third. If they are both Nicaraguans (heavily weighted in the index), they have many more, and so on.

Geographic proximity, if it dates from birth, often unites its subjects into many subcultures. The "American culture" is a combination of thousands of subcultures shared by people who have lived together. But geography is not enough. Professors of economics would be hard put to find conversation with electronic engineers, if they did not share the subculture of people who get wet in the rain. Harlem residents share many subcultures with their neighbors on Riverside Drive, but not enough to avoid problems.

Strictly speaking, there is no such thing as "cross-cultural" communication. Any communication at all depends on the sharing of *some* subcultures. The term therefore refers to communication between members of two "cultures," or nuclei of subcultures, who have few subcultures in common. It may be used internationally, as between "Americans" and "Vietnamese," but it may also be used intranationally, as between "landowners" and "feudal peons."

Before takeoff, subcultures may exist intranationally for many years without forging the instruments of communication among them. Especially in ascriptive societies, where communication consists of the minimum giving and receiving of orders, few experiences are shared among subcultures. The feudal landowner with a paternalistic feeling toward his peons can communicate with them in the limited way that defines their relationship. But he has never been a peon, nor they landlords, and all they have in common is their association with the same hacienda. So there is much they cannot exchange. He may be totally incapable of comprehending their susceptibility to the demagogue who excites them to demand agrarian reform.

CONTRAST: UNITED STATES AND SOVIET UNION

We now propose that the system of institutions providing cross-cultural communication in the United States performs some of the same functions as central planning in the Soviet Union. It would, of course, be interesting to rate each of them on its effectiveness. In that case, the American institutions would suffer for their failure to achieve complete communication among racial groups or even between generations. The Soviet institutions would lose points for failing to achieve consensus between government officials on the one hand and literary figures who have proposed institutional change on the other. However, our present concern is not with ratings, but with functions.

In the United States, the expanded communality of subcultures facilitates the creation of such institutions as parent-teachers' associations, the League of Women Voters, and the Committee on Political Education of the AFL/CIO. There are also informal institutions. For example, the oft-criticized conformity of suburban inhabitants of "ticky-tacky" nevertheless generates a capacity to communicate that is common to Los Angeles and Baltimore—among people who know what "ticky-tacky" means. It moves the apparent solution line upward, toward congruity with the physical, for the many conflicts that fall within its scope. Though advocates of states' rights in the United States may disagree with proponents of central authority, nevertheless their large number of shared subcultures enables them to define the conflict in mutually understandable terms as well as to set the rules—via Congress and the courts—for resolution. Thus each side knows the price it must pay for culture change. Conformity also facilitates the mobility of factors of production. Transport a suburbanite from San Francisco to Boston, and he hardly knows he has moved!

The same applies to some of the problems of civil rights. Despite the convulsive riots in northern cities, nevertheless the past two decades have seen important advances in civil rights in the United States. How have they come about? Institutions must have evolved either to blunt the excess demand for civil rights or else to stimulate supply.

These institutions include government agencies on all levels, courts of law, school boards, committees for community action, chambers of commerce concerned with the image of strife-ridden cities, and others sprung up or adapted to the challenge. That they have been possible is explained by the increasing participation of blacks in the subcultures of educated persons, of labor unions, of professional men, of politicians, and so forth. That they have not averted violence is testimony to the fact that masses of blacks not only do not share a large number of subcultures with neighboring whites, but have begun to insist upon different institutions, created and managed by themselves.

Counteracting the growing (excessive?) conformity in the United States are the new subcultures that are constantly emerging. Economic development is not a unifying, one-way street, but depends on the continuous creation of new tensions. The greater communality of subcultures facilitates the formation of institutions; the creation of new subcultures provides issues for them to resolve. The problem is one of balancing the conflict-resolving capacity with the volume of emerging issues.

While in the United States such institutions operate primarily on a decentralized, horizontal basis, their counterparts in the Soviet Union tend toward vertical relationship of groups with the central authority. Although official Soviet sources stress the "classlessness" of society and therefore presumably the free communication among individuals, nevertheless American literature on the Soviet Union focuses more on relationships between government and local groups. There is less need for horizontal communication than in the United States, since a horizontal conflict is often converted into two vertical ones, each between one of the groups concerned and the central authority. Inkeles and Bauer refer to a "definitely stratified" society in which different groups have "markedly different views on basic social and political issues."[3] On conflict-resolving institutions, they report:[4]

> Assuming that the level of class hostility is as high in the USSR as in our sample, or even higher, would this be a critical problem for the system? Our answer, in general, is "no." To begin, it seems unlikely that such sentiment could find a political channel for expression. In the nature of the case, the one-party system in the Soviet Union does not allow the significant political expression of class feeling through the organization of a distinctive class-based party functioning in opposition to other parties. Furthermore, the sharp restrictions on free discussion and on the development of factions or other formal divisions within the one legal party largely preclude the effective expression of this sentiment within the Communist Party as it is now organized.

Ploss contrasts the United States with the Soviet Union more specifically:[5]

[3] Alex Inkeles and Raymond A. Bauer, *The Soviet Citizen* (Cambridge, Mass.: Harvard University Press, 1961), p. 299.

[4] *Ibid.*, p. 317. The sample referred to was of Soviet émigrés, who were interviewed by the Harvard project on the Soviet social system.

[5] Sidney I. Ploss, "Interest Groups," in *Prospects for Soviet Society*, ed. Allen

In the United States, perhaps fifty major organizations, and ten times as many minor ones, attempt to satisfy particular needs that the consensus-oriented political parties cannot routinely advocate. The organizations do not fit any simple pattern of membership or unity, but are aggregates, shaped in large measure by the internal cleavages of labor, agriculture, business, the professions, and other bodies. . . .

In the Soviet case, authoritarian theory obscures the existence of a comparatively narrower circle of interest groups which struggle behind the scenes to wield influence within the single-party structure. . . .

Communication among the interest groups is essential to their functioning, and will be examined from the standpoint of how dialogues are conducted and access gained to the locus of decision making. . . .

As Ploss continues his analysis of interest groups, he stresses "Kremlin decision-making" and the Politburo as "the foremost theatre of political operations," hence a vertical type of conflict resolution.

Not surprisingly, there is a void in the literature on horizontal intergroup communication in the Soviet Union. The automobile, advertising, chambers of commerce, nongovernment political-education committees, and other privately developed arrangements for such communication are far scarcer in the Soviet Union than in the United States. Physical mobility from job to job has been limited at various times in Soviet history, for example in restrictions on members of collective farms and in the freezing of jobs that began during World War II. In the fifties these restrictions were substantially reduced, and now the Soviet worker may change jobs at his own initiative. Even so, "his freedom of movement, like that of other Soviet citizens, depends on the willingness of the police to register him as a resident of the city he wishes to reside in."[6]

Kassof (New York: Frederick A. Praeger, 1968), pp. 76-78. It appears to me that Ploss has vastly underestimated the number of "minor" organizations at work in the United States.

[6] Alec Nove, "The Worker and his Livelihood," in "The State and the Wage-earner," *Soviet Survey* (October-December 1958), reprinted in *Soviet Society: A Book of Readings*, by Alex Inkeles and H. Kent Geiger (Boston: Houghton Mifflin Co., 1961), p. 385.

Each of these deficiencies is readily explained: there are few automobiles because scarce resources have been allocated more to heavy industry, the military, and outer space; physical mobility is limited so that factors will conform to the national plan; there is no advertising because it is "nonproductive" in the Marxist ideology, and no chambers of commerce because they are "bourgeois." But these explanations are half or less than half of the story. Rather, we ask whether, given the Soviet ideology of production, the institutions cited are more effective than their alternatives in promoting the cultural cohesion necessary for collaboration among the factors of production and for the evolution of clear rules of order within business enterprises and between them and other social institutions.

Latin American Values

We have argued that in the short run institutional structure must conform to national values. But what are these values? And how must it conform? In the present state of knowledge, the answers can only be intuitive. There is no clear-cut, objective way of stating that institution *X* conforms to value *A*, while alternative institution *Y* conforms to alternative value *B*. While it is possible to correlate values and institutions in narrative form on an item-by-item basis as we have done for the division of labor in the United States and the Soviet Union, no grand theoretical design has been as yet evolved.

Let us nevertheless take the narrative form one step further. Let us consider a set of values for middle sectors in Latin America, together with a set of institutions that appear intuitively to conform to them. Fortunately, Gillin has examined the values of these middle sectors, though in general terms rather than with a focus on their impact on growth.[7] Some Latin Americans would disagree with Gillin's list, others would acclaim it with pride. Most would argue that values differ in relative intensity from one country to another. We have no reason to be other than neutral, citing the values only as potential illustration of the highest level of culture in any social system, to be examined for the extent to which they influence the selection of institutional structure.

The values listed by Gillin are the following:

[7] John P. Gillin, "Some Signposts for Policy," in *Social Change in Latin America Today,* by Richard Adams *et al.* (New York: Harper & Row, for the Council on Foreign Relations, 1960), pp. 28-47.

1. *Personalism.* Personalism is a central value to Latin cultures. While the North American credo emphasizes equal rights and opportunities, Latin Americans stress "the inherent uniqueness of each person" and the accompanying *dignidad.* The result, Gillin argues, is that "words or actions interpreted as insults to the person's inner worth are highly explosive in their effects."

2. *Family ties.* Family ties, including the extended family and intimate friends honored by the system of *compadrazgo* (godfathers), are a weighty influence in both social and commercial dealings.

3. *Hierarchy.* The uniqueness of the individual, Gillin argues, leads to the acceptance of hierarchy. The relationship of a person to someone who is not his equal yields a *patrón* system of protector-dependent, which influences social, commercial, and government relationships, and partly explains a propensity toward welfare statism.

4. *Tangible materialism.* "Tangible materialism" is the pattern of trusting and seeking "only those kinds of property 'one can put one's hands on.'" It is exemplified by the propensity toward landowning as a prestigious form of investment, and it implies that economic return is not the sole criterion for selecting one's portfolio.

5. *Transcendental values.* Transcendental values, Gillin argues, are integral to the Latin American personality. "Just as, to them, an individual has an inner sense and a dignity that may not be immediately apparent, so the universe and human experience are believed to have deeper, not always manifest, meaning."[8]

6. *Emotion as fulfillment of the self.* According to Gillin, Latin Americans believe that "when one feels an emotion one should express it." This value is manifest in their "love of life," their *fiestas*, songs, and storytelling. The negative includes an abhorrence of boredom or ennui.

7. *Fatalism.* Fatalism, Gillin proposes, explains both the "heroic defiance" and "passive resignation" of Latin Americans. The former occurs when deterministic history confronts the sense of

[8] *Ibid.*, p. 41.

personal value; it is man's duty to die with *dignidad*. Yet the theme of resignation is ever present, with its own peculiar dash of sadness.

This summary is much too brief. One cannot adequately deal with a culture, or many cultures, in seven short paragraphs. Nevertheless, all the values in Gillin's list might be related to the characteristics of Latin American business administration mentioned in Chapter 3. Personalism impedes institutional loyalty and even loyalty to the state, both of which have been found essential for effective use and mobility of factors of production—the former in capitalist countries and the latter in socialist. Family ties impede the development of the nuclear family and the transformation of family enterprise into large corporations. Hierarchy and its *patrón*-dependent system cause embarrassment to the department head who seeks advice from his staff. Tangible materialism limits investment opportunities, while transcendental values and fatalism interfere with scientific positivism, promoting instead the mañana philosophy and inexactness of timing. The need for emotional fulfillment may cause individuals to react explosively to each other, focusing on immediate conflicts while blinding themselves to ultimate goals in common.

The Relationship of Institutions to Values

Let us accept, *ex hypothesi*, Gillin's catalog of values for middle sectors in Latin America. We now ask whether the ineffectiveness of Latin American institutions of administration (discussed in Chapter 3) and pricing (discussed above) has been caused by the transplant of formal structures not congruous with Latin value systems. This question implies a more serious one: whether the value systems are incompatible with economic growth regardless of which institutions are selected, or whether growth could have been achieved through some other set of institutions of primarily indigenous origin, which might have found the values compatible.

In general terms, the question is whether values *must* be changed in takeoff countries or whether the judicious selection and structuring of institutions will facilitate growth without value change.

The answer lies in the middle. That certain values, such as fatalism, are incompatible with economic growth, no matter what the institutional structure, is evident from their decline or disappearance in all post-takeoff societies. But other values, such as paternalism, may well be consistent with economic growth provided proper institutions are selected.

Personalism is a value that need not be abandoned with economic growth provided other values with which it interacts are themselves revised. While personalism may have declined in more developed countries, it has not completely died. Personal friendship is a factor in employment in the United States, as well as the technical capacities of the employee. But personalism has a different meaning in a country where friendship is based on professional respect rather than on school and family ties. A successful business administrator in the United States is likely to select his friends from among those with equal administrative capacity. Consequently, the hiring of a friend is more likely to bring high technical qualifications to his enterprise than would be the case in a culture where friends are selected on other bases. To this extent, personalism need not die for development to be promoted, provided other values, such as the nature of friendship, change.

In conclusion, *some* values must change if growth institutions are to be promoted at all, while *other* values may remain intact so long as compatible institutions are selected and complementary value changes occur. Furthermore, the extent to which value change is necessary depends on the range of alternative institutions that might equally well resolve the conflicts encountered. Since value change is costly, the appropriate choice of institutions becomes a crucial element in growth promotion.

Let us consider three institutional systems whose development in Latin America has been, or might be in the future, relatively independent of transplants. Because foreign influence is pervasive, it is not easy to find such institutions. Nevertheless, the collective-bargaining system in many countries, the government and electoral systems in Mexico, and the agrarian reform in Chile offer interesting examples, which we consider below. All these institutions show some compatibility with the value systems outlined by Gillin or with other potential values not so clearly defined, yet all of them also demonstrate the potentiality to achieve high effectiveness ratings by our three criteria.

THE COLLECTIVE-BARGAINING SYSTEM

Collective-bargaining systems in Latin America depend more heavily on government participation than do their counterparts in the United States. In the United States, primary reliance is on direct negotiation between union and management, with government intervention confined to protecting the bargaining power of the union and to clarifying rules of election and voting on strikes. In addition, the Department of Labor offers its negotiating services and even puts pressure on both unions and management in disputes of national importance.

In many Latin American countries, however, the Ministry of Labor plays a leading role through the whole process. Collective bargaining in Peru, which with minor differences is typical of most Latin American countries, consists of the following steps.[9] First, any complaint initiated by the union must be discussed with management. Both parties are required to make reports of their discussions to the local labor authority, usually by submitting minutes of meetings signed by union and management representatives. Secondly, if direct negotiations fail, the Regional Inspector of Labor acts as conciliator, but his views are not binding. Thirdly, if this conciliation fails and both parties agree, they submit to arbitration. A tribunal of three is appointed, one member by the Ministry of Labor, one by the union, and one by management. The decision of the tribunal is final, and no strike is permitted. If, however, the parties do not agree to arbitration but have followed all preceding steps, a strike may be legal. It must be decided upon by a majority of union members, with voting results submitted to the labor authority together with proof that constitutional procedures have been observed. A new vote must be taken every four days, to determine whether the strike will continue.

In many Latin American countries workers must be paid for periods in which they are on legal strike. In Peru, whether they are paid or not is a matter for bargaining. Nevertheless, the labor authority generally argues that declaring a strike legal is tantamount to considering the claims of labor as just; therefore the workers are usually paid for the period of the strike.

The widespread practice of paying workers for days on strike is sur-

[9] Melquiades Castillo, *La Contratación Colectiva en el Perú* (Lima, 1957).

prising to most North American observers, who argue that the Latin American union has "all to gain and nothing to lose" by striking. However, payment is normally deferred until after the strike has ended. Since the union usually lacks the finances to support idle workers, it may still feel strong financial pressure for settlement.

Any strike that contravenes established procedures is illegal. In most Latin American countries, illegal strikes may occur without any deterring action on the part of the authorities. But the union is denied those good services of the Ministry of Labor that often spell the difference between victory and defeat.

Latin Americans defend their systems of collective bargaining on the ground that they balance the struggle between weak unions and powerful business. The strike could never be won, they argue, if the union were not supported by the Ministry of Labor. North Americans find this argument incomprehensible. In the United States, even the most powerful of employers are prostrate if a well-organized union, with no more government help than guarantee of the right to organize and to strike, simply decides to walk out.

But the North American argument is not necessarily valid in Latin American conditions. Given the *patrón* system of protector-dependent, the problem may well be to transfer the dependent relationship of the worker away from the owner-manager and to the union leader. This same paternalism has led to the selection of union leaders not from among the ranks, but from among university-trained professionals. Personalism also makes the transfer difficult, especially in feudal farms and small industries where loyalty is to the person of the owner. Given these factors, it is likely that the Latin American systems will achieve higher effectiveness ratings than a transplanted North American system whose instructions would clash with well-entrenched personalist and hierarchical values.

THE GOVERNMENT AND ELECTORAL SYSTEMS IN MEXICO

The government and electoral systems in Mexico are a peculiar mixture of transplanted and indigenous institutions. Formally, the government is divided into three independent branches—executive, legislative, and judicial—just as in the United States. In fact, however, the presidency is the most powerful of the three, and policy-making is conducted largely in the councils of the leading political party, the

Partido Revolucionario Institucional (PRI). Formally, also, there are other political parties, but the PRI always dominates the voting and wins the presidency by a wide margin.

The electoral system would not rate so high on the rules criterion as would its counterpart in the United States. Mexicans are not agreed on the extent to which local elections are manipulated. There is widespread belief that a certain number of local offices and seats in the national legislature are rationed to opposition parties, though the official word is that these are determined by free and secret elections.

The selection procedure for the PRI's presidential candidate is also debated. Though in final analysis he is chosen by the preceding president, there is some discussion on the extent to which the president must yield to pressures from local and national politicians and powerful party members. The president must keep party unity, for his survival depends on it. Lesser officials have less degree of dependency, and this fact may provide the leverage they have over the president.

Despite these shortcomings, which would lead to lower ratings than the maximum technologically possible, the Mexican electoral system may be the most effective of which the country is capable. It surely conforms to the values of personalism and hierarchy mentioned by Gillin. In its vote-gathering ability, this system may also appeal to other values such as fatalism and the transcendental nature of human experience, but if so, the relationship is indefinable and beyond our capacity to analyze.

Many of the functions (or conflict resolutions) performed by competing parties in the United States are done within the party structure in Mexico. The PRI is divided into three sectors: labor, agriculture, and popular, the latter representing general business. Each sector has a formal organization through which its interests are communicated to top-level party officials. Candidacies for political offices are divided among the sectors in ways agreed upon by the sectoral leaders meeting jointly. The sociological origins of this structure, or the explanation of why it was selected rather than a multiparty system, may lie partly in the peculiar combination of Mexican individualism and collectivism. Mexicans are so individualistic that equal competing parties would find no ultimate values in common to conduce to consensus-based institutions. Yet the formation and accession to political power of growth-sensitive groups has led to the necessity for instruments of cooperation that would have been impossible without a centralized framework such as that of the PRI.

Another difference between the PRI and its counterpart multiparty system in the United States lies in its role as consensus builder. We will have more to say on this in the following chapter, in the section on nationalism. The numbers of people falling outside the national value-system in Mexico (e.g., Indians) is far greater proportionately than the corresponding number of outsiders (e.g., the black community) in the United States, and the degree of isolation is greater as well. The PRI leadership is aware that continued economic growth, on which its own survival depends, in turn depends on the inclusion of an increasing number of Mexicans within the consensus. This task, which differs in both magnitude, intensity, and appreciation of its need in Mexico and the United States, would lead to different types of party structure in the two countries.

THE CHILEAN AGRARIAN REFORM

When serious agrarian reform occurs in most Latin American countries, as ultimately it must, choices will be made among potential forms of landholding. These include the family farm, the corporate farm, the cooperative, the nationalized farm, and variants of these. The experience of Chile with agrarian reform in the 1960s offers some interesting perspectives on the choice.

In November 1962 the government of Chile adopted an agrarian-reform law authorizing the expropriation and subdivision of certain large holdings, depending on size, efficiency of use, and technical conditions such as soil and irrigation.[10] Though development policy was vested in the Ministry of Agriculture, the direct responsibility for carrying out the reform program was assigned to the new Agrarian Reform Corporation. By July 1967, when a new law was passed, some 479 properties had been expropriated for the benefit of 8,051 rural families.[11]

The 1962 law contemplated the division of expropriated lands into three basic types of holdings: garden plots for artisans, who would raise food for family sustenance and also produce handicrafts for the

[10] Inter-American Development Bank, *Social Progress Trust Fund Report* (Washington, D.C., see any year, section on Chile).
[11] *Ibid.*, 1967, p. 98.

market; greater acreage for commercial farmers; and lands allocated to cooperatives and for other communal services.

This law failed in important respects. First, the unclear division of responsibility among the agencies administering the reform (the agrarian reform corporation, housing agency, and finance agency) led to confusion and high cost in house construction and the operation of technical assistance, as well as to inefficiency in lending operations. Secondly, the garden plots proved unviable, since the artisans assigned to them were not trained in production and marketing, and studies of marketing possibilities had been inadequate. Thirdly, technical assistance was not provided in sufficient quantities for the farmers on commercial holdings.

These inadequacies led directly to the law of 1967. Under this law, further land expropriated is not immediately divided, and no more housing is built. The same peasants employed on the land before expropriation are left there, at first to cultivate it in much the same way as before. On each expropriated hacienda, now referred to as a "settlement" (*asentamiento*), the farmers elect an administrative council to determine the deployment of land and people among crops. Trained agronomists are assigned to regional offices of the Agrarian Reform Corporation, from which they visit the settlements regularly, participating in the meetings of administrative councils. Though they carry a veto over council decisions, they try hard not to use it in the hope that sensible decisions will be reached by consensus. After a three-year test period of operating on these lines, the members of each settlement will determine the institutions by which they wish to continue to be organized, whether on individual tracts or by cooperatives or joint individual and collective arrangements.

This process is one of intuitive institution-selecting. Private family farming, which has been so successful in the United States, was tried under the law of 1962 and failed. Presumably other institutions more compatible with the value structure will be chosen.

But it is not necessary for the Chileans to identify their values and specify the correlation between them and institutions. Indeed, they may argue that values are irrelevant. To them, the need for cooperatives may arise from the farmers' lack of technical knowledge. It would seem, however, that this could be provided in other ways, such as by a county-agent system, that would conform to private holdings. It is

135

much more likely that the value structure conduces to the selection of other institutions more effective than the family farm.

Complex Institutions

Our analysis of institution selection has been absurdly simple. We have assumed that each institution performs a single function (i.e., resolves a single conflict or conflict-type) and that alternative institutions performing the same function are perfectly substitutable for each other. In practice, alternative institutions have overlapping functions, and they are not completely substitutable. The system of cross-cultural communication in the United States provides goods and services demanded by the American people, quite apart from efficiency in allocation of the factors of production. The Soviet Union needs some cross-cultural communication for these same purposes, even though questions of the division of labor are resolved through other institutions.

Nevertheless, we do not elaborate this point now. Our approach to institution-selecting has been essentially economic, in terms of benefit, cost, supply, and demand. The treatment of complex institutions can be resolved in ways similar to that of complex products in economics, through substitutability functions and the theory of imperfect competition and differentiation of products. It is not an easy theory, and the counterpart treatment in economics leaves much to be desired. We sidestep the problem not because it is simple but because it is complex. Just as economists evolved the laws of competition and monopoly before tackling imperfect competition, so also are we content at this moment, to rest with the basic principles involved in the selection of simple institutions.

Summary of the Micro-Theory

The following principles of institution-selecting follow from the discussion in this and the preceding chapters.

1. Institutions are selected by those groups capable of establishing them and for whom the institution's product has a greater value than its cost. Value and cost are both subjectively determined.

2. In a takeoff nation where growth-sensitive groups are achiev-

ing power, the new institutions will presumably be those directed toward increasing the national product. We presume that the more effective the institution, the greater will be its capacity to increase national product.

3. Two types of cost are involved: the sacrifices (subjectively evaluated) of the growth-sensitive power groups who perceive benefits from the new institutions, and the losses (also subjectively evaluated) of other groups. The costs to the former will include the sacrifices they entail in either persuading or coercing the other groups, whose cooperation they need. The cost to the other groups (other "suppliers") will be the values they must sacrifice. If they are coerced, then they sacrifice values because the opportunity cost of defending them becomes too high. If they are persuaded (or deceived), they sacrifice values because they believe the compensation is worthwhile. In the latter case, they probably become growth-sensitive groups.

4. Where two institutions of equal effectiveness are substitutable for each other, the one less costly to the power groups will be selected.

5. While cost may be economic (e.g., resources spent on propaganda for an institution), the greater cost will doubtless consist of value sacrifice. Certain values, such as family ties, hierarchy, and fatalism, will yield in favor of others, such as close personal relationships with business acquaintances and less close with family. Each individual will subjectively evaluate the pain he feels in the sacrifice compared to the benefits expected from the new institution.

6. Each value sacrifice thus involves both cost and benefit. Values that are more cherished are more costly. They will be sacrificed only if the benefit is great. Less cherished values are easy to give up, but they may or may not yield much increment in product.

7. Ideology lies among the values difficult (hence costly) to change. Since institutions conforming to divergent ideologies may be equally effective, it is sometimes not necessary to sacrifice an ideology; rather, the institution conforming more closely to it is selected. We will treat ideology in greater detail in the next chapter.

137

8. Where two institutions are not perfectly substitutable for each other, the one with the greater marginal output in proportion to its cost will be selected. For example, institution *A* will be selected over *B* if its benefits (as perceived by the power groups) are three times as much as those of *B* but its cost (as perceived by the same groups) is only twice as high.

CHAPTER 5

A Macro-Theory of Institution-Building

> Any economic system requires a set of rules, an ideology to justify them, and a conscience in the individual which makes him strive to carry them out.[1]

BECAUSE of its greater time-perspective, the macro-theory of institution-building permits a broader focus than the micro-theory. While the choice between institution A and institution B still interests us, we transfer our emphasis to institution types, and we relate these in turn to national values, now variable in the long run. We surmise that if an institution of one type is chosen, the probability will increase that another of the same type will follow. Thus if one industry is nationalized, it is easier (cheaper) to nationalize another. If legal disputes are settled by juries, it is easier to establish arbitration boards for labor disputes. If the president of the Republic is chosen in a free election, it is the easier to establish a corporate board of directors elected by the stockholders. Finally, if there exists an *ideology*, or vision of society, that leads its members to *believe* that institutions of a certain sort are more desirable than others, then these institutions *will* function more effectively. (This is a self-fulfilling prophecy.) Indeed, without such ideological preference, it may be impossible to establish any institutions at all.

In a formal sense, the macro-theory is the same as the micro-theory. Those institutions and institution types will be selected whose demand and supply as we have defined them are equal. The only difference is that in the short run (micro-theory) we ruled out value change as a cost. In the long run, an institution need not conform exactly to existing values; its changing functions and structure over time may whittle them away. Any inconsistency in values, however, may be a cost to be counted in the supply schedule and affected by the law of relatively rising cost of coercion.

The Law of Relatively Rising Cost of Coercion

This "law" was introduced in Chapter 1: as national income increases in coercive societies where growth-sensitive groups are in

---

[1] Joan Robinson, *Economic Philosophy* (Chicago: Aldine Publishing Co., and London: C. A. Watts & Co., 1963), p. 13.

power, the cost of coercion and consensus both rise, but after a certain point that of coercion rises more rapidly. Ultimately, the marginal cost of coercion to power groups exceeds both the marginal cost of consensus and the marginal value of economic growth itself. As a result, either consensus institutions are substituted for coercive or growth stops. The process may be revolutionary or evolutionary. Coercive societies are those whose institutions, for the most part, would receive low ratings by the consensus criterion. They are not necessarily identical with totalitarian societies, whose ratings, like those of "democratic" nations, may be either high or low.

Coercion is not the same as control. By our definition, a slave society is coercive if the slave is dissatisfied with the master's control over him. He would substitute another system if he could. But if he has been indoctrinated into believing that God made him to be a slave and he is best off in his station, then the society becomes consensual. Since the slave's dissatisfaction may be to a degree, so also the coercion-consensus axis is measured in degree.

The distinction is thus subjective in the mind of the person or group whose collaboration is sought. It might seem intuitively that armed robbery is coercive. But it is a consensus institution if everyone is an armed robber, willing to accept the benefits and consequences. If an employer fires a misbehaving employee, is he coercive? The question is beside the point. The distinction depends not on an objective description of the act but on whether the employee is satisfied with the institution of hiring and firing or whether he would prefer another to accommodate the same conflict.

The law of relatively rising cost of coercion was first perceived by Durkheim, though he expressed it differently. To him, "repressive law" was associated with primitive and undifferentiated societies, while "cooperative law" emerged from the links forged through social differentiation and the division of labor.[2]

Empirical demonstration of the law, however, would be exceedingly difficult. First, it would be necessary to select a sample of coercive societies in which growth-sensitive groups are or have been in power. To identify these societies, studies of the degree of consensus on their major institutions would have to be made. This type of research is

[2] Emile Durkheim, *The Division of Labor in Society* (New York: The Free Press, 1933), chs. 4 and 5.

usually not permitted by coercive power groups. Secondly, it would be necessary to identify alternative institutions that would perform similar functions on which the power groups must decide, and to rank them ordinally according to how the power groups subjectively assessed their cost. Again, research is implied with which coercive power groups would not cooperate.

We might be tempted to select sample countries deemed to have been subject to coercive power groups for many years, say two decades or more, but which were ultimately "liberated." We then might observe whether the institutions created during the coercive regimes were capable of sustaining increases in gross national product afterward. We would observe, for example, that a military government can achieve high rates of growth while it is in power, but we would question whether it created the value consensus and institutional base for growth to continue once constitutional government had been restored.

Such a case might be the Dominican Republic, which achieved high rates of growth under the Trujillo regime (1930-1961). Statistics of gross national product are lacking before 1950, but other evidence of growth exists. Between 1935 and 1956, first-class highway mileage doubled, and second- and third-class increased even more. Before 1935 there was only coastwise commerce, but then it became possible to travel between the north and south coasts by car or truck. There were heavy expenditures on social welfare programs, such as disease control, housing, education (chiefly for literacy), and social security. Commercial and export crops (such as rice, peanuts, bananas, cotton, and sisal) increased greatly, and sugar production doubled between 1950 and 1960. The expansion of truck farming, however, did not keep up with population growth. Capital accumulation increased: from 1950 to 1957 average investment was 17.9 percent of gross national product, though it declined in ensuing years. Gross national product increased at an annual rate of 5.6 percent from 1950-1952 to 1957-1959, which in Latin America was exceeded only by Mexico, Nicaragua (under Somoza), and Venezuela.[3]

Trujillo's assassination in 1961, however, was followed by a series of military coups and revolution leading to armed intervention by the United States and an election imposed from abroad. The average in-

[3] Organization for Economic Cooperation and Development, *National Accounts of Less Developed Countries, 1950-1966* (Paris, 1968), p. 20.

crease in gross national product declined to 3.0 percent from 1957-1959 to 1964-1966, a rate exceeded by fourteen Latin American countries for which data are available and superior to only three.[4] One might be tempted to conclude that the coercive society of Trujillo did not promote institutions capable of sustaining economic growth.

While such a conclusion would support our thesis, nevertheless it is not necessarily valid. Though many would rate Trujillo as ruthlessly coercive, the evidence is inconclusive. Southern, on the one hand, writes of him as follows:

> The Trujillo regime had no political or ideological content whatever; the doctrine of *Trujillismo* was mere word-spinning. Far from being ostensibly based on a totalitarian theory, the regime scrupulously preserved the external forms of democratic institutions and legal procedures. There was a constitution providing for separation of powers and other traditional safeguards, and an all-embracing bill of rights. But the apparatus of repression was systematic and ruthless, and pervaded every aspect of Dominican life. It was completely effective in stifling all opposition within the country, and even Trujillo's critics abroad were not safe from his agents.[5]

On the other hand, there is alternative evidence that some Trujillo institutions were consensus-based. Trujillo made great effort to win over the working groups, both urban laborer and farmer. With some success he popularized his slogan, *mis mejores amigos son los hombres de trabajo*. His rural-improvement programs won him great support in the country. The wild celebrations over his assassination which broke out in Santo Domingo and the monument memorializing the scene of his death do not in themselves indicate gross lack of consensus on his regime. Unless tests are made, it is impossible to generalize on consensus. Furthermore, even ten years of political convulsion following the overthrow of a dictator do not provide sufficient grounds to argue conclusively that an institutional base had not been forged, however apparent it may seem to be. Though the Dominican Republic is probably in fact an example of our "law," nevertheless we are unable

[4] *Ibid.*, p. 20.
[5] Richard Southern, "The Dominican Republic," in *Latin America and the Caribbean*, ed. Claudio Veliz (New York: Frederick A. Praeger, 1968), p. 260.

to prove it. Similar problems would beset any other country we might choose.

We are therefore led to a different kind of observation. We note that all countries that have achieved and sustained high rates of economic growth have surrounded their institutions by an aura of ideology on which they have achieved consensus. This applies to socialist and capitalist societies alike. We also note the strength of nationalism in the early stages of all post-takeoff countries. Indeed, political scientists have argued that nationalism is a prime cohesive force in the achievement of consensus. Now, it is not possible successfully to promote nationalism and ideological consensus in less developed countries except at some cost, a fact demonstrated, for example, by the expenditure on propaganda of centralist nations like the Soviet Union and of less centralist ones like Mexico and Japan. We surmise that these expenditures are willingly undertaken because consensus is cheaper than coercion. (Remember that cultural revulsion to the instruments of coercion is treated as part of its cost.) From this we are led to our "law."

At the same time, we come upon some macro-principles of institution selection. Just as ideological consensus is characteristic of more developed countries, so conversely do we attribute ideological conflict to the less developed. (We intend to demonstrate this dichotomy with respect to Latin America and the United States in the present chapter.) From this we surmise that ideological consensus is a prerequisite for adequate institution-building. Not a particular ideology, but consensus on *any* ideology. Then the kinds of institutions to be selected will depend on that ideology.

We do not call for unanimity of ideology. On the contrary, a certain measure of ideological disagreement may be an ingredient of growth. So long as there is enough consensus to keep production institutions alive and healthy, those outside the consensus may provide the needle-pricks for change. Because they are not powerful enough to be unfriendly critics, they must be friendly ones. While Franklin Roosevelt was a prime mover of change in the thirties, Norman Thomas was a stimulus. The International Workers of the World were unsuccessful as a labor union, but they stimulated ideas on social security which were accepted over a half a century later. There may well be an

143

optimum degree of ideological consensus, which social scientists might some day seek.

The cost of ideological consensus is an overhead cost of institutions. It corresponds in every way to the overhead cost of any economic good. There are even advantages of scale, in that the greater the ideological consensus the less the direct cost to produce conforming institutions. It is even likely that there is a law of diminishing marginal productivity on the basis of which calculations of the optimum expenditure on ideology creation could be made.

We consider ideology only in relation to economic growth, with no reference to its desirability on other grounds. Clearly Germany's economic growth in the thirties was fostered by the consensus on Nazi ideology that the Hitler government was able to achieve; it therefore fits our model. But it was a highly undesirable ideology, since the consensus was attained at the cost of murdering nonconsensus groups and by infringing the territories, values, and concepts of liberty of neighboring nations.

We now turn to a detailed consideration of the relationship between ideological consensus and institution-building, with illustrations from the economic ideology now being formed in Latin America.

Ideology

"Ideology" has suffered in sociopolitical literature for being used pejoratively, and associated with falsehood. Kenneth Boulding once commented that ideology is like a ski: long, narrow, and pointed. Mannheim, whose work is one of the classics, wrote of it as follows:[6]

> But it is only when the distrust of man toward man, which is more or less evident at every stage of human history, becomes explicit and is methodically recognized, that we may properly speak of an ideological taint in the utterances of others. We arrive at this level when we no longer make individuals personally responsible for the deceptions which we detect in their utterances, and when we no longer attribute the evil that they do to their malicious cunning.

To many, ideology stems from Marxism or from disparity in wealth and income. Or it relates to Utopia, as is suggested by Mannheim's

[6] Karl Mannheim, *Ideology and Utopia* (1929), trans. Louis Worth and Edward Shils (New York: Harcourt, Brace & Co., 1946), p. 54.

title. It is then an ideal construct demonstrating how society *ought* to function. This led some scholars in the early sixties to question whether there has not been a decline in ideology as economic growth and egalitarianism have "triumphed" in the West.

The question is attributed to Shils. His title, "The end of ideology?" was borrowed by Lipsit in a postscript to his *Political Man*. Lipsit argues that "the fundamental political problems of the industrial revolution have been solved: the workers have achieved industrial and political citizenship; the conservatives have accepted the welfare state; and the democratic left has recognized that an increase in over-all state power carries with it more dangers to freedom than solutions to economic problems."[7]

He distinguishes, however, between the internal problems of more developed countries, where ideology is presumably dying, and the international struggle for the minds of men in the less developed world:

> Ideology and passion may no longer be necessary to sustain the class struggle within stable and affluent democracies, but they are clearly needed in the international effort to develop free and political institutions in the rest of the world. It is only the ideological class struggle in the West which is ending. Ideological conflicts linked to levels and problems of economic development and of appropriate political institutions among different nations will last far beyond our lifetime, and men committed to democracy can abstain from them only at their peril. To aid men's actions in furthering democracy in then absolutist Europe was in some measure Tocqueville's purpose in studying the operation of American society in 1830. To clarify the operation of Western democracy in the mid-twentieth century may contribute to the political battle in Asia and Africa.[8]

The tone of Lipsit's writing implies his belief that Western institutions are universally superior and the opposition tainted with "ideology," and battle lines are drawn. But he may be a victim of Mannheim's Paradox—that social scientists are not impartial or "scientific" because they cannot divorce themselves from the subject of their in-

[7] Seymour Martin Lipsit, *Political Man: The Social Bases of Politics* (New York: Doubleday & Co., 1960), p. 406.

[8] *Ibid.*, p. 417.

vestigations. Lipsit, of course, is defending his own system. This itself is paradoxical, because he also implies that Mannheim's Paradox may no longer apply in the Western world, where left and right are converging. He was writing, of course, about the "old left," before the "new left" had received much public notice.

LaPalombara takes issue with Lipsit, disagreeing—it seems to me— primarily on definition. While Lipsit accepts the pejorative, LaPalombara takes a more neutral stance:

> But if one elects a definition that is based too heavily on the notion of wilful or unintended deception or distortion, much of what social scientists generally identify as ideological would simply have to be ignored, or called something else. . . . My usage of ideology is quite close to the definition suggested by L. H. Garstin, in that it involves a philosophy of history, a view of man's present place in it, some estimate of probable lines of future development, and a set of prescriptions regarding how to hasten, retard, and/or modify that developmental direction.[9]

But can one's ideology be "true" or "false"? In Pilate's old question, is it possible to know what is truth? Sartori contributes to this point by distinguishing between ideology and pragmatism.[10] To him, ideology is the political branch of a person's *belief system*. He distinguishes between persons with "open" and "closed" systems, as well as between ideologies that are "strongly held" and "weakly held." If initially fixed elements become open or weakly held, then the person's belief system tends toward the open and flexible. According to Sartori, this marks the end of ideology and its conversion into pragmatism.

I accept, with Sartori, the inclusion of ideology in an individual's belief system. But in a sociopolitical context, the metaphysical concept of truth, or even pragmatism, eludes me. I accept, with LaPalombara, that ideology should be removed of taint. But while a philosophy of history may be a component of some people's ideologies, I do not believe it is required. Many hold ideologies without having the slightest concern for history. Finally, I find a psychological content to ideology.

[9] Joseph LaPalombara, "Decline of Ideology: A Dissent and An Interpretation," *American Political Science Review* (March 1966), p. 7.

[10] Giovanni Sartori, "Politics, Ideology, and Belief Systems," *American Political Science Review* (June 1969), pp. 398-411.

Everybody has a *need* for an ideology. To hold an ideology is *universal*. What Lipsit saw as the "end" of ideology in the West was really *consensus* upon it, a consensus which I believe is now diminishing as our once takeoff societies now approach landing. Ideology flourishes and always has. If all this is acceptable, then ideology is not pejorative, and it does not contrast with pragmatism. It is now time to set out my own definition, upon which the macro-theory of institutions depends.

DEFINITION OF IDEOLOGY

Ideology is the individual's view of society that best enables him to fit into it. It combines a myth (of how society does function) with an ideal (of how it ought to function). We reject any metaphysical concept of the "true" nature of society; therefore, it is as each person sees it. This sociopolitical concept of ideology implies a psychological reason for the individual's selection. He must create his niche in society. Either he must shape himself to fit society, or he must form his concept of society to fit his concept of himself. Most of us do a bit of each.

ECONOMIC IDEOLOGY AND POLITICAL IDEOLOGY

Ideology has an infinite number of dimensions corresponding to the infinity of ways of viewing society: economic, political, sociological, cultural, and other. Most or all of these dimensions are related to economic growth, since society is a system and they are among its elements. Nevertheless, we select two dimensions as being the most pertinent to growth, and for simplicity we refer to these as *economic ideology* and *political ideology*. Economic ideology is the individual's view of the creation and distribution of wealth, while political ideology is his view of the attainment and use of power.

Since our purpose is to relate ideologies to institutions—*if* ideology A, *then* institution X—we must not beg the question by employing the same name for the ideology as for the institution type. To us, "capitalist" and "socialist" are institution types—private and government ownership of business respectively—and we must invent different names for the ideologies.

Economic ideology. Economic ideology focuses on the right to material possession. Why are some people rich? Why are others poor? Whether we are satisfied with the answers we *perceive* to these questions profoundly affects the values and institutions (e.g., centralized

147

or decentralized) we find acceptable. Private property, definitions of liberty, the role of government, all reflect on the individual's right to seek and attain material possession. A society whose members agree on the causes of wealth and poverty has a running start on ideological consensus.

Let us hypothesize that most will agree that a person has a right to wealth he produces but does not have a right to take away, without compensation, what someone else produces. This statement does not apply to societies that have distinguished between their own members and others, accepting as moral the dispossession of others. Some Latin Americans feel it does not apply to North American society, whose rules and monopoly power (they believe) permit them to pay Latin Americans less than they deserve for primary products. But we hypothesize that most North Americans do not agree. And more, we hypothesize that in the modern world few see *themselves* as believing they have the moral right to take what others have produced without giving appropriate return.[11]

Once we are agreed on this point, the search for economic ideology "narrows" to the definition of what is production and what is appropriation. How *ought* product to be divided in a world where two or more persons must cooperate as factors of production? Neoclassical economic thought has one set of answers, based on marginal productivity, and Marxist thought another, based on the labor theory of value.

Both are narrow, simplistic explanations. Marginal productivity theory ignores slavery, feudalism, and conquest. It was intended only to demonstrate, with no moral connotations, how product is divided in an exchange society. But its adherents adopted the posture that to divide output according to marginal productivity is moral, and an ideology is based on this belief. The Marxist theory, on the other hand, has moral and ideological connotations from the start.

Let us define the two extremes of economic ideology as the *appropriationist* (approximating Marxist) and *productionist* (embracing marginal productivity theory). Productionists see an unfettered society—i.e., one without government controls or socialist direction—as awarding its product to those who have produced it. The wealthy are productive, the poor lazy and fun-loving. Appropriationists, on the other

---

[11] We except, of course, the young, the old, the infirm, and others whom society has agreed to support.

hand, view the same society as yielding its output to the powerful. The wealthy are those with the physical power to take, the poor are the weak, who are forced to work but must give up what they have produced.

To productionists, wealthy families are those that have invented useful technology, achieved scientific breakthroughs, discovered minerals, written best-selling novels, produced great movies, or—mainly—have had the administrative capacities and vision to organize factors of production efficiently. Conversely, the poor are physically or mentally incapable, or if capable, have lacked ambition. Productionists place more value on administrative capacity as a productive force than do appropriationists.

Political ideology. Power is to political ideology as material possession is to economic. Let us again define two poles and invent names for them. The *popularist* believes that, by and large, those persons with power and influence over social decisions, such as government officials, business executives, and labor leaders, act on behalf of their respective constituencies. The *selfist*, on the other hand, believes that those same persons wield power to their own advantage only, and care little or not at all about the aspirations of their constituents. The ideology-holder himself defines the constituency; he may view the constituency of the president of the Republic as the whole people, that of businessmen as employees and customers, that of labor leaders as members of their unions, and so on. Whoever sees mutuality in that power groups promote their own advantage by serving their constituents is popularist. To be selfist, one must presume divergence of interest.

Like economic ideology, political ideology must be distinguished from institutions. One may be either popularist or selfist in a totalitarian state. Whoever believes in the "white man's burden," arguing that colonial governments do indeed assume the responsibility to promote the best interests of their benighted subjects, is a popularist. On the other hand, one may be selfist in a democratic state, believing that selfish demagogues are elected by deceiving illiterate voters.

Both political and economic ideology relate only to those groups whose behavior impinges on the ideology-holder or on others who concern him directly. Alien power groups are either irrelevant or they are reference groups. For example, an American who believes that the United States government represents only the "military-industrial complex," and manipulates income in its favor and to the exclusion of the remaining electorate, is selfist and appropriationist, regardless of his opinion of the Soviet Union. Indeed, selfists in the United States may use the Soviet government as their desired reference group. On the other hand, popularists in the United States may consider that the Soviet government is totally unrepresentative of its people. Selfists in Latin America frequently use Cuba as their reference government.

A SUSPECTED CORRELATION

We now suspect a correlation between economic and political ideologies: that in general, appropriationists are selfists while productionists are popularists. In any research program, we would not take this identity for granted; each ideology should be investigated separately, and a correlation should be run. At present, however, we are seeking hypotheses that we hope will lead to research, and the correspondence we have indicated appears to be a reasonable one.

Our theory of institutions presumes a relationship between an individual's political and economic ideology on the one hand and his choice of institutions on the other. From this we deduce that ideological *consensus* is essential to agreement on institutional forms, and we have defined such agreement as an element in institutional effectiveness. But we do not argue (yet) that any particular ideology is associated with any particular set of institutions, since these relationships remain to be discovered. Both because of this latter limitation and for the sake of simplicity, it is appropriate for us to accept temporarily the correlation between economic and political ideology. For brevity, we therefore drop the terms for political ideology. Wherever "appropriationist" is used, we mean "appropriationist-selfist"; wherever "productionist" is used, we mean "productionist-popularist."

THE RELATIONSHIP BETWEEN MATERIAL WEALTH AND POWER

To appropriationists, wealthy families are (or were) slaveholders or *conquistadores*. The politically powerful always become the economically affluent, and vice versa. The poor, on the other hand, are the exploited, the slave, the peon, the class or race that is discriminated against.

Whatever the definitions of production and appropriation, there are

150

few who do not recognize that some wealth is gained in one fashion and some in the other, that some poor are exploited and others have not produced. Also, production and exploitation may be part of the same process. Likewise, the difference between self-seeking politicians and those who represent their constituencies is one of degree.

Despite the intellectual recognition of middle-of-the-road complexity, ideologies tend to polarize simplistically. Particularly is this so when political implications are reached. Soviet Communists may recognize intellectually that workers are well paid in the private-enterprise system of the United States, yet ideologically they favor *universal* systems of state ownership to protect the exploited. North Americans may understand intellectually that many Latin American haciendas are inefficient and feudal, initially acquired by conquest and now held by the grace of socially inconscient governments. Yet these same North Americans stubbornly oppose confiscation without full compensation.

What causes ideological polarization? Let us conjecture that without it consensus would not be so easily achieved. Values and institutions appropriate to the dominant ideology (and therefore *any* values and institutions) might not be readily formed, or if formed would be vulnerable. If this is so, private enterprise had to be idolized in the United States in order to survive at all. To admit that it is not universally optimal (e.g., not the best for Latin America) opens the United States itself to question. The same, of course, applies to the Soviet view of Communism. While we decry ideological polarization for its consequent parochialism in international affairs, nevertheless we are gratified by its contribution to domestic institution-building. We wonder whether polarization has a historic role. Perhaps it should be spurred during takeoff and reined in when major institutions are solidly formed and the nation becomes an international power.

IDEOLOGY AND GOVERNMENT

The extreme ideologies are distinguished by their views of government. To productionists, government has its own personality. Just as the corporation in the United States is a separate being, not only legally but also morally and personally, so also is government. As soon as it has personality, it can gain power. If the people do not control government, it will control the people, doing for them the things they ought to do for themselves. To productionists, a powerful though benevolent government is dangerous, for people will rely on it, and individual initiative will weaken. To appropriationists, on the other hand, the government "after the revolution" is not a personality apart. Rather, it is a collective venture of the people, who do in cooperative form what they cannot do individually.

Each ideology must explain how the social order implied by it would prevent members from taking more than they have produced. Productionists rely on competition in a social system where "all men are created equal," or else they look to the countervailing power of large groups, like labor, manufacturers, and farmers, strong enough to stand up to each other. It is assumed that everyone belongs to a group that will defend his interests. Government is the balancer, shifting power only as necessary to redress excesses. Appropriationists, on the other hand, cannot permit private groups to compete among themselves, for some will become more powerful than others. To assure appropriate income distribution, a superpower is needed as arbiter. The government is able to redress periodic imbalances by its active and continuous intervention in the affairs of participant groups.

THE FORMATION OF IDEOLOGY

Ideology is primarily learned from others, particularly those who are admired, such as friends and teachers. It must, however, be confirmed by "experience." This experience consists of interpreting events in a way that conforms to the ideology learned.

Each person's perception of an event is partial only. A Latin American viewing foreign investment by a North American business or the invasion of the Dominican Republic by the United States marines cannot have a complete concept of the motivation for these actions. Nor can a North American perceive all that enters the mind of Cuban government officials as they train combat guerrillas for service in other Latin American countries.

In order to digest an event, however, an observer must satisfy himself with a complete explanation. He therefore makes a *fact-completing assumption* based on his ideology. A Latin American appropriationist will likely conclude that in both foreign investment and the Dominican invasion the Yankee's motive was to maximize economic gain by transferring cost to those weaker than himself. The payment of lower wages to Latin Americans than are earned in the United

States is not viewed as resulting from lower marginal productivity but from this propensity to exploit. A North American productionist likewise may view the Cuban guerrilla not as a liberator of the peasant from exploitation but as one who tries to compromise his freedom of enterprise.

Once the fact-completing assumption has been made, the observer believes he has all the facts and the interpretation of the event corresponds to his vision of reality. As he observes a subsequent event partially, he interprets it with even greater conviction because of his previous experience. Each time a fact-completing assumption hardens into "fact" in the mind of the observer, the ideology hardens as well. A change in ideology is exceedingly difficult.

IDEOLOGIES IN LATIN AMERICA AND THE UNITED STATES

A study of economic ideologies in Latin America and the United States by this author in 1966 revealed the likelihood that North Americans then possessed a high degree of consensus on productionist ideology while Latin Americans were sorely divided between productionist and appropriationist.[12] The methods and results of this study are summarized in the present section. Since research was done before the full-blown emergence of the "new left" (back in the days of the "end of ideology"), it is possible that if it were repeated, the same degree of consensus would not be found today among North American students.

Over 2,000 questionnaires were distributed to businessmen, government officials, and students in Latin America and the United States, of which 400 were circulated by the National Research Organization of Colombia and the rest by selected government and university officials. There were 563 replies from Latin America and 285 from the United States.

In testing for adherence to the productionist or appropriationist ideology, respondents were asked (among others) the following question:

Think of someone you consider to be wealthy—either someone you know personally, or else a famous person of the nineteenth

[12] John P. Powelson, "Economic Attitudes in Latin America and the United States," in *Values and the Future*, by Nicholas Rescher and Kurt Baier (New York: The Free Press, 1969), pp. 233-61.

153

or twentieth century. *Do not mention his name.* (Though your answers should relate to a specific person, please try to select someone you consider more or less typical of wealthy people.) Check all the words in the following list that apply to this person.

The answers to this question were reported as follows:[13]

Sixty adjectives were selected and listed in random order in the questionnaire. In the compilation, however, they were divided into the following groups:[14]

1. *Productive* (presumably deserving of wealth because he created it): eager, imaginative, creative, innovating, showing qualities of leadership.

2. *Shows high-order positive qualities* (economically beneficial to others): helpful, just, honest, trustworthy, benevolent.

3. *Shows low-order positive qualities* (attractive, but not necessarily beneficial to others): virtuous, kind, friendly, honorable, courteous, respectful, humble.

4. *Lucky* (either with or without risk): lucky, fortunate, speculative, venturesome, showing tendency to win.

5. *Skillful* (can be used either in production or appropriation): intelligent, shrewd, genius, wise, discerning, skillful, cunning.

6. *Shows low-order negative qualities* (unattractive, but not necessarily harmful to others): covetous, pompous, vain, hypocritical, ostentatious, arrogant, odious.

7. *Shows high-order negative qualities* (economically harmful to others): bad, conquering, bloodsucking, criminal, murderous, deceptive, oppressive, unjust, offensive, pitiless, vengeful, inhuman.

8. *Elitist*: powerful, military, oligarchic, aristocratic, intellectual.

Questionnaires were scored in the following way. The number of checks after all words in a group was counted separately for Latin American and North American respondents. Each group total was then divided by the number of words in the group and again by the number of respondents (563 for Latin America and 285 for the United

---

[13] The text from this point, up to but not including the last line of p. 155, is quoted from *ibid.*, pp. 245-47, with permission of the publisher.

[14] Seven words were not put into any group.

States). The result was a score, ranging from zero to one hundred, applicable to each group.

In view of the large number of words in the list (60) and the tendency of respondents to check only a certain number (some checked as few as four or five, very few more than twenty), a score above 40 is high for a group.

The scores, by North American and Latin American respondents, appear below:

	United States	Latin America
Productive	55	38
High-order positive qualities	41	27
Low-order positive qualities	38	29
Lucky	48	38
Skillful	49	42
Low-order negative qualities	10	30
High-order negative qualities	6	14
Elitist	3	3

From this compilation, the picture one gathers is roughly the following. To North American respondents, the dominant characteristic of wealthy men is that they have been productive. Their wealth is coupled with a high degree of luck and skill. They have also served in benefit to others, and they are personally attractive as well. They are not thought of as oligarchic or elitist, and they have few negative qualities.

To Latin American respondents, skill, luck, and productiveness were about equal in importance, with skill leading slightly over the others. Some felt that wealthy men have been economically beneficial to others, but many others did not. A smaller number (but large compared to North American respondents) felt that wealthy men have acted in ways harmful to others. Wealthy men divide about evenly between those with attractive and those with unattractive personal characteristics. Surprisingly enough (at least to me), few Latin American respondents thought of wealthy men as oligarchic or aristocratic.

The survey is not conclusive in itself; it suffers from various statistical defects which were discussed in the original article. Nevertheless, the conclusion on ideological division in Latin America is amply supported by evidence from the literature as well as the many confrontations between labor and student groups on the one hand and military and conservative governments on the other, as we will discuss immediately below. If the two ideologies are conceived as extremes in a continuum, North Americans cluster at the productionist end but Latin Americans are strung out along the line. There are dissensions among the North American ranks, including not only the few socialists and Communists but perhaps the more important groups of radical students and "black-power" advocates. Nevertheless, the hypothesis appears valid.

With respect to the United States, the hypothesis is reasonable when tested against the backdrop of writings and traditions that include Weber's "Protestant ethic," Benjamin Franklin's sayings, Westerns, and Horatio Alger. It is also reasonable with respect to Latin America, when one views the extremes of left-wing sentiment in the universities and the unbending traditionalism of those occupying the narrow base of power in many countries. Let us turn to Latin America, where we consider the extremes in more detail.

Left-wing ideology. Economics and law students in Latin America are notorious for left-wing extremism.[15] Though they may not agree

[15] My attempts at formal research on opinions of left-wing students in Latin America have generally failed. Where they succeeded, it was mainly because I knew personally either the students or a professor in whom they had confidence, a factor that hardly makes for a random sample! University students in Bolivia and Argentina refused to fill out my questionnaires, even when asked by their own professors, on the grounds that they smacked of Project Camelot. Students in the Central University of Venezuela did fill them out, however. Some twenty students in Mexico filled out questionnaires, but only because of a personal relationship; they would not circulate them among their fellow students for fear of being dubbed agents of the "imperialists."

More than the results of the questionnaires, the views of left-wing Latin American students cited in the present paragraphs are syntheses of conversations I have had with them during the following assignments: a year's course at the economics faculty of the University of San Andrés, Bolivia, in 1960; five two-week seminars yearly, 1964-1969, with a total of fifty students from economics departments of universities in Mexico, mainly the National University; and individual lectures (followed by discussion) in the economics schools of the universities of Guadalajara (*Autónoma*), Monterrey, and the Americas in Mexico; the National Universities of El Salvador, Costa Rica, Argentina, and Colombia; Javeriana University of Colombia; and the Central University of Venezuela.

on details, nevertheless their opinions coincide remarkably on essential points. Their ideology is basically imported. They believe, along with Engels, that the political and social posture of any country, at any time, depends on its economic structure; that the "Wall Street–Pentagon axis" dominates United States government officials from the president down; that elections are not free in the United States or their own countries, because public opinion is molded by a wealthy, bourgeois press and votes can be bought. Left-wing students have their own jargon. "Neocolonialism" is the subjugation of one country by another not through a traditional colonial office but by economic pressure, foreign aid and advisers, and military threat. The "metropole" (subjugating power) is strong in some ways but weak in others. Without neocolonialism it would be utterly helpless, for its economic progress—some say its survival—depends on keeping the "periphery" weak.

This is so for two reason. First, the industrial machines of the metropole need raw materials, generally produced in the periphery. If wages should rise in the latter because of economic growth, costs would increase in the former, "surplus value" (profits) decline, and the power groups would not be pleased. Secondly, the industrial machines of the metropole grind out products far in excess of the capacity of its underpaid workers to consume. Chronic unemployment and a balance-of-payments deficit lead to the necessity to export. For the periphery to have its own competitive industry would be unthinkable to the industrial giants of the metropole.

From this it follows that the economic development of the United States is attributable entirely to capital accumulated through slavery and low wages at home and exploitation by private investors abroad. The removal of mineral wealth from Latin America by United States businessmen, their repatriation of profits and reluctance to invest in industries for domestic consumption, their monopoly status permitting them to pay low for Latin American primary products and charge high for the manufactured exports of their home companies, all have con-

---

Other sources are informal conversations with students during nonlecturing visits to the University of the Valley (Cali, Colombia), National University of Ecuador, University of San Simón (Cochabamba, Bolivia), and Instituto Getulio Vargas (Brazil). In addition, of course, there have been conversations with Latin American exchange students in the United States.

tributed to a capital drain which underlies that continent's economic backwardness.

The image is both *appropriationist* and *nationalist,* the former because it distinguishes between exploiter and exploited, the latter because the exploiter is primarily foreign. Left-wing ideologists recognize the domestic elite also as exploiters, but they assume they would have been powerless had it not been for foreign financing and military support. Rather, they see an unholy alliance between foreign and domestic power blocs impeding national economic development and justice for the poor.

Right-wing ideology. The productionist ideology in Latin America has also been imported. Its adherents have traditionally been the intellectual elites, the military and the church, groups that until recently have held political power in all of Latin America and still do in most. Their education and culture ties have been European and North American, and through these they have been exposed not only to the ideology but also to the panoply of values and institutions evolved around it. Influenced by classical economics, they are culturally international. Like their counterparts abroad, however, they willingly accept tariff and other protection to cultivate national economic interests. Their internationalism thus lies in the fact that they view foreigners as competitors and purveyors of capital and technology, not as exploiters.

Because these groups have held power, they have been able to transplant institutions intact. Hence arise the *surface* similarities between Latin America and the United States, in such systems as three-branched government, "free" elections, political parties, labor unions, and private enterprise.

Grafted into a culture of ideological conflict, institutions that have survived have had to adapt. We have seen how the price system, whose single goal in countries with productionist consensus is to allocate resources efficiently, takes on the secondary goal in Latin America of income redistribution. This mixture of goals, with its attendant uncertainty, reflects the ideological conflict. The same is so for private enterprise, a productionist institution which, yielding to appropriationists, has taken on many of the characteristics of a socialist society, with subsidized housing and other social services.

To assure survival, transplanted institutions have sought the aid of

158

indigenous cultural instruments. Among these, paternalism has been able temporarily to bridge the gap between the two ideological extremes. It has always been compatible with the productionist ideology, whose wealthy adherents have accepted the "burden" of "protecting" the poor. It is also consistent with the appropriationist ideology for its view of government as active intervenor in economic affairs and redresser of grievances.

We have seen the two extremes in Latin America. Neither is likely to yield to the other. Paternalism is a flimsy common ground that may help the temporary survival of productionist institutions, but it is not the basis for efficient contributions to economic growth. Growth-sensitive groups have therefore set out to seek ideological consensus as the foundation for a workable set of values and institutions.

This search has led to a third ideology. Somehow, constituents have been attracted from both extremes and melded into a working ideology that shows promise of consensus in some countries. Its founders arose from the left, appropriationists from the universities who grasped the fact that growth depends on intergroup collaboration and who have been flexible enough to compromise with social elements that in younger years they damned. They are the ones that Hirschman has referred to as "reformmongers."[16] They have been joined by splinter groups of businessmen who, not seeing eye to eye with their productionist elders, have been willing to form associations with government and economic planners. In some countries these businessmen have thrived through the new association, their prosperity being caused by a mixture of new productive effort and government benevolence. In their desire for protection from foreigners, they have found common ground with their appropriationist colleagues. Mosk refers to these businessmen as the "new group" in Mexico, while Friedmann writes of soul-wrenching struggles in the Venezuelan Chamber of Commerce as younger businessmen seized control.[17] This third group,

---

[16] Albert O. Hirschman, *Journeys Toward Progress* (New York: Twentieth Century Fund, 1963).

[17] Sanford Mosk, *Industrial Revolution in Mexico* (Berkeley, Calif.: University of California Press, 1950); and John Friedmann, *Venezuela From Doctrine to Dialogue* (Syracuse, N.Y.: Syracuse University Press, 1965).

initially a *coalition* of left-wing intellectuals and "progressive" businessmen, has become virtually a *union* in Mexico under the institutions of the revolutionary party. It is perhaps still a coalition in Venezuela and an embryonic attempt in some other countries.

The third ideology selects from both extremes. From the appropriationist, it takes the view that society is historically exploitative. While believing government to be an instrument of justice if in proper hands, its adherents nevertheless do not accept the argument that the productive process can be adequately managed in total collectivity. From the productionist, it accepts the view that individual initiative is an essential ingredient of growth. But it regards individuals with high suspicion, believing they will not act for the good of all if left to their own devices. Perhaps it was originally through pragmatic compromise that its holders came to accept private enterprise as a dynamic force under the close observation and benevolent direction of government. To holders of the third ideology, business–government cooperation is the shibboleth corresponding to "private initiative" for the productionists and "Communism" for the appropriationists.

Internationally, the voice of the third ideology is the United Nations Economic Commission for Latin America. Many *técnicos* in the governments of Venezuela, Chile, and Mexico had their early training as functionaries of ECLA. As they filled the vacuum in the economic thought of Latin America through their writings in *Trimestre Económico* and other publications, their thinking spread throughout the continent. New institutions such as the Inter-American Development Bank and the Inter-American Committee for the Alliance for Progress are led by believers. As an international institution, therefore, ECLA has contributed to the blending of the third ideology with a strong degree of Pan-Latin Americanism.

"IDEOLOGICAL" ECONOMIC THEORY—A UNIFYING FORCE

Largely through ECLA, the third ideology has generated some contentious economic thought. Its adherents have issued theories of the terms of trade, of economic integration, of inflation, of foreign investment, and of the relationship between development and the balance of payments.[18]

---

[18] Economic Commission for Latin America, *Development Problems in Latin America*, with a foreword by Carlos Quintana, executive secretary of ECLA (Aus-

These theories have gained but scant currency in the United States and Europe. More than that, they have been rebuked and rejected. In article after article, economists (principally North American) have pointed to serious omissions and errors in the theoretical framework and to biased statistics in the empirical validation. In the more sophisticated world, the ECLA theories are widely known for their lack of rigor and their ideological base.[19]

The greatest value of the ECLA-type thought, however, may lie not in whether or not it is correct, but in what it reveals about the ideology of growth-sensitive groups in Latin America. Hirschman has suggested that ideological theories play a special role in the political economy of development.[20] He distinguishes between privileged problems (on which the legislators are willing to act), such as the balance of payments, and nonprivileged ones (on which they are not willing to act), such as agrarian reform. An ideological theory is one that demonstrates that the solution of a nonprivileged problem is a condition for solving a privileged one. Its purpose is to evoke legislative action.

By extension, ideological theories may be designed to stimulate big-power action. For their own security, big powers are concerned for the economic development of the less developed world, which therefore becomes a privileged problem. Now, it is debatable whether deterioration of the terms of trade is a *necessary* concomitant of development or even a deterrent to it, though the ECLA theory proclaims it is both. If this theory is accepted, it calls the big powers to action to preserve growth, through, for example, commodity agreements or unilateral tariff preferences, both of which have been urged by the United Nations Congress on Trade and Development, an institution formed largely through efforts of adherents to the third ideology. Were it not for the relationship to development, commodity prices and tariffs would surely be unprivileged problems.

---

tin, Tex., University of Texas Press, 1970) is a compendium of articles intended to demonstrate the development of ECLA's economic thought over its first two decades.

[19] In an earlier article I selected several "ECLA-type" theories and showed, with specific references, how they have been rebutted by economists from the U.S. See John P. Powelson, "Toward an Integrated Growth Model—The Case of Latin America," in *Constructive Change in Latin America*, ed. Cole Blasier (Pittsburgh, Pa., University of Pittsburgh Press, 1968).

[20] Hirschman, *Journeys Toward Progress*, p. 231.

There are, however, two other reasons for ideological theories. First, the theories united the once-divergent ideologies of their adherents. Secondly, by *erroneous* economic logic, they have led to *correct* policy conclusions. We treat these separately, below.

Uniting of divergent ideologies. We have seen that the third ideology springs from a coalition formed mainly of two groups: erstwhile left-wing intellectuals (formerly students and now government and international *técnicos*) and erstwhile right-wing businessmen. We may even add the church and the military, to the extent that they are also defecting from pure productionism. Now, coalitions in Latin America have all too often been temporary alliances formed in mutual opposition to something. The third ideology, however, is the basis for a new kind of union, formed not because its members have enemies in common but because they recognize the common goal of growth. They also recognize that a common goal cannot be achieved unless it is grounded on a common theory, leading to a common policy. A theory that the terms of trade have moved and necessarily do move against newly developing countries satisfies all their interests: the intellectuals because it is appropriationist, the businessmen because the policy implications (higher price for exports, protectionism) are in their favor, the military because the resulting policy may bring greater revenue to the government that supports it financially, and the church because greater national revenue will assist the programs of social justice that it is beginning to espouse. Transcending all these, however, is the fact that *the theory will be in itself a unifying force* for the third ideologists.

Correct policy but erroneous logic. This explanation is illustrated by the attitude of the third ideologists toward foreign investment. Let us accept that foreign investment has both positive and negative effects on economic growth. The positive effects are well known—the resources, the technology, and the training that it brings. The negative effects depend largely on the policies followed by investing companies. The more they pressure (or dominate) the host government, the less that government can develop independent, national institutions (such as the legislature and courts of law); the more they refuse to employ nationals in policy-making positions, the more they impede the development of managerial capacity; the more they suppress labor, the less likely it becomes that unions will develop, and so on. Foreign-owned

162

firms may also monopolize fields of activity, thus discouraging entry by nationals.

Let us suppose that the marginal positive effects of foreign investment on value added (through the output of all direct investment firms) are reflected by the curve *MP* in Figure 5-1, whose negative slope implies diminishing marginal productivity. The negative effects (on the output of all firms, including national) are depicted by the curve —*MP*, whose positive slope implies an increased negative marginal impact as investment increases. To the extent that the policies of the firm are "enlightened," more national-centered, —*MP* shifts downward and to the right. It follows the horizontal axis for a short distance from the origin because it is presumed that the negative effects do not begin with the first dollar invested.

FIGURE 5-1. MARGINAL PRODUCT OF FOREIGN INVESTMENT.

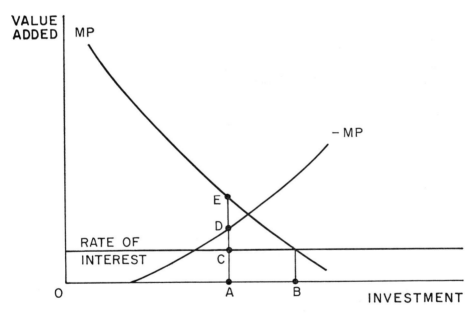

Classical economic theory accepts only the *MP* curve and tells us that the optimum amount of investment is *OB*, where marginal productivity equals the rate of interest. If we consider the —*MP* curve as well, however, then the net marginal impact on national product is measured by the difference between the two curves. The optimum amount of investment then becomes OA, where $AC = DE$.

But economists of the third ideology could not admit that their purpose in restraining foreign investment depends on the cultural cost implied by AD in Figure 5-1, for then they would be admitting that they were incapable of forging domestic institutions to protect the people while at the same time accommodating the full output increment of which foreign investment was physically capable. Instead, the economists invent "economic" reasons why investment should not be increased beyond OA, a limit they sense intuitively. They argue, for instance, that foreign investment is bad for the balance of payments. Over time, the income debits build up to a point where they exceed the investment credits.[21] In this explanation, they ignore the effect of foreign investment on exports and import substitutes. They also ignore the inefficiency of fiscal and monetary institutions in their attempts to correct balance-of-payments deficits. Alternatively, other theories are fashioned to demonstrate that such correction is impossible because of high marginal propensity to import and low elasticity of demand for exports.

The manifest function of ideological theories is to explain the rate of economic growth, but their latent function is to muster consensus on the third ideology as the basis for institutional development.

Nationalism

Consensus on ideology is no mean achievement. In countries characterized by deep ideological conflict, it may be costly indeed. A strong nationalism, however, will help lower its price.

Nevertheless, even growth-sensitive governments are not impelled toward nationalism by a conscious search for ideological consensus. The primary basis for nationalism lies in psychological drives such as the need for identity. Furthermore, nationalism has been encouraged and manipulated by governments for other reasons than economic growth. But the fact that sometimes governments distant from each other (e.g., Meiji Japan and present-day Mexico) actively promote both economic development and nationalism, leads one to suspect a causal relationship.

[21] Helio Jaguaribe, "A Brazilian View," in *How Latin America Views the U.S. Investor*, by Raymond Vernon (New York: Frederick A. Praeger 1966), pp. 67-94.

The fact that nationalism is demanded and supplied for other reasons than development makes it an inexpensive input for economic planners. We do not argue that it is intrinsically cheap. In many countries, such as Mexico, France, the United States, and Soviet Russia, much of the cost of nationalism was paid in bloody revolution. But the revolution was not ordered by the economic planners; to *them*, the nationalism that it fostered was free. When we speak here of the cost of nationalism, we mean only the increment paid by those who promote it for the specific purpose of achieving economic growth.

NATIONALISM AND POLITICO-ECONOMIC SYSTEMS

Among "liberal" economists and "internationally minded" political scientists, nationalism has long been anathema. Four decades ago Hayes described it as a fanatical religion related to war, militarism, and intolerance. Furthermore, it contained a basic contradiction (since two or more objects cannot all be superior to each other) in "the belief that one's own national state has such intrinsic worth and excellence as to require one to be loyal to it above every other thing and particularly to bestow upon it what amounts to supreme religious worship."[22] To liberal economists, nationalism establishes "artificial" (political) boundaries impeding the free flow of resources, thus creating market imperfection and other inefficiencies costly to production and trade. There is a pronounced tendency in more developed countries for businessmen to discount their nationality, basing investment and other decisions on objective political and economic realities. Witness, for example, the growth of the multinational corporation.

But nationalism is neither monolithic nor purposeless. Later political scientists, including Hayes and Deutsch, and sociologists such as Wilbert Moore, have pointed to its role in the achievement of consensus. Moore, for example, writes that "nationalism presents an essentially non-rational unifying force that may ease and rationalize the hardships of personal change."[23] Deutsch writes of national consciousness, or the awareness of symbols of nationality, as a means of enhancing communication and predictable behavior within a society, thus promoting

[22] Carlton J.H. Hayes, *Essays on Nationalism* (New York: Macmillan 1933), p. 245.

[23] Wilbert E. Moore, "The Social Framework of Economic Development," in *Tradition, Values and Socio-Economic Development*, by R. Braibanti and J. J. Spengler (Durham, N.C.: Copyright © 1961 by the Duke University Press), p. 63.

its cohesion. He proposes several tests of nationalism, based on the degree to which the society has achieved communication capacity, predictability, and common behavior patterns, including language (slang, figures of speech, and dialects).[24] Most of these tests would not serve the theory of institutions well. We need, rather, a test of the intensity of awareness of nationality, such as might be indicated in fantasies (thematic apperception tests) or the frequency with which one mentions one's country. We theorize that such awareness correlates with capacity to communicate and predictability, and these in turn stimulate a common ideology and capacity for institutional effectiveness. But we must not anticipate our point by defining nationalism in terms of the variables we expect it to correlate with.

Hayes, Whitaker and Jordon,[25] and others have classified nationalism according to types. Whitaker and Jordan relate different types to the purposes of different ruling classes in Latin America, such as the "old bourgeois," who are associated with the attraction of foreign investment and enterprise as a means to build up the nation's cultural and economic strength.

Two of the Whitaker–Jordan classifications are especially relevant to government promotion of economic development in some Latin American countries.[26] One, "new bourgeois" nationalism, which is particularly applicable to Mexico, Brazil, and Argentina, is supported by "a new upper middle class, primarily industrial-entrepreneurial, whose interests are rooted in the country, in contrast to the foreign-oriented, old middle-class. . . . It stands for economic nationalism and for a modified statism that still allows a wide role for private capital and private enterprise." The other, "populistic nationalism" (corresponding to Hayes's Jacobin type) "represents the most complete form of the fusion of nationalism with social revolution." The authors assign

[24] Karl W. Deutsch, *Nationalism and Social Communication*, 2nd ed. (Cambridge, Mass.: The M.I.T. Press, 1966). The testing procedures are outlined in ch. 5.

[25] C.J.H. Hayes distinguishes five types of European nationalism: Humanitarian, Jacobin, Traditional, Liberal, and Integral (*Nationalism: A Religion* [New York: Macmillan, 1960]). Arthur Whitaker and David Jordan apply other classifications for Latin America—Traditional-rural, Old Bourgeois, New Bourgeois, Populistic, and Nasserist—in their *Nationalism in Contemporary Latin America* (New York: The Free Press, 1966), pp. 14-15.

[26] Whitaker and Jordan, *Nationalism*, p. 15.

166

it to Mexico in the revolution of 1910, Péron's Argentina, Paz Estenssoro's Bolivia, Castro's Cuba, and Goulart's Brazil.

The modern tendency to classify nationalism and assign it a purpose reflects the growing belief that it does not spring *solely* from uncontrollable psychological drives. It is controlled and promoted by governments to serve their aims.

In Latin America, the nationalism that is most successful in promoting ideological consensus is a combination of the new bourgeois and populistic, appealing to different groups in a unifying way. We have already seen how the third ideology has opened communication among businessmen, left-wing intellectuals (ex-students), politicians, and labor leaders—in short, the most powerful groups for organizing economic rules of conduct—in Mexico, Venezuela, and possibly elsewhere. The military has been brought into the consensus in Venezuela and omitted as a political force in Mexico. New bourgeois-populistic nationalism has in all cases underlain this ideology.

Every six years in Mexico, the presidential candidate of the leading *Partido Revolucionario Institucional* makes a whistle-stop campaign covering the entire country. To many North Americans, it is a source of wonderment that a candidate whose election is not the least in doubt should campaign as vigorously and comprehensively as one in the United States to whom the votes of some far-off state might provide the margin of victory. Though institutionally his campaign appears similar, the objective of the presidential candidate in Mexico is not to be elected but to unify the nation through its association with his image. Thus every *campesino*, every laborer, every student, and every businessman from the Pacific to the Caribbean coast and from the United States to the Guatemalan border would know that he is Mexican and would identify himself personally and individually with the goals of his government.

The Mexican government disseminates nationalism in other ways as well. Cinemas (whose prices are controlled and low) regularly present lengthy documentaries on the accomplishments of the revolutionary government in housing, hospitals, and other social services. Primary and secondary schools, both public and private, use uniform textbooks distributed free, and these promote respect for the country's traditions and history. These and other means constitute a conscious effort to promote respect for Indian culture as the cornerstone of Mexican civilization.

In many less developed countries, there is a concerted effort to substitute nationals for expatriates in important positions in business and government. In Mexico, no position may be held by a foreigner unless the employing institution can prove that there is no capable Mexican available, a task which becomes increasingly difficult over the years. Thus Mexican nationals occupy virtually all posts in foreign-originated enterprise, from the president of the board on down. In Kenya, the government increasingly denies operating licenses to foreigners who own commercial establishments in important cities such as Nairobi. As a result, many "Asians" (persons of Indian ancestry, born in Kenya, but holders of British passports) have been forced to sell to Africans (blacks born in Kenya). Since the Asians find it difficult to move elsewhere, being denied the right to live in Britain, their only recourse is to move their commercial activity to villages, where the authorities are less stringent, or to enter into manufacturing. Thus the Kenyan government kills two birds. It upgrades the Kenyan citizenry, and it forces Asian entrepreneurial talent into manufacturing. In both the Mexican and Kenyan cases, it can be argued that strictly economic results are sought, for opening new positions to nationals will enhance their earning power. In addition, however, is the feeling of pride, that productive facilities are increasingly controlled and operated by citizens.

Yet remaining to be studied by interdisciplinary social scientists are the forms of nationalism most likely to promote consensus on ideology, the extent to which such nationalism arises spontaneously out of certain levels of income and rates of growth and in expectation of higher levels and rates, whether it is overtly recognized and rational or intuitive and quasi-rational, the extent to which the chain (nationalism → consensus on ideology → effective values and institutions → income growth) is successful (provable?), and whether noneconomic forces that inspire nationalism, such as psychological drives, are detrimental to growth, growth-promoting, or growth-neutral.

NATIONALISM AND LANGUAGE

The government of Tanzania has selected Swahili as the national language. It is taught in the schools and spoken in the Parliament. But the decision was not an easy one. Swahili (or Kiswahili) is the language of the Swahili people, who have historically occupied the East African coast along Tanganyika and on up into Kenya, as well as the island of Zanzibar. Their language is a combination of the Bantu tongues and Arabic, with other foreign influence as well. In the interior of Tanzania, and in Kenya and Uganda, other tribal languages are primary. But because the Swahili traded extensively in the interior, their tongue has become a second language for tribes from Malawi in the south to southern Sudan in the north, and extending westward into the eastern part of the Congo.

Economic development is not dependent on the adoption of a single national language, as Switzerland and Canada amply testify. Nor is it necessary to speak an indigenous tongue; witness the United States and Latin America. But nationalism requires certain artifacts of unity, and language—though not indispensable—is a reasonable candidate. The Tanzanians did not select Swahili for its growth-promotion qualities; national unity and dignity were doubtless more in their minds. But as we have seen, unity and economic development are not unrelated.

In East Africa (Tanzania, Kenya, and Uganda), each child first learns the language of his own tribe, and only if and when he goes to school does he ordinarily learn Swahili or English or both. English remains the language of the educated and internationally minded people; its use is widespread in the universities. It is still the language for government business in Kenya and Uganda, and many prefer English rather than Swahili as the second language.

Two questions emerge. First, for the theoretical social scientist: why did Tanzania, and not Kenya and Uganda, opt for Swahili? Was the decision historically determined, or did it stem from the personalities of President Nyerere and other high government officials? Second, for the practitioner of development: what are the benefits and costs of the decision, with respect to economic growth? If our theory of institutions is acceptable, the adoption of a national language, and particularly an indigenous one, may well have positive effects on the rate of economic growth. But there may also be costs. Language (like nationalism and ideological consensus) ought to be part of economic growth models. That it is not is the result of narrowness of disciplines and disciplinary approaches, as well as of the difficulties of measurement.

Why Tanzania? Let us examine first the question of history versus personality. There are important historical differences among the East

African countries. Tanganyika was a German colony before World War I. The Germans, far more than the British, promoted Swahili as a means of communication between colonial authorities and tribal governments. The British colonized Kenya and Uganda in the late nineteenth century to secure the route to India by protecting the southern approaches to the Nile and ultimately to Suez. British colonies were self-financing. To obtain revenues from illiterate and non-monetary tribes, the British drafted Africans into forced labor, paid them in newly introduced money (at first rupees, later shillings), and then levied a hut tax. But they also encouraged colonization by British farmers, who were already enculturated to modern tax methods. Since the Kenyan highlands, north and west of Nairobi, were the most agreeable lands climatically and the most adaptable to British agricultural methods, the bulk of the colonization took place there, with considerably less in Uganda and Tanganyika. The city of Nairobi, located (like Denver, Colorado) at the end of the dry plains where water first becomes available from the highlands, became the commercial and industrial capital of East Africa, leaving Dar es Salaam (the capital of Tanzania) and Mombasa (the port serving Nairobi) as centers for foreign commerce. These developments may account in large part for the industrial ascendancy of Kenya over the other two countries. Even after independence, most Kenyan industries remain owned and managed by Europeans (whites, usually of British ancestry) while smaller commercial establishments are owned by Asians, as we noted earlier. The economic predominance of these groups may well have promoted English as a lingua franca rather than Swahili. Whereas Swahili is spoken extensively in Tanzania, in Kenya it is used primarily in Nairobi and other large cities, where migration from the countryside has brought together peoples of different tribes who could not otherwise communicate. But in the Kenyan countryside—outside of the Swahili-speaking areas of the coast—other tribal languages predominate.

While all three countries are ostensibly fostering nationalism, Tanzania alone has outspokenly adopted an ideology, which it is promoting both by overhead methods (teaching the ideology per se) and by successive institution formation (of institutions conforming to the ideology). It is here that historical facts (e.g., the lesser industrial position of Tanzania than Kenya) combine with personality (Nyerere's fervent belief in cooperative methods) to yield a new "third ideology" with respect to both foreign and domestic affairs. For the former, the institutions include acceptance of economic assistance from both European powers, the United States, and China. On the domestic front, they include cooperatives and nationalized enterprises and the adoption of an indigenous language to unify the people.

Benefits and costs. The economic costs of adopting Swahili as opposed to English are high. First, Swahili is not so precise a language. It lacks vocabulary and richness of expression. (This criticism must not be overdone, for—contrary to the arguments of some detractors—Swahili does possess a literature, both prose and poetry. Furthermore, words can be invented as needed; a language develops with its people.) Secondly, English is an international language; those who engage in foreign trade must learn it; technical books are written in it. Thirdly, elementary school books exist more abundantly in English. Swahili, which was earlier written (among those who wrote it at all) in Arabic symbols but later was put into Roman by missionaries, has only recently adopted the standardized spelling and grammar formed by the East Africa Swahili Committee, which was established by the colonial governments of Tanganyika, Kenya, and Uganda in 1930.[27] If solely economic criteria were considered, the benefits in incremental national product resulting from enhanced national cohesion would be weighed against the costs of employing linguists to enrich the language; of propagating the words and expressions they would construct; of either sacrificing internationalism or causing traders and scholars to learn English or an alternative second language; and of developing and printing textbooks and educational materials in Swahili for elementary schools as opposed to importing them or reproducing them in English at low marginal cost.

The willingness of the Tanzanians to pay these costs reflects their belief that the benefits are worth the while. How to substantiate and measure the feeling of national pride that arises from having a language of one's own, as well as the increment of gross national product yielded by the national cohesion that that pride makes possible, remains a substantial challenge to social science investigators.

Institutional Ideology

Values, especially economic and political ideologies, are associated with institution preferences. Appropriationists will favor socialism,

[27] Wilfrid Whitely, *Swahili, The Rise of a National Language* (London: Methuen & Co., 1969), pp. 79ff.

productionists capitalism. Thus an ideology-holder does not have a value-free choice among all conceivable institution-types. He may select only among those that conform to his ideology.

We now create a taxonomy of institutions. This is a multidimensional scale by which *any* institution may be measured. If our assumptions are correct, then holders of a certain ideology will limit their choices to institutions falling within a certain range on the dimensional scales, while holders of another ideology will select a different range. Such ranges may or may not overlap. We refer to the range to which an individual limits himself as his "institutional ideology."

INSTITUTIONAL DIMENSIONS

Unfortunately, "socialist" and "capitalist" are not adequate descriptions of institutions. We suspect they are special cases of the generalized dimensions we seek. We now tentatively select the following dimensions, all of them conceived as continua:

1. *Centralized versus decentralized.* Institutions will be centralized or decentralized depending on whether decision-making (conflict resolution) is concentrated in a small elite or is dispersed over many participants. For example, decisions on the allocation of national resources would be centralized if done solely by a planning board, less centralized if certain elements were decided by business enterprises (private or government), and completely decentralized if done only by impersonal market forces.

2. *Authoritarian versus nonauthoritarian.* An authoritarian institution is one where decisions involving the cooperation of other individuals are made without their participation; they are directed to comply. A nonauthoritarian institution is one where all who participate in an activity have a role in determining how that activity will be selected and implemented.

3. *Formal versus informal.* The institution is formal if it is contained within an organization whose structure is defined by constitution, bylaws, or other such arrangements that govern the manner in which the decision is made. It is informal if formal arrangements either do not exist or are not operative: if, for example, there is a *modus vivendi* or some pattern of human relations which has developed over time.

172

4. *Incentive versus penalty.* This dimension depends on the extent to which the institution enforces its decisions through incentive or penalty. Penalty is distinguished from coercion, which implies forcible action against one's will. An individual may participate without coercion in an institution that imposes penalties upon him. The traffic-control system, for example, applies fines to motorists who do not stop at red lights and does not give lollipops to those who do.

5. *Neutral versus interested in specific resolutions.* This dimension depends on whether the institution is biased or neutral toward potential solutions. Some organizations (e.g., lobbies) are designed to achieve specific solutions to specific conflicts; others (e.g., courts of justice) are presumed to be impartial between contestants. In this dimension, especially, differences of opinion may occur if there is a poor rating by the rules criterion. For example, some may believe that a development corporation well organized and staffed to analyze capital-intensive projects may be biased against projects that are labor-intensive.

These dimensions are selected for several reasons. First, they are salient features. Not only are they fundamental to structure and function, but they are an obvious way by which one type of institution can be distinguished from another. Secondly, they constitute alternative modes of resolution applicable to a wide variety of conflicts. While any specific conflict, by its nature, may tend toward a set of dimensional points different from that tended to by another conflict, nevertheless for any such conflict there is usually *some* choice. Within a limited range, there may be no technological reason why one institution would not function as well as another. Thirdly, and most importantly, we hypothesize that choices among the points will tend to correlate with the political and economic ideologies of groups exercising the option.

For example, a hypothesis worthy of investigation is that appropriationists *in general* prefer centralized, authoritarian, formal, penalty-invoking institutions designed to foster specific solutions, while productionists by contrast prefer decentralized, nonauthoritarian, informal, incentive-providing institutions that are neutral toward proposed solutions. Alternatively, appropriationists (productionists) who have lived under one set of institutions may favor quite a different set

173

from appropriationists (productionists) with experience under another. Thus appropriationist students in the United States might favor decentralized universities while their counterparts in the Soviet Union would be content with highly centralized ones. The theory of institutions does not predict which institutional ideology will conform to which set of economic and political ideologies. Rather, it suggests that economic and political ideologies are the basis for institutional ideology, and—most important—consensus on all three ideologies is essential to institutional effectiveness.

MEASUREMENT OF THE DIMENSIONS

Let an institution be measured by the points it occupies on these dimensions (or others to be selected). For example, suppose each dimension might be scaled from zero to one hundred: an institution might be rated (say) 90 for centralization, 60 for authoritarianism, 30 for formality, and so on. Two institutions might occupy the same points even though their functions are different; they are nevertheless *similar* institutions. For instance, a nationalized steel mill might be similar to a nationalized textile mill and different from a private steel mill. More curiously, one family might be similar to an army headquarters and different from another family.

Measurement of the dimensions would require the following steps. First, a conflict would be specified. (See, for example, the statement of the conflict between the economist and the engineer in Table 3-5, page 75.) Secondly, a textual description of formal and informal rules and procedures would be set forth. ("The bill is first presented in the Ways and Means Committee and after certain procedures goes before the whole House.") Thirdly, the rules would also be specified according to cues such as those listed for the computer on page 78 (rules criterion) with general agreement on weighting presumed. Finally, both the textual description and the computerized cues would be examined for their effects on the five (or more) dimensions. In the conflict illustrated in Chapter 3, a high rating on technical characteristics (cue no. 1) would tend toward high ratings for decentralized (because many technicians contribute), nonauthoritarian (because each technician consults his staff), formal (because procedures are outlined and followed), incentive (because loan applicants are rewarded for preparing good plans and not penalized for not doing so),

174

and neutral (because the loan committee presumably has no axe to grind). On the other hand, a high rating for cue no. 3 (prestige of the protagonists) would militate toward authoritarian, informal, and biased toward specific solutions.

The rating scale cannot avoid being subjective, since it will depend on the opinion of the assessor. It will be easier to compare alternative institutions which perform the same functions than institutions performing different functions. Ratings will probably be more meaningful if several investigators agree on them, and if certain ratings are assigned in advance to certain institutional characteristics in the abstract. Meaningful ratings will probably also require that the same investigators rate all institutions that are compared in a given study.

THE BOUNDARY OF THE INSTITUTION

We emphasize the uniqueness of our definition of institution (introduced in Chapter 1). The institution is the means by which a conflict is resolved. Thus the conflict sets the boundary of the institution, and many institutions may exist and overlap in the same organization. As we study whether decision-making is more centralized in one society than another, we are not confined to organizations with formal structure. While one business enterprise may be more centralized than another, so also may the general procedure for allocating resources in a nation. Both concern us.

For practical reasons, institutional dimensions must frequently be investigated at an organizational level. But the organization as such is not classifiable. Many organizations do not serve the same mix for all participants. A corporation may be a means of income to its stockholders, a source of power, prestige, and high salaries to its officers, a producer of necessities to its customers, a taxpayer to the municipal treasury, and a source of employment and fraternization to its workers. In each such function conflicts will abound, and each conflict is associated with a separate institution. The president of the Republic may make the final decision on whether a criminal will hang and he may also influence the allocation of resources under the national development plan. He operates as a different institution in each case.

In existing institutions, a dimensional measure is possible only where the effectiveness rating is high by the rules criterion. There must be agreement on the formal and informal decision procedure as well as on the foci of power and influence. If our theory that the institutions of economic growth become more effective by all three criteria after takeoff is valid, then the quality of the dimensional measure should improve as the post-takeoff period proceeds. And it is during this period that we are concerned with which types of institutions are selected.

COMPARISONS WITH PARSONS' PATTERN VARIABLES

The institutional dimensions bear some similarity to the famous pattern variables of Talcott Parsons, dichotomies that Parsons has employed to classify social action. These are the following.[28]

1. *Affectivity versus affective neutrality*: to distinguish social relations according to whether they embody emotion and gratification (as between husband and wife) or are businesslike and disciplined (as between sales clerk and customer).

2. *Specificity versus diffuseness*: to distinguish the scope of a social relationship: whether A orients to B as a total person or only with respect to some particular activity.

3. *Universalism versus particularism*: to distinguish whether the quality of an object or social role is judged on universalistic criteria (e.g., an honor-roll or marginal student) or by some subjective feeling of the actor (e.g., friendship).

4. *Quality versus performance* (or *ascription versus achievement*): to distinguish whether an object or activity is judged for its intrinsic characteristics or the way it functions.

5. *Self-orientation versus collectivity orientation*: to distinguish between those activities and roles in which the actor responds to imperatives of the social system (subsystem) and those where he responds to his own needs only.

The similarities lie in the fact that we try to do for institutions what Parsons did for social action: establish dimensional measures applicable regardless of function or type. But Parsons' purpose was different from ours. An institution encompasses social action, and therefore the kinds of activity taking place within it could be rated according to the Parsons variables, but the institution itself could not. It is possible,

[28] Talcott Parsons, *The Social System* (New York: The Free Press, 1951), pp. 58ff.

however, that additional institutional dimensions might be derived from the pattern variables.

Hoselitz has observed that three of the Parsons variables (specificity versus diffuseness; universalism versus particularism; and quality versus performance) might help classify the degree of development of a nation.[29] He sees development as a process leading toward greater specificity, universalism, and performance. The same might be said with respect to the institutional dimensions. Development might lead toward greater formality and the increasing use of incentives rather than penalties. But it also might not. There is no need to investigate this point now. Rather, the question lies in the institutional differences between two (or more) nations at approximately the same stage of economic growth (same GNP per capita and rate of increase). Why did one choose one set of institutions and the other another?

The Relationship between Institutions and Values

We now propose that for any given conflict in a specific time and space, there exists a solution line farther from the origin than any other, representing all those maximum positions whose achievement is technologically possible. This is the physical solution line. However, an institution capable of achieving a position on this line may not be acceptable to all contestants, for it may conflict with the personal values held by one or more of them. In that case, the solution line farthest from the origin (but ordinarily not so far as the physical) that is achievable through an institution acceptable to all contestants is the apparent solution line. We call the institution capable of achieving this line the *optimal institution*, for it is more effective than any other that is acceptable. There may, however, be more than one optimal institution. Of course, if the physical solution line can be achieved, then the institution capable of doing so is the optimal.

In some cases, the optimal institution will be determined more by the nature of the conflict than by the personal values of the contestants. A university by the nature of its functions will be more decentralized than an army. A scientific agency whose purpose is to discover the most efficient means of putting a man on Mars will probably be constructed in similar fashion whether it is in the Soviet Union or the

[29] Bert F. Hoselitz, *Sociological Aspects of Economic Growth* (New York: The Free Press, 1960), pp. 29ff.

United States. Scientists with conflicting theories will put them to test in similar ways. Of course, the institutional structure depends on scientific positivism as a value, but it makes little difference whether the scientists adhere more to the appropriationist or to the productionist ideology.

In other cases, the optimal institution will depend more on the personal values of contestants than on the nature of the conflict. These institutions will differ according to time and place, and their apparent solution lines are likely to be far from the physical. Highly centralized institutions may be optimal for contestants strongly imbued with the appropriationist ideology. They cannot trust decentralized ones, which they fear will lead to inequitable power distribution. Conversely, adherents to the productionist ideology may prefer decentralized institutions, fearing that a strong central government will destroy their concept of personal liberty. The choice between compulsory and "indicative" instruments of economic planning is a case in point.

The exact points occupied by any institution therefore depend on the relative pulls of two forces: (1) its functions, which would lead it toward the same points anywhere in the world, and (2) the values held by those participating in it, which would lead it toward the same points occupied by other institutions, regardless of function, which service the same participants. Some institutions respond more strongly to the first force and some to the second.

Any society that has achieved a fair degree of consensus on its economic and political ideology will therefore contain institutions ranging over the limits of its corresponding institutional ideology, but the institutional ideologies of different societies may differ. If the United States and the Soviet Union should choose an identical institution for a given conflict, it would be because (1) the choice of that institution probably depends more on its inherent characteristics than on societal values, and (2) the Soviet and American institutional ideologies overlap at that range.

At present, we are concerned only with the second force, or the question of why some cultures tend toward one institutional ideology and others toward another. We find ourselves deep in territory of inadequate empirical research. What is necessary is first to identify and catalogue national values relevant to economic growth, including of course nationalism and ideology; secondly, to measure the degree of consensus achieved on these values; and thirdly, to relate them to the dimensional ratings of the institutions selected to resolve the conflicts of economic growth or to ideal constructs that individuals would select if given free choice.

Anthropologists have prepared catalogues of national values, as, for example, the one by Gillin cited in the preceding chapter. Another, by Lasswell and Holmberg, has attempted to relate values and institutions to economic growth, but not in the sense that we suggest here. The Lasswell–Holmberg model proposes eight value-institution groupings (power, enlightenment. wealth, well-being, skill, affection, respect, and rectitude) which the authors associate with institutional development and for which they suggest measurements by means of interactions (symbols, signs, and resources).[30] Their purpose, however, is to demonstrate that *if* (say) the enlightenment value is strongly held, *then* enlightenment institutions (e.g., schools) will tend to be formed rather than institutions associated with other values less strongly held.

Another interesting approach is that of Kluckholn and Strodtbeck,[31] who propose that the qualities of five different value orientations are related to a people's economic growth. These are man's relations to nature, to activity, to time, to human relations, and to human nature. Those countries showing high rates of growth tend to orient these values respectively in the following manner: control over nature, actively doing, looking to the future, individualism, and perfectibility of that which is bad (or neutral). Those countries showing low rates of growth tend to orient these values respectively as follows: subject to nature, passively being, looking to the past, relationship to ancestors, and acceptance of good and evil mixed.

Our present objective is different from those of the authors cited above. Though we recognize the likelihood that some values may be more closely related to economic growth than others, we do not try to identify them. Rather, we examine the process by which growth-sensitive groups seek to alter the value structure, either by "overhead"

[30] Harold D. Lasswell and Allen R. Holmberg, "Toward a General Theory of Directed Value Accumulation and Institutional Development," in *Comparative Theories of Social Change*, ed. Hollis W. Peter (Ann Arbor, Mich.: Foundation for Research on Human Behavior, 1966), pp. 12-59.

[31] Florence R. Kluckholn and Fred L. Strodtbeck, *Variations in Value Orientations* (New York: Row Peterson and Co., 1961).

attack (as through nationalism and ideology) or through the direct formation of institutions. We do agree that certain values—say, enlightenment (of the Lasswell–Holmberg classification) or future-orientation (of the Kluckholn–Strodtbeck classification)—may be associated more closely with institutions of certain dimensions than with those of others. Failing adequate measures and correlations, we can only suggest the following hypotheses. First, without consensus on a set of values (including ideology), it is difficult to form any consistent institutions, and conflict resolutions will be *ad hoc*. The failure to establish predictable institutions is a serious obstacle to economic growth. Secondly, the kinds of optimal institutions in any society depend on the values on which the society is able to achieve consensus, and especially on economic and political ideology. We have already suggested that the appropriationist ideology is associated with centralized institutions. So also a paternalistic or hierarchical society (in the Gillin classification) may opt for authoritarian and penalty-invoking institutions; it may prefer formal over informal. While nations with more developed enlightenment values (in the Lasswell–Holmberg classification) may have more effective educational institutions, they may also opt for less authoritarian institutions in all categories. The important point is that successful institutions require the confidence of all contestants. Those that do not conform to national values will not command confidence.

The Path of Successive Institution Formation

Now, economic growth generates *new* conflicts, which continuously call for *new* institutions. In a static model, the choice of optimal institution-types depends entirely on existing values. But institutions so chosen are likely to be ineffective (apparent solution lines far below physical), since the values to which they conform were not evolved with the new conflicts in mind. Contestants will be vaguely aware that a physical solution line lies "somewhere out there," and they will seek more effective institutions.

Any new institution will occupy a different set of points on the dimensions from its predecessor. Since the old institution conformed most closely to currently held values, the new institution will conform less so. It will differ from the old by small shifts in the dimensional measures. Some dimensions will have to yield. But which?

Let us suppose that a new conflict x arises in a growth situation. An institution X_1 is formed, which lies within the range of currently held institutional ideology. It is defined by a certain set of dimensional measures. But we presume that it is ineffective, and the contestants seek modifications to increase its effectiveness. Let us suppose that another institution, X_n, with a different set of dimensional points, is capable of achieving the physical solution line, but that it lies outside the range of currently held institutional ideology. There are, however, a series of modified institutions, from X_2 to X_{n-1}, each successive one of which yields an increment in one or more dimensions and approaches those of X_n. The contestants will accept institution X_2 as optimal at such time as its increased effectiveness is worth the cost of the personal value forgone (in subjective evaluation of sacrifice) to that participant least willing to relinquish it and powerful enough to block the institution. After X_2 has been selected and has proved, through its operations, that it is not so ugly as its enemies had supposed, *the range of institutional ideology itself has been moved*, and a new situation is created. Of course, as institutional ideology moves, so also do political and economic ideologies. Indeed, the union of divergent political and economic ideologies into a new consensus may shift the range of institutional ideology; they react upon each other mutually. With the passage of time, X_3 becomes optimal, and so on until X_n is both included within the range and achieved. However, the process may stop at any point along the way if the cost of some institutional modification is deemed too high to a contestant capable of blocking it.

This analysis casts a new light on some traditional ways of viewing institutions. For example, a corrupt civil service may be the optimal institution for managing government operations, corresponding to X_1, even though an uncorrupt one would be most effective (and efficient) in maximizing national product, corresponding to X_n. But the uncorrupt service may be unattainable because it may clash with deeply ingrained values of personalism and distrust for the government. In their eagerness to abolish corruption, foreign public administration advisers may, it is feared, have left a vacuum in their host countries that has delayed the orderly evolution of effective institutions.

A corrupt system has the following advantages. First, it provides a progressive system of "taxation." The peasant who is too poor to pay bribes is never expected to do so. The motorist, who palms a small note while handing over his driver's license has at least sufficient resources to own a car. The industrialist seeking an import license must pay a higher sum, commensurate with his firm's capacity. Likewise the most wealthy, who benefit from legislative favors such as highways past their property and government contracts for their firms, must reward the highest political officers, paying in proportion to their affluence.

Secondly, corruption provides a scale of emoluments roughly proportionate to the civil-service rating of the government official. A policeman, low on the scale, must be content with the pittance in the motorist's palm. The minister who issues the import license makes higher-level decisions than the policeman, and he rightfully deserves a greater "salary." But the highest officials, who control national policies, should obviously be compensated according to the seriousness of their responsibilities. So they have access to the national treasury. Clearly, both corrupt and uncorrupt systems tax and reward in roughly the same proportions; the flows of funds simply follow parallel channels.

In those countries where corruption is the optimal system, the attempt to eliminate it suddenly may make rules and their enforcement even less clear than before. Earlier (page 95) we discussed how the tax system in some Latin American countries probably rates very low according to the three effectiveness criteria, because enforcement is spotty and taxpayers are unclear as to what is really expected of them. While the uncorrupt system (X_n) would be the most effective if it accorded with institutional ideology and expectations of compliance, nevertheless it can be approached only step by step. Each sub-institution must be changed only as the immediate demand for reform is perceived as greater than the cost. Each change must be followed by a pause (which it is hoped will be short) until national values catch up with it.

Nye sees additional benefits in corruption, including its contribution to capital formation, the cutting of red tape, entrepreneurship and incentives, national integration, and governmental capacity.[32] He offsets these against costs, which include waste of resources and skills, instability, and reduction of governmental capacity in certain ways. His

[32] J. S. Nye, "Corruption and Political Development: A Benefit-Cost Analysis," *American Political Science Review* (June 1967), pp. 417-27.

general conclusion is that "the costs of corruption in less developed countries will exceed its benefits except for top level corruption involving modern inducements and marginal deviations and except for situations where corruption provides the only solution to an important obstacle to development."[33]

The inconsistency resulting from the imposition of institutions oriented to foreign culture-patterns was examined by psychologists Sanchez and Saavedra in a study of regional centers of the University of Chile formed to promote professional training in fields needed for economic development. These institutions were in large part financed and staffed from the United States, and therefore had a tendency toward the infusion of North American values.

Sanchez and Saavedra used the Kluckholn–Strodtbeck techniques, consisting of twenty-two items in a questionnaire, each depicting "a typical life situation and then (posing) alternatives of solution for the problem which derive from the postulated alternatives of the value orientation in question."[34]

The authors concluded that the student population was not undergoing the kinds of value changes that their teachers were promoting or that Kluckholn and Strodtbeck would associate with economic development; a working population which they also sampled demonstrated greater achievement in value change. They suggested that professional training centers staffed and financed from abroad not only fail to promote value change but set up unhealthy strains and emotional disturbances among the students:[35]

> It is apparent that the Agencies created to bring about change . . . do not actually fulfill their purpose. They rather superimpose stereotypes which seem irrational and sometimes disturbing. At the same time, they obtain a change in the expectations and level of aspirations of the individuals concerned.

> The structural characteristics of the country do not provide at present the necessary channels to satisfy the new roles, expecta-

---

[33] *Ibid.*, p. 427.

[34] Vicente Sanchez and Patricio Saavedra, "Programmed Change in Values," mimeographed (Santiago: University of Chile, 1970), p. 24; the authors are Professor of Psychology and Personality and Consultant Psychologist, respectively, at the University of Chile.

[35] *Ibid.*, p. 46.

tions, and level of aspirations, and therefore a series of consequences can ensue: maladjustment, emigration, conformity towards foreign models which are not adaptive to our reality and even authoritarian solutions.

It may well be that the institution selected (regional centers of the university) is the appropriate X_n for maximizing economic growth, but on the basis of the study by Sanchez and Saavedra it would seem not to be the appropriate X_1.

In some situations, a certain X_n may be the only institution capable of achieving the physical solution line. In this case, any society accepting and retaining *maximum* economic growth as a dominant goal will ultimately move to that X_n. Such, for example, *may* be the case of the free-price system, which is decentralized, nonauthoritarian with some formal organization (markets), and based far more on incentives than penalties. The Soviet Union has recently moved toward this system, which had previously been adopted by the United States. Let us hypothesize that free pricing is the most effective institution for allocating economic resources, regardless of time or place. In the years immediately following their revolution, however, the Soviets, seized by the appropriationist ideology, believed that free pricing would be abused by the powerful. Had it been adopted, it would have required elaborate controls, such as budgetary justifications to ensure it against monopoly or to control its effects and audits to prevent cheating, and the high cost of these controls would have made the system less effective than central government pricing, which therefore became the optimal institution. As ideological consensus increased, the apparent effectiveness of central government pricing even improved. Conversely, the effectiveness of free pricing, had it been employed at all, would have decreased as the Soviets became more convinced of its injustice. Only when the confidence of the contestants (government bureaucrats and plant managers) in their institution had been transferred to confidence in each other was it possible for them to change their values and accept a free-price system, which they decided was more effective on technological grounds. If this interpretation is correct, that decision was not an "error corrected" but the outcome of an orderly evolution toward maximum institutional effectiveness.

But it is also possible that two or more institutions, very different from each other, are equally capable of achieving the physical solution line. There is no *technological* reason why a nationalized and a private enterprise might not be equally efficient in their input–output relationships. The nationalized enterprise might be centralized, authoritarian, formal, with more penalties than incentives, while the private enterprise would be moderately decentralized, less authoritarian, a bit less formal, and heavily weighted toward incentives.

In contrast to opinions freely circulating in the United States, a report based on a visit to the Soviet Union by steel executives from the United States found that the heavy steel industry there was just as efficient (possibly more so) than its counterpart at home.[36]

Veliz and Adams have argued that Latin American countries are a "conforming" society and that modification of major institutions is extremely difficult.[37] For example, they say that a middle class—so often deemed an engine of change in the Western world—is not emerging. Rather, lower-class individuals move directly into the upper class, adopting its values and way of life. Upper-class people are motivated not principally by a desire for material advancement (a characteristic of middle classes) but more by a need to control others, possibly through the exercise of wealth, but more subtly through a network of obligations such as the extended family, the granting of favors, or the control over employment or other objects that their subjects value. But, they go on to argue, the intractability of Latin American society does not prevent economic growth. Rather, this occurs amid a broadening of the network of obligations, through (for example) a redefinition of the functions of the military, or through a new, mechanized agrarian capitalist class, or through a resurgent church hierarchy, and the like. This observation is consistent with our own theory, that economic growth is possible without a change in those institutions that are difficult to change, provided other institutions where change is less costly are appropriately modified. In contrast to what is often supposed, the two sets—of change-possible and change-impossible institutions—are *not* unique the world over.

[36] American Iron and Steel Institute, *Steel in the Soviet Union* (New York, 1959).

[37] Claudio Veliz, ed., *The Politics of Conformity in Latin America* (New York, Oxford University Press, 1967). See esp. the introduction by Veliz and the article by Richard Adams, "Political Power and Social Structures."

Where two institution-types are equally capable of maximum effectiveness, the set of optimal, successively modified institutions will be selected whose cost at each point along the way (in terms of value sacrifice) is least. Clearly, the earliest choices will be telling, since later institutions of the same type will be cheaper than others of a different type. Frequently the successive steps will lead, without reversal, to one of the most effective institutions. Nevertheless, it is possible that midstream shifts will be required, if for example the costs of early modifications are less in the direction of effective institution path X, but the costs of later modifications become much greater. This may well occur in the coercive society at the point where coercion, previously less costly than consensus, now becomes more so. The society may then choose to retrace its steps, at some cost, and set out on the path of effective institution Y.

Finally, it is possible that the most effective institution will never be reached, for its cost becomes ultimately too high, and the society opts for less economic growth rather than making the necessary value sacrifice. This would be so, for example, if the most effective institution were nonauthoritarian, but the society was unwilling to relinquish authoritarianism as a value. Furthermore, at time of takeoff the optimal institutions selected by a society may not lead toward maximum effectiveness. For example, these optimal institutions may be either socialist or capitalist, or some mixture, depending on the value consensus. But it is by no means proved that ultimately either socialist or capitalist institutions are capable of greater effectiveness in production and income distribution than the other. If society opts for whichever of these is ultimately less effective and constructs its ideology on that basis, it may later discover that the cost to reverse itself is too great. If the Soviet authorities should decide that capitalist institutions are, after all, capable of exacting greater output per unit of input than socialist, they might still be unwilling to change. The same would probably be so for the United States with respect to socialist institutions.

I am not sure whether the macro-theory of institutions conflicts or does not conflict with Levy's concept of the modernized society. Levy is an exponent of convergence theory, that societies become more and more alike the more they modernize. He states, for example, that "as the level of modernization increases, the level of structural uniformity among relatively modernized societies continually increases regardless of how diverse the original basis from which change took place in these societies may have been. In other words, the more modernized modern societies become, the more they resemble one another."[38]

I say I am not sure, because Levy's examples of structural similarity are on so general a level that it is often difficult to disagree with them. For example, all modernized societies have market structures, they use money, the role of government increases, and so on. His theme is that the social interdependence of modern societies is such that the same component parts will be evolved and will fit together by the same ecological conditions everywhere. If the same theory were applied to biological evolution, it would require that all modernized animals would tend to become the same. In fact, there are similarities in the body structures of all mammals, and so long as one remains on a sufficient degree of generality, it is correct to say they are all alike.

Levy does recognize variations, though he attributes them primarily to differing degrees of development. But it is precisely those variations, as they apply to societies of the *same* degree of modernization, to which the theory of institutions addresses itself. Nations with the same levels of GNP and the same rates of growth are patently unlike in many ways. Moore elaborates on this point, disagreeing with Levy on convergence theory and distinguishing between those elements of similarity and those of dissimilarity in modernizing nations.[39]

Ends and Means

We have now touched on two related questions of deep concern to promoters of societal change. One is how fast it can occur. The other is whether culturally abhorrent means (e.g., killing) are justified in achieving desirable political solutions (e.g., more egalitarian distribution of income and power).

The theory of institutions makes no general prediction with respect to the first. However, by outlining the minimum conditions of institutional change, it provides a basis for predicting the speed of that change under particular circumstances. These conditions of change are a concerted effort to achieve ideological consensus as well as suc-

---

[38] Marion J. Levy, Jr., *Modernization and the Structure of Societies* (Princeton, N.J.: Princeton University Press, 1966), p. 709.

[39] Wilbert E. Moore, "The Singular and the Plural: The Social Significance of Industrialism Reconsidered," mimeographed (Denver, Colo.: University of Denver, 1970).

cessively formed institutions that are always consistent with society's capacity to modify its institutional ideology. How rapidly these changes occur depends on the demand schedules of the individuals who seek them and the supply schedules of those who resist them. These differ from time to time and from place to place. The theory does not rule out convulsive change, but it does imply that successful convulsions require special circumstances. Among these might be large masses of individuals with little or no stake in existing institutions, who therefore not only do not join the consensus upon them but can be readily persuaded of the value of other institutions. Their low opportunity cost of change makes it cheaper for growth-sensitive power groups to pay the price of upheaval. These conditions would seem to have applied in pre-Castro Cuba.

Whether the changed institutions in Cuba are sustainable depends on the government's success in maintaining ideological unity. In this, it has been assisted by three forces. One has been the possibility of exporting those who refuse to join the consensus, via the airlift to Miami which came to an end in September 1971. Another has been the persistent threat of invasion by the United States, which, believed by most Cubans, is a powerful integrative force. The third has been the personal charisma of Fidel Castro. It is interesting that the United States is responsible for maintaining two of these supports. The big test before the Cubans will be to see whether they can preserve unity once these three integrative forces have disappeared.

The conditions of convulsive change would not, however, appear to exist in the United States. The poor and discriminated-against are numerically weaker there than in pre-Castro Cuba, and the ideological consensus on existing institutions is much stronger. The price of convulsive change is beyond the budget of those who propose it.

The second question—that of ends and means—implies that it is possible to obtain the same quality of society by different methods, for instance through violence or peaceful change. But what is meant by "quality of society"? Clearly a particular political solution, such as egalitarian income distribution, access of unprivileged groups to social organizations, or antipollution laws, can be attained either way. But no political solution is final. Hence the most pertinent value judgment is on the institutions by which a solution is reached and sustained. A student of revolutions in Latin America is bound to be struck by the number of times that reforms achieved violently are again taken away violently. Bolivia since its revolution of 1952 has been a murderous seesaw, in which concessions to workers and miners made by one government have been rescinded after the next coup d'etat, only to be restored and rescinded several times over. Similar histories can be recounted for Argentina, Brazil, Ecuador, and a host of other countries, many of them involving suppression of liberties, imprisonment, and torture, of which no one side possesses a monopoly.

Quality of society, it would seem, should be assessed not in terms of particular political solutions but of the kinds of institutions through which these solutions are reached. The law of relatively rising cost of coercion warns against violent and repressive measures taken in the name of change and justice. If one believes this, then there is no controversy between ends and means. Indeed, the means are the ends.

Summary

The conformity of institutions to national values is both positive and negative. Negatively, values act as constraints, making certain institutional forms too costly. For example, private enterprise is unthinkable in a nation polarized on the appropriationist ideology. Positively, values are the foundations of institutions. Institutions cannot survive without value support.

Since takeoff imposes conflicts a country has never known before, new institutions are required. Characteristically, no institution capable of resolving these conflicts with the maximum effectiveness known to man will be consistent with the existing value structure. The nation must at first depend on ineffective institutions that do so conform. Growth-sensitive groups that achieve power will act to increase institutional effectiveness.

We define an optimal institution as one capable of achieving a solution on the highest (apparent) solution line that is both possible and consistent with national values. During early takeoff, optimal institutions are usually ineffective.

Institution-types are defined according to the dimensions we have mentioned and, it is hoped, according to others that other authors will add. In seeking more effective institutions (an outward shift of optimality as values change), power groups ordinarily choose among many directions, for there is no unique path to effectiveness. Normally they select those institutions that yield the greatest marginal economic growth per marginal unit of sacrifice (to the power groups themselves) as they push out on the dimensional continua.

The cost (sacrifice) to the power groups is twofold. First, there are values that they themselves forgo. Secondly, they must secure the cooperation of other groups, either by consensus (persuading them to be growth-sensitive groups), by coercion, or by both. We surmise that over time the cost of coercion rises relative to that of consensus, since we observe that *all* modern societies that have achieved and maintained high rates of growth have *ultimately* employed largely consensus institutions. Indeed, some have expended great sums on that consensus. It follows, therefore, that the cost of economic growth to those societies that opt for coercion early may be far greater than to those that early adopt consensus.

Growth institutions will ultimately conform to national consensus on economic and political ideology (appropriationist, productionist, or mixed), or else they will not be formed. This consensus may come about in one of two ways, or a mixture of them: successive institution formation or direct pursuit of ideology.

Successive institution formation leads to selection of an ideology because each choice makes easier a subsequent choice of the same kind of institution. To justify all choices, a nation is led into an ideology. By direct pursuit, on the other hand, power groups select an ideology and form economic and political theories to support it. Since it is difficult for a nation to form consensus on ideology until it has had experience with other types of consensus, and since popular nationalism is a relatively low-cost object on which to form consensus and one that fits in closely with ideology, takeoff countries usually expend great sums on the promotion of nationalism. Some of these sums represent resource sacrifices that physically retard economic growth (as, for example, the rejection of foreign investment). These sacrifices, which puzzle foreign intellectuals of other ideologies, may nevertheless constitute the least costly path to maximum *net* economic growth. A benefit-cost analysis of nationalism as promoter of economic growth is sorely needed.

The cost of ideology and nationalism corresponds exactly to overhead in manufacturing, and greater expenditures upon them are analogous to the higher cost of building a larger-size plant. Overhead is a way of reducing direct cost. The selection of one ideology rather than another is analogous to selecting one production process (to which a larger plant structure will conform) rather than another.

It cannot be said, in some final authoritative way, that any one ideology will lead to the greatest institutional effectiveness possible, as it might be argued (for example) that production of synthetic rubber based on polybutadeine is more efficient than that based on alcohol. But it can be said that one ideology is less costly than another, in that it conforms more closely to a nation's concept of itself, its values, and its historical experience. Nations that have been subject to more conquest and exploitation than others find the appropriationist ideology more satisfying than the productionist. So also do nations that have not achieved the economic or social progress they now deem desirable, for the appropriationist ideology allows them to blame their failures upon the rest of the world rather than themselves.

Possibly the optimal institutions successively selected will lead some day to a dead end, in that even greater effectiveness could be achieved only by retracing one's steps and selecting a different route. While maximum institutional effectiveness is surely not beyond their capacity, nevertheless for some nations it will be very costly indeed.

PART II

Implications of the Theory

Introduction

THE theory of institutions has been completed in Part I. The hope that others will improve it and research upon it was a principle motive for publishing it at this time. We now turn to the implications of the theory.

Chapter 6 presents ideas on how the concept of institutional effectiveness may influence the manner in which economic planning is viewed: how macro-plans are formed and projects analyzed. It argues that institutional effectiveness ought to be a principal criterion in project selection. We suggest that maximum economic growth may be achieved not by choosing those projects with the highest benefit-cost ratio but by selecting those most likely to increase the nation's capacity for effective decision-making.

In Chapter 7 we ask the important question: has the theory of institutions contributed anything to the theory of economic growth? For the answer to this question I await the judgment of colleagues in all disciplines, a judgment which will best be reflected in the use that they make of the theory. It is hoped that it will form a bridge between economic and sociological models of growth, for the chasm is yawning and there are many who yearn to cross. I propose that *aggregate* institutional effectiveness is a measurable concept that will take on different values in different nations and ought to contribute to the explanation of their differing rates of growth.

Chapter 8 is a brief essay in speculation. Economic growth models usually predict an indefinitely increasing gross national product. But no organism, social or biological, will grow forever. Thus we consider the forces that may ultimately stop growth. We conclude that the end will come not for the reason given by the classical economists that the earth exhausts its capacity to supply. Nor will it happen because man cannot form adequate conflict-resolving institutions. Rather, we boldly and optimistically predict that economic growth will end for no other reason than that man no longer wants it.

CHAPTER 6

The Effectiveness of Economic Planning

THE concept of institutional effectiveness ought—I believe—to influence the manner in which economic planning is undertaken, the macro-plans formed and the projects analyzed. We now turn to this concern, and select Latin America as our area of attention.

The State of Planning in Latin America

After a decade of the Alliance for Progress, there is widespread dissatisfaction with the state of economic planning in Latin America. In June 1969 a report to a ministerial-level meeting of the Inter-American Economic and Social Council stated the following:

> It is repeatedly discovered that long-term plans were either not put into effect, or they were implemented officially for only a fraction of their time, or they were simply ignored at the moment of governmental decisions. The conditions of political support for the plan, changes in the government, the permanent attention demanded by oppressing short-term problems, the administrative inflexibility in its execution and lack of operative mechanisms that might have translated the goals of programs into immediate actions, are among the complex of factors that provoked the relative failure in the realization of long-term plans. . . .
>
> The lack of greater administrative efficiency is basically a manifestation of economic underdevelopment. Many public functions are not filled, or else their performance presents considerable gaps, because of the scarcity of material and human resources in the public sector and in the economy as a whole. Apparently this is also related to the scarcity of fiscal revenues and tax reforms.
>
> But this absence of functions is not the only danger of this sort that confronts the execution of plans and projects. Frequently there is inadequate distribution of public responsibilities, lack of definition of jurisdiction over lines of authority and no way to carry out inter-institutional relationships.
>
> Stemming from a broader concept of the role of the State in economic welfare and development, during the present century a large number of new tasks and organisms have been added to

the traditional structure. Different influence groups or historical circumstances have given birth to these agencies, which—though they may have performed their functions and contributed to development—have been superimposed on the classical State apparatus in a disperse and disorderly way, such that now they diminish the possibilities of applying a programmed application of economic growth policy.[1]

In fourteen out of twenty countries listed by the Organization of American States the central planning office is an arm of the presidency of the Republic. In two it is a ministry, and in the others it is at a lower governmental level. Its principal duty is the formulation of planning budgets. While in some cases (e.g., Mexico) this consists of no more than a coordination of the investment expenditures of the various ministries, in most countries it extends to a forecast of all national expenditures, both public and private, together with recommendations of policy designed to bring about desired levels. Several planning offices are also involved in reforms of the public administration system. Most offices are subdivided into regional agencies concerned with sectoral plans and project formation.

In all Latin American countries funding is done by financial institutions that are distinct from the planning office. These include development corporations (*corporaciones de fomento* or *financieras*), industrial banks, agricultural credit agencies, and the like. This separation of funding from planning is appropriate for control purposes; nevertheless, the inability of planning offices and funding institutions to coordinate their efforts is a serious impediment to implementation.

The ineffectiveness of Latin American planning stems from two major causes. One is that many institutions are transplanted and are not optimal for local conditions. The other is that even optimal institutions are restricted by national failures to achieve consensus on ultimate goals. As a result there is little pragmatic agreement on the institutional objectives, inter- and intrainstitutional commitments are

[1] Inter-American Economic and Social Council of the Organization of American States, *Estado de Planificación en América Latina*, document of the 6th annual meeting of IA-ECOSOC at the level of experts and ministers, Port of Spain, Trinidad and Tobago, June 14-23, 1969; OAS document series H/X.14, CIES 1383, May 22, 1969, pp. 2-3, 44-45; translation mine.

difficult to achieve, and those that do emerge require elaborate safe-guards to overcome the lack of confidence.

We consider these factors below, separately for macro- and micro-planning. Sectoral planning (in between macro- and micro-) is omitted because it has only recently become widespread in Latin America in presumed answer to the deficiencies of the macro- and the micro-theories. The experience with sectoral planning has therefore been too limited for us yet to offer valid comments on it.

Macro-planning

Macro-planning was à la mode during the fifties. Less developed countries the world over were working out macro-models based on national product identities, input-output tables, and projected techno-logical and psychological functions that presumably could be read from the accounts of past years, with data modified as necessary by engineers and policy-makers.

The form of these models was imported. It had matured in the more developed world during the depression and Second World War. There the instruments of macro-economics served three purposes. First, they contributed to an intellectual understanding of the structure and process of the economy. Secondly, they were the basis for macro-policy, consisting of indirect influence through such variables as rate of interest, taxation, and government spending and (during wartime) through direct controls over certain prices and expenditures. Thirdly, during the war input-output tables helped forecast industrial short-ages in the United States, which might have developed into bottle-necks and weakened the nation's military or civilian effectiveness.

With the postwar focus on economic growth in the less developed world, macro-accounting models rushed to fill the vacuum of planning instruments. Yet after a decade of five- and ten-year plans based on them, planning offices began to retrench. The crystal ball had been too dim for the long range. Macro-models had largely failed in all three purposes.

In the first, *understanding*, the accounting models were inhibited by their alien origin. On the supposition that great revelations would arise from international comparability, the United Nations and the Inter-national Monetary Fund had urged standardized national-product and balance-of-payments accounts upon member governments. The selection of sectors and classification of items were based on those of more developed countries. But countries with diverse financial institutions, different corporate structures, and varying degrees of centralization or decentralization of decision-making were thus portrayed uniformly. Possibly the efforts of international organizations resulted in making the member governments statistics-conscious, so that they published data where none would otherwise have been compiled. Whether the data were the most appropriate, however, is open to question.

The accounting models were also inhibited by the institutional ineffectiveness of data-collecting agencies. Interagency jealousies prevented the sharing of data. In one Latin American country, the staff of the central bank became incensed because researchers in the national university used data from the central bank without citing reference. The anger was great enough to cut off communication, causing duplication of effort. In another country the central bank refused for many years to disclose its methodology for national income accounts, information which would have been useful to planners in judging their accuracy. The apparent reason was that when methods had been disclosed earlier, the staff had been bitterly criticized (especially by professionals from the development corporation) for the high probability of data error. The staff agreed with the criticism but believed the error could not be decreased under its present budget. In a third country, the central bank and the planning office prepared conflicting statements of national accounts, one based on indices of real production and the other on deflated estimates of current output. Jurisdictional jealousy prevented them from reconciling these differences for several years, until they were settled through the arbitration of an international agency. In many countries ministries of agriculture do not believe that their duties include the compilation of data on agricultural output, which are needed by the planning office but which the ministries are in the best position to collect. All these are cases of institutional ineffectiveness in resolving technical conflicts.

In their second purpose, *macro-policy,* accounting models proved deficient for their assumption of universal institutional adequacy in policy implementation. For example, macro-models would show the degree of monetary restriction or taxation required to contain inflation to specific rates. But they would not predict the point at which restrictions would become intolerable to identifiable groups, or the political abilities of those groups to thwart them, or the kinds of concessions needed to buy them off.

Particularly vulnerable was the concept of homogeneous or even predictable functional relationships among the macro-variables. These relationships may well be predictable in countries where institutions are "thick"—that is, capable of absorbing wide variations in the volume of conflicts they are called upon to resolve. A "thin" institution, on the other hand, is one that cannot handle a much greater volume of conflicts than it is currently doing without losing jurisdiction over them or else radically changing its own character. Central banks in less developed countries have often proved to be thin, in that the setting of high discount rates or credit ceilings has led to the adoption of other forms for rationing bank reserves or loans, through special permissions, exceptions, or other means of avoidance.

Forecasts of the capital-output ratio have been particularly erroneous, and investing institutions have proved to be thin. Development corporations have been unable to compel fulfillment of obligations on the part of borrowers and corporate administrators of their investments. Such failures, many of which are statistically hidden through loan extensions or failure to enforce reporting requirements, become evident through long pipelines (loans authorized but not disbursed) or through repayment by other guaranteeing institutions.

The inability of exchange controls to achieve their objectives has been notorious. These controls, including multiple rates, are usually intended to ration scarce foreign exchange, applying it to imports essential to economic growth, such as machinery, and denying it to luxury consumption goods. The problem has often been that the price of luxury goods would rise, making them attractive to domestic producers. While foreign exchange was conserved, domestic factors of production would be "wasted."[2] Furthermore, institutional inadequacies and corruption frequently made it difficult for the authorities to enforce reductions in the consumption of popular items, and because it was unthinkable to restrict the import of materials or semi-manufactured goods that would affect current output adversely, the restrictions ended up by excluding the very imports that were supposed to be fostered, those of capital goods.

[2] Margaret de Vries, "Multiple Exchange Rates: Expectations and Experiences," *Staff Papers* (Washington, D.C.: International Monetary Fund, July 1965), p. 305.

In their third purpose, *identification of shortage areas,* macro-models were not accompanied by adequate tools of project selection and development. Many of the earlier plans included computations of amounts to be invested in various sectors with no indication of what, or whether, specific projects would be available. Techniques of project analysis were considered a field apart in micro-planning, but the link between macro- and micro-plans has never been precisely defined. We deal with micro-planning at greater length below.

The failures of macro-planning have not led to its abandonment. Rather, five- and ten-year plans have been reduced to one and two years, and macro-variables have been employed more in monetary and fiscal policy than in project selection. In many Latin American countries planning has become increasingly decentralized, through regional and sectoral programs. A multitude of middle-level institutions have been formed (such as development banks identified with producing sectors or geographic regions) whose formal links with a central planning office tend to be attenuated over time.

Micro-planning

The heart of development planning ought to lie in projects. No development plan, however finely tuned, has any significance except insofar as it is implemented through projects, such as power plants, farm credit, highways, and factories. Yet over the past decade development planners in Latin America as well as international agencies operating in that area have paid progressively *less* attention to instruments of project analysis. This observation is based on the following points:

1. The criteria for project selection are unclear. Agencies financing projects generally list several criteria (e.g., profitability, balance-of-payments impact, employment impact, etc.), but none, to my knowledge, has published either a set of weights or trade-off functions among them.

2. In their final approval of projects, the managements of development institutions frequently pay little attention to underlying economic and social studies, if indeed these studies are made at all. Economists and business analysts have prepared shiny instruments (e.g., benefit-cost studies and linear programming) which

either are not used or their results are not taken into account when project selections are made.

3. The number or money value of projects "in trouble" is not generally known to academic economists or to the professional public. Development agencies try to cover them up, and none, to my knowledge, has ever published a comprehensive list of major projects that have either gone bankrupt or whose financing is being repaid by government or other guarantors because the project itself does not generate the revenue expected of it. Likewise, no information is available on projects whose execution is delayed on account of input failures, structural inadequacies, or shortage of administrative skills. The exceptions to this statement lie primarily in small, short-term credits (e.g., agricultural) where a few defaults are not considered to bring shame on the lending institution.

The legitimation of self criticism, so essential to scientific advances, has not been extended to the operations of development corporations.

4. Development-financing institutions often pay little attention to the managerial capabilities of project administrators, in that they do not know (or care) whether they possess decision-making skills, whether the proper information systems (e.g., budgeting and cost accounting) are instituted, or whether the appropriate officials know how to advertise and market their products.

Over the past eight years, the Agency for International Development (AID) has shifted the bulk of its financing from a "project" to a "program" basis. A "project" loan is, of course, awarded for a specific project. A "program" loan, on the other hand, covers the general input requirements of macro- or sectoral plans (as in agriculture) but is not tied to this project or that. The public justification for program-lending is the greater responsibility for project selection and execution vested in the borrowing government and the wider flexibility provided to planners. Privately, AID officers admit that it may also lie in the shortage of well-developed projects, the reluctance of AID to give its endorsement to those that may not succeed, and the political dynamite that might be fired if AID "interferes" with project management, which is deemed a purely national matter. Officials of other agencies that lend internationally, such as the World Bank, Inter-American Development Bank, and Export-Import Bank, also admit privately that well-developed projects are in short supply and that officials of different institutions have been known to "compete" with each other for them.

Economists are normally unable to study the *process* of selecting and implementing projects in less developed countries and to make their findings public. Those concerned with pure research are not admitted to the inner decisions of development-financing institutions.[3] Consulting economists are so admitted, but they are considered professionals, like lawyers and accountants, who respect their clients' confidences. During my absense from the university, I have been primarily a consulting economist. I believe, however, that my clients and other contacts have been sufficiently diverse for me now to be able to publish observations that will not violate the confidence of any of them, though examples of specific cases will be disguised. In general, my sources are those mentioned in the footnote on pages 91-92. Because I am constrained from citing institutions and cases more specifically than as indicated, the academic community cannot judge my observations on the basis of scientific testing, but only according to whether they appear reasonable and whether there is any evidence to the contrary.

LACK OF APPROPRIATE WEIGHTING IN SELECTION CRITERIA

Adopting recommendations by the Stanford Research Institute, the United Nations Economic Commission for Latin America includes among its criteria for project selection such items as net return (social and private), integrated development, stability and growth, balance-of-payments effects, socioeconomic desirability, and experience and competition.[4] Not only are the criteria unclear and sometimes overlapping, but no trade-off function is suggested.

When I asked the staff of one institution operating in Latin America what were their criteria of project selection, the replies included

[3] The World Bank is an exception. Cf. Albert O. Hirschman, *Development Projects Observed* (Washington, D.C.: The Brookings Institution, 1967).

[4] United Nations, *Manual on Development Projects*, E/CN.12/426/ Add. 1, Rev. 1 (New York, 1957), pp. 239-40; and Stanford Research Institute, *Manual of Industrial Development with Special Application to Latin America* (Washington, D.C.: Institute of Inter-American Affairs, Foreign Operations Administration, 1954).

profitability (either net return on investment or benefit-cost ratio), employment impact, contribution to Latin American economic integration, multiplier effects (forward and backward linkages), balance-of-payments effects, fiscal effects, and value added to the gross domestic product. None was able to state either weights or trade-off functions or even general guidelines to the conditions under which some weights would apply instead of others. Furthermore, studies of small samples of individual loans of various government-related financing institutions operating in Latin America have led me to believe that only rarely are any of the mentioned criteria seriously taken into account. Examples, and guesses as to why they are not, follow.

Profitability criterion. Theoretically, the profitability criterion has two justifications. First, unsubsidized project loans depend on profitability for amortization and servicing. Secondly, profitability presumably measures the net social contribution of a project to the nation's economy. The first justification is self-evident; only the second needs examination.

Whatever the measure of profitability (economic, private, or a combination), economic theory presumes that revenues from the sale of a product measure its social value, while costs are the sacrifices, or other products forgone. Profit, the excess of revenue over cost, therefore gauges the net social value increment. This is so no matter to whom (e.g., government or private) or how (e.g., dividends, taxes) the profit is distributed. Where the product is not sold, other measures of benefit substitute for revenue, so that the resulting benefit-cost ratio still weighs the net increment.

Nevertheless, time and again financing institutions set aside measures of profitability or else consider them only up to the point where amortization is assured, not where benefits are maximized. Profitability is sometimes obscured by the merging of separable, unprofitable units with profitable ones, so that a positive, though not maximized, net return is forecast for the project as a whole.

The scant attention given to profitability might be explained by attacks upon its legitimacy as a measure. In cases of widely skewed income distribution, profitability would allocate resources to production for the rich while the poor went without houses. But there is an even more likely explanation. The principal usefulness of the profitability criterion lies in its ability to select the maximizers out of large numbers of potentially profitable projects. Few development institutions possess the trained manpower to seek, identify, and analyze such an inventory. Far more often the problem is to find enough acceptable projects to employ available resources fully. The seeming contradiction between this statement and the concept of a less developed world short of capital lies not in the improbability that capital can be used there wisely but in the fact that the identification of wise uses requires skills that are in short supply.

Macro-type variables. Most of the remaining variables cited (e.g., employment, integration, fiscal, balance of payments, and value added) have in common the fact that they are abstractions from *macro*economic accounting. While wise businessmen have always taken into account the state of the overall economy in their decisions on investment, marketing, and the like, nevertheless the extent to which *macro*-variables are now reputedly being employed in *micro*-decisions is unprecedented. Unlike most banks and businesses in the more developed world, the institutions I have studied call on macro-economists rather than business-school specialists in administration, marketing, and forecasting to analyze their projects.

Project implementers, however, are unable to provide the data sought. Such data would require, for example, a distinction between goods procured from abroad and those bought locally as well as between foreign and domestic sales. But industrial corporations do not usually make this distinction in their accounting records. Especially is this so when the purchase or sale is intermediate; that is, not bought from the original producer or sold to the final user. Often the macro-effects depend on how resources would have been used had they not been employed by the project, something that the borrower does not know and for which the financing institution cannot spare the staff to do original research. In one national industrial bank in Latin America, I was shown elaborate forms that borrowers were asked to complete, providing impact data on balance of payments and gross domestic product. The bank economist complained that customers would rarely fill them out, and when they did he suspected the figures were fabricated.

LACK OF MANAGEMENT CONTROL OVER TECHNICIANS

When a lender calls for macroeconomic data, the borrower produces them, reliable or no. The data then become sanctified because of another characteristic of development-financing institutions: the widespread feeling that management should not question the conclusions of the institution's own professionally trained technicians. Accountants, economists, engineers, and agronomists are supposed to possess specialized skills that "generalized" managers need not comprehend. When project documents are presented for approval, management frequently questions only the interpretation of the data, not their accuracy. More important, supervisory chains to determine that all work is done professionally do not extend upward into management; they are broken off at a lower, technical level.

The supposition that management should have no technical competence is contrary to accepted administrative theory. According to this theory, managers should combine a talent for quick thinking and decision-making with enough knowledge of the technical skills of their staffs to challenge opinions and demand technical explanations *to a certain degree.* Any technical reporting truly beyond their capacity to question should be test-checked by independent professional reviewers, such as auditors, who determine that appropriate standards are upheld.

The lack of management controls results in inadequate substantiation of data on project documents. Over and over again, I discovered that technicians would accept estimates made by the hopeful borrower, including them in the project document as if they themselves had done the calculations. An example is the following (with products and figures changed to obscure the real case).

Company S requested a loan of $3 million at 6 percent interest from the national industrial bank to produce synthetic fibers that had previously been imported. After studying the application, the bank's technicians recommended approval, provided that company P, a German enterprise that owned company S outright, would contribute equity investment of $1 million. It was argued that company P could not finance the entire project from its own resources because of competing financial commitments in Europe and elsewhere. In the project document, the bank's economist estimated that sales would be sufficient to yield a return of 25 percent (net profit on both borrowed and equity investment). The document stated that the sales estimate was based on projections of market trends, personal interviews by technicians from company P with customers of company S, and knowledge of concrete expansion projects to be undertaken by domestic textile companies if a new source of synthetic fiber were available. Furthermore, the estimate also took into account an expected expansion of sales owing to price reductions, since import tariffs would no longer apply. The bank's management was convinced, and the loan was approved.

Later I asked the economist to show me the working papers on which his market estimates were based: data on the sample of company S's customers, the list of known expansion projects, and the calculation of increased sales due to price reduction. He replied that all those studies had been done by the economist from company P, with whom he had discussed the results but whose data he had not seen. He argued that company P, being German, was already sophisticated in the ways of market analysis and that P's interest in the project was identical to that of the industrial bank. If the project should fail, both would lose; therefore, company P would not be motivated to exaggerate the sales forecast.

The economist was wrong. With an investment of only $1 million as opposed to $3 million of borrowing, company P had the leverage to earn a return of 82 percent on its equity if the project did indeed yield 25 percent on total investment. Even if it yielded only 10 percent, company P's return would be 22 percent of equity. On the other hand, if the project failed, company P's loss would be only $1 million, less its tax write-off and less royalties collected from company S in the meantime. The industrial bank, on the other hand, would have lost $3 million. The opportunity for such high gains at minimum risk gave company P the incentive to exaggerate its sales forecast, which the bank management had accepted unquestioningly, possibly in the belief that the forecast had been performed by the bank's own economist on the basis of his specialized skills.

MANAGERIAL CAPACITIES OF PROJECT ADMINISTRATORS

It is scarcely odd that development institutions with communication gaps of their own will not be rigorous in demanding skilled administrative performance of managers of the projects in which they invest.

Often the administrative structure and principal officers of these projects have not even been selected when funds are committed. In addition, the transfer of funds is frequently contingent on certain performances, such as the negotiation of subcontracts, the installation of an accounting system, or the construction of employee housing, whose successful completion will depend on the skills of the project manager finally selected. If he does not possess those skills, then "long pipelines," or funds committed but not yet invested, will result, tying up the resources of the development institution. This malady is not confined to national lending corporations; it is even known to more sophisticated international agencies, including AID.

The Three Concepts of Project Selection

From the above observations let us distinguish three divergent concepts of project selection, which for want of better names we will call the expansionist concept, the maximizing concept, and the reformist concept. Often all three are *apparently* held by the same individual or development institution. Only when they conflict is it possible to determine which dominates the others.

THE EXPANSIONIST CONCEPT

The expansionist concept regards a development institution as one engaged in maximizing the flow of capital into development projects. Its sources of funds are government, international, or private, the latter source being at interest rates judged by market standards or better. Its objective is to commit all the funds it can obtain, the quality of technical and economic studies being no higher than is necessary to select the target volume of projects.

Projects are selected *ad hoc*. Usually they are initiated by groups or organizations known to the development institution, including government agencies, local authorities, and private businesses. Political pressure may or may not be a factor.

Normally, the projects so selected would not be eligible for financing through regular channels. Yet "expansionists" believe (intuitively) that a large percentage of such projects would be successful on their merits, say 80 percent or so. They are eligible for financing through regular channels because no one knows in advance which will be the 20 percent to fail, and private capitalists are unwilling to take the risk.

Private investors insist on a much higher rate of probability, say 95 percent.[5]

But it would be a pity, argue the expansionists, for the 80 percent to go undone, for surely they would contribute greatly to the nation's economic and social goals. Expansionists therefore play down their concern for problem projects, arguing that if a development institution does not have them it is not a development institution. Instead they point with pride to achievements: roads that have been paved, farmland that has been cleared, successful plants that have been built, and universities that have been equipped, all of which would not have been done had the loan projects been subject to truly professional scrutiny.

THE MAXIMIZING CONCEPT

The maximizing concept views a development institution as a maximizer. Certain desiderata are projected, such as increased national product, employment, or balanced international payments. Consistent and attainable levels are selected as goals, with appropriate trade-off functions. Projects are then selected for their maximum contribution to those goals. Not all that can be funded are necessarily chosen, for sometimes the preferred alternative to a project is no project. The development institution does not have to invest all the funds it can find; it might decide that available savings would be better invested by others.

THE REFORMIST CONCEPT

The reformist concept views a development institution as active participant in reforms on the part of project-implementers. "Reformists" differ on the extent to which the institution should urge, cajole, reward, or threaten. But they unite in their belief that borrowers with (say) only 80 percent chance of success must possess some operational deficiency, such as poor management or lack of technical capacity. These, they argue, the institution should fill with technical assistance.

CONSISTENCY OF THE THREE CONCEPTS

Many technicians in development institutions argue that the three concepts are compatible and indeed complement each other. Presum-

---

[5] The figures of 80 percent, 20 percent, and 95 percent, are purely hypothetical.

ably the institution can provide funds only to those projects with a chance of success (say 80 percent), can select them according to maximizing criteria, and can provide technical assistance for reforms. There is apparently no reason why decisions based on maximizing criteria cannot exhaust available funds if the development institution so desires. There is, however, an annoying dilemma. The maximizing and reformist concepts demand clear-cut rules of decision-making, with universal criteria, but the expansionist concept does not. Borrowers and other project implementers are notoriously expansionist; they resist studies and reforms. It is when the development institution faces the awesome reality that there are a large number of projects with high potential for success for which funds are available, but it is neither possible to study them fully for economic efficiency nor to design acceptable reforms to the extent necessary, that it must make up its mind whether it is primarily expansionist, primarily maximizer, or primarily reformist.

Should social psychologists be inclined and permitted to study the staffs and techniques of development institutions, they could, with the tools indicated in Chapter 3 (Hammond's policy tests), determine and weigh the motivating concepts. To date, however, these institutions have shown no inclination to permit psychologists to experiment upon them. Intuitive and heuristic though they are, the observations from my own consulting experiences are the only evidence I have on which to form a judgment.

EXPANSIONISTS VERSUS MAXIMIZER-REFORMISTS

These observations lead me to believe that in many development institutions the expansionist criterion dominates the others. Management has not built in controls over professionalism in technicians' studies because it believes that professionalism, by the standards of more developed countries, is not relevant to project selection. Thus it would be useless for an administrative expert to propose hiring project auditors who would review and report to management on the professional base of data collection.

The maximizing criterion, on the other hand, dominates the thinking of professional economists. To them, projects should be selected according to their capacity to maximize national product or other goals. Their weapons are benefit-cost studies, linear programming, econometric models, and other quantitative techniques. Technical assistance may be a necessary input, and in this way the reformist criterion complements the maximizing.

To maximizer-reformists no country should invest beyond its capital absorptive capacity. This capacity is not a fixed amount but a marginal productivity function, which is *presumed* to drop sharply where administrative skills are in short supply. Adler, for example, has drawn it in this manner, citing as justification the lack of knowledge, administrative skills, and managerial experience, the institutional limitations, and social and cultural constraints.[6] Presumably administrative reforms should be undertaken to increase absorptive capacity before capital is invested beyond a certain point.

Yet no one to my knowledge has demonstrated that the marginal productivity of capital (MPK) does drop precipitously in less developed countries. In fact, there is every reason to suspect that it does not. Abundance of labor (underemployment) is characteristic throughout the less developed world, and there are many countries, especially in South America, where land is plentiful. Under these circumstances one would expect MPK to be high. To accept that lack of administrative skills causes it to be low, it must be shown that these skills and capital are complementary and *not* substitutable. I will argue the opposite, that they are substitutable for each other. Two cases, drawn from the files of development institutions, illustrate this point.

In one case, a loan was requested for the purchase of new locomotives. The economist from the development institution discovered, however, that locomotives already in service were not pulling all the cars they could because station platforms were not long enough. Larger stations would relieve the shortage with less investment. Had the railroad company had the administrative skills to reach this decision, it might not have requested the locomotives.

In the second case, a company received a foreign-exchange permit to acquire equipment even though it did not have the funds to construct a factory to house it. Rather than lose the permit, it ordered the imports, which stood unused on the docks for several years. Only later was the development institution able to lend funds for the factory. Had the greater administrative coordination been available on a

[6] John H. Adler, *Absorptive Capacity: The Concept and its Determinants* (Washington, D.C.: The Brookings Institution, 1965), pp. 31-34.

national level, it would have been possible to build and equip the same factory with less investment.

Similar cases are legion. A company lacking strict inventory control can avoid running out of stocks by keeping more on hand. Standard cost systems to control material wastage can reduce input requirements. Both are instances where the same product would result from either more administrative skills or more investment.

My opponents, of course, will argue that output will be attained at higher cost where administrative skills are scarcer, and that marginal funds have alternative international opportunities and will tend to go where other-input costs are lowest. So be it. But if labor and land are cheap in the less developed countries and if capital is substitutable for administrative competence, then there may well be much room for increased investment before the MPK falls below current interest rates. For this reason, I believe the expansionists are right, and that absorptive capacity limitations have been a red herring for development planners.

Where two inputs are substitutable, the amounts of each to be employed depend on their relative marginal costs. Now, maximizing-reformist concepts were born in more developed countries where the supply of administrative skills has been elastic. These skills are produced cheaply by business and public administration schools as well as through on-the-job experience. It is only natural for economists from those countries to suppose that input shortages should be solved by supplying more skills, not by "wasting" capital. In countries where goals are unclear, and where personalism, hierarchical rigidity, failure to communicate cross-culturally, and other items of hard-to-change culture capital make administrative skills costly of culture sacrifice, it may be that capital is the cheaper input.

We are not equipped to undertake benefit-cost studies where the culture sacrifices of improved administrative skills are compared with the economic sacrifices of investment, for as yet we have no common scale. But if both kinds of cost are considered, we can now accept that the expansionist concept of project analysis may well be the logical route to maximizing the national product.

Having attacked the maximizer-reformist, I now turn my guns on the expansionists. The managements of many development institutions have discovered that raising funds is so much easier than improving administrative skills that they have totally ignored the latter. Indeed, the absence of these skills in their own institutions blinds management to the possibility of imparting them to projects. Yet available funds will have a higher marginal product if administrative skills are improved. But what is even more perilous is that the management is not gaining experience against the day when the supply price of funds will be higher than the cost of upgrading skills. For the elasticity of substitution of capital for skills is not infinite over time. It becomes lower and lower as more and more capital is acquired.

From all the above, I am led to the following recommendation on project selection:

1. The exact procedure for picking projects should matter little. Selection may be done by means of regular negotiations between project promoters (private or government) and lending agencies, through planning-board exercises in the identification of sectoral deficiencies, or by other means deemed desirable by the planning authorities. (*We reject the maximizing concept as the principal vehicle of selection.*)

2. The planning authorities should seek the maximum quantity of sound (noninflationary) financing consistent with reasonable interest cost, and the volume of investment projects should be limited only by this maximum. (*This is an endorsement of the expansionist principle.*)

3. Project-feasibility studies should be carried out to the maximum capabilities of the development institution, in terms of human resources, subject only to the provisions laid down in no. 2. (*We reintroduce some elements of the maximizing concept, but subject to the expansionist constraint.*) No project should be selected unless the development institution foresees a *minimal* opportunity for success. The project should pay its way if this was intended, or the government should have the financial capacity to subsidize it if that was intended. No project that the management intuitively feels will be successful should be rejected because the institution does not have the requisite manpower to forecast confidently that it will yield a greater rate of return than any alternative.

4. Once the project has been selected, the development insti-

tution should devote major attention to designing for it an administrative system that would achieve the highest possible ratings in the three criteria for institutional effectiveness: identification, rules, and consensus. Administrative skills would be required to improve the ratings for these criteria. (*Subject to the expansionist and maximizing principles cited above, we propose that development institutions consider themselves primarily reformist.*)

Let not the radical implications of this proposal escape. *Out of the large number of unanalyzed potential projects that will probably achieve minimum profitability, it does not matter which are selected. Most of the tools of maximization based on comparisons of solely economic inputs and outputs are of limited usefulness. What does matter is that the goals (and trade-off functions if there is more than one goal) should be clearly stated and that the development institution should follow project execution closely, insisting on the highest-order administrative system possible to achieve those goals.*

CHAPTER 7

Toward a Social-Science Model of Economic Growth

FOR growthmen, the pot of gold at the end of the rainbow is a complete theory of societal development. It would be at the same time both a theory of history and a theory of the social system. It would draw on all the social and behavioral sciences, and even these would not be enough; the humanities and physical sciences would have to participate as well. Despite the compelling works of Toynbee and Parsons, whose disciples may believe they have come close to such a theory, nevertheless the dream is so elusive that most would argue that it will never be fulfilled. It would be something like finding the secret of life.

I use such strong terms in order to be completely sure that no reader believes I have any intention of accomplishing that distant goal in the present chapter. I rested my case for theory in Part I. Nevertheless, I believe that the theory of institutions has something to offer in the search for an interdisciplinary theory of growth. The value of such a search lies not in the hope that the object will be found, but in the search itself. I believe that economics has run its course in the explanation of growth, and that it has little more to offer. The same may well be true for sociology, but I shall speak only for my own discipline. The next step, it seems to me, is to merge sociological and economic models. I do not even plan to do that in this chapter. But I do propose that the concept of institutional effectiveness will be a useful variable in the pursuit of integrated socioeconomic growth models. I shall now set forth my reasons for this assertion.

In Chapter 1 we suggested that the division of labor is limited not only by the size of the market but by the capacity of people to cooperate. In succeeding chapters we attempted to clarify "the capacity to cooperate" by defining institutional effectiveness and developing a theory of its evolution after takeoff. To date, however, we have been considering individual institutions. We now question whether there is an overall tendency for some nations to have superior institutions to others. If so, then *aggregate institutional effectiveness* (AIE) should be defined and measured on a national basis. Next, we question whether

215

AIE correlates positively with economic growth during certain periods (takeoff and thereafter) in a nation's history.

Let us introduce two possible definitions of AIE. First, it might be the mean effectiveness rating of a specified list of formal institutions associated with the growth process, including political systems, markets, business enterprises, and agencies, such as planning boards and development banks, whose purpose is to promote growth. Secondly, it might be the mean effectiveness rating of all institutions, formal and informal, in a nation. In either case, the measurement would be by sample.

The first definition has the advantages of aiming specifically at growth institutions and of being more easily measured than the second. But only the second definition implies the existence of a general level of social cohesiveness which should be more representative of the nation's capacity to cooperate than the ratings for a specified list of institutions. I would suggest adoption of the second definition provided it can be demonstrated empirically (by large numbers of samples) that the ratings of many institutions tend to cluster around national means and that the cluster for one country can be distinguished from that for another. The standard deviations should be small for a given country but large if data for several presumably dissimilar countries are assembled. Only if this is so does the concept of a national aggregate make sense, and only then would it be logical to search for a correlation between national AIE (second definition) and economic growth. If this fails, it would be better to seek the correlation between the effectiveness of growth institutions (first definition) and economic growth.

There is sound theoretical ground to support the existence of AIE by the second definition. Institutional effectiveness is probably contagious, for the following reasons:

1. *Practicality.* Individuals in a community participate in many institutions. Procedures found effective in one will be transferred to others if it is believed they will also be effective there.

2. *Values.* Institutionalized forms of behavior affect the value structure. Values are objects or modes of behavior deemed desirable at all times and in all places. Quite apart from practicality,

modes of behavior adopted in one institution will be passed on to others as they become values.

3. *Influence of common culture objects.* In addition to values, other agencies and norms will exert a common influence on large numbers of institutions. For example, the education system will teach a certain level of effectiveness, both implicitly (through its influence on values and norms) and explicitly (in courses on administration, for example).

4. *Dying institutions.* Institutions incapable of increasing their effectiveness *pari passu* with others or whose effectiveness decreases after takeoff will tend to die because others will perform their functions better or because their functions become obsolete. Though they will have lower effectiveness ratings than other institutions, their demise will remove this exception to the principle of contagion.

Much needs to be studied about the contagion process. Does effectiveness spread more easily from certain institutions to others? How rapidly does contagion occur? These questions have direct policy implications. Will effectiveness fostered in growth institutions spread more rapidly to others, such as the family and friendship systems, or is there greater speed in the reverse direction? If the latter, expenditure of national resources on overhead—nationalism and ideological consensus—would have a greater marginal productivity than direct intervention to improve the effectiveness of institutions controlled by the government.

Let us hypothesize that AIE exists. If empirical results by the second definition are not satisfactory, we will use the first. In either case it would be useful to examine the relationship between AIE and economic growth.

Sociologists have expressed concepts similar to AIE under various rubrics, such as solidarity, social cohesion, integration, cooperation, and community organization. Each of these is both more comprehensive than AIE and more difficult to define and measure. Yet sociologists have long presumed that one community may have "more" or "less" of these than another. Oscar Lewis refers to the "culture of poverty,"[1] or

[1] Oscar Lewis, *Five Families: Mexican Case Studies in the Culture of Poverty*

217

the disdain shown by poverty-stricken people for each other and the casual, unfeeling relationship they develop among themselves—hence negative effectiveness. Another case of negative effectiveness is Banfield's concept of "amoral familism,"[2] a culturally approved mode of behavior that the author observed in Montegranaro, Italy, in which the maximization of short-run benefit for the immediate, nuclear family prevents the strengthening of communal cooperative ties. Finally, AIE is closely related to the integrative system developed by Talcott Parsons.[3]

All these sociological concepts are useful in attempting to answer the oft-debated question of why some nations can settle intergroup rivalries and get on with economic growth while others become so bogged down in civil strife that they grow but slowly. What is the secret of the Japanese, whose apparent AIE in the early twentieth century was much greater than that of virtually all other countries at comparable stages of growth?

AIE AND EMPATHY

AIE does not comprehend all the components that sociologists would include in the above-mentioned concepts. It does not measure, for example, the ability of people to identify with each other's roles, which Lerner refers to as empathy: "We are interested in empathy as the inner mechanism which enables newly mobile persons to *operate efficiently* in a changing world. Empathy, to simplify the matter, is the capacity to see oneself in the other fellow's situation. This is an indispensable skill for people moving out of traditional settings."[4]

There is reason to believe, however, that empathy is closely entwined with AIE and that the causal relationship works *both ways*. The proposition that increased empathy promotes institutional effectiveness is obvious on its face, but the reverse causation is not. It is justified as follows. Man without his culture is an amoral being, ruled by

---

(New York: Basic Books, 1959). Lewis, however, has also argued that the culture of poverty is confined to capitalist countries and does not exist in socialist Cuba.

[2] Edward Banfield, *The Moral Basis of a Backward Society* (New York: The Free Press, 1958).

[3] Talcott Parsons, *The Social System* (New York: The Free Press, 1951).

[4] Daniel Lerner, *The Passing of Traditional Society: Modernizing the Middle East* (New York: The Free Press, 1952), pp. 49-50.

biological desires and with no sense of feeling toward his fellow men. Only through action and interaction with others does he define common and conflicting goals, forming institutions to resolve differences and realize cooperation. The more effectively these institutions function, the more each participant becomes aware of common experiences in joy and suffering. Repeated awareness causes him to learn to experience himself the joy and suffering of others close to him.

Examples are legion. Empathy toward brothers and sisters is promoted by the institutional effectiveness of the family. Soldiers in war often feel little empathy toward the enemy, with whom they have little experience in common. Though no one to my knowledge has investigated the matter quantitatively, frequently cited incidents reveal that American soldiers probably feel less empathy toward the Vietnamese in the current war than they did toward the Germans in World War II, a factor presumably deriving from the greater number of institutional and cultural relationships (as well as racial similarities) held in common with the latter than with the former.

Empathy often emerges only after one has lost an institutional battle against it. The invention of modern plumbing was not sufficient reason for employers in the United States automatically to provide lavatory facilities for workers; these came only after unions had won them through labor negotiations and strikes. If an employer now considers it unthinkable, on humane grounds, to deny bathrooms to workers, this empathy was not born within him; it is the direct result of institutional effectiveness in labor relations. The institutions, furthermore, were effective because the parties perceived mutuality of benefit. Employees who are provided with bathrooms work more efficiently.

Many in the present student generation are deeply frustrated because "the establishment" *reacts* to pressure instead of *acting* out of a sense of moral values. They believe the war in Vietnam will end not because the president sees it as immoral but because a population impatient with its failure has exerted pressure; and that businesses will adopt antipollution devices not because they value fresh air and water but only as they bow before social repugnance and the law. Many modern students then argue that "the capitalist system" is evil and ought to be replaced by something else.

The problem is that in any system—capitalist, socialist, or other— the reaction-action process is similar. Behavior that is a reaction to pressure in one generation becomes acceptable as a value to the next, as in the case of bathrooms in factories. Indeed, *this process is probably the only way by which new values emerge.* Awareness of this fact might relieve considerable tension in the younger generation as well as direct tension toward fruitful positive action.

The Quasi-Rationality of AIE

We recall that AIE is constructed from the Hammond policy tests on *quasi*-rational thought. (Quasi-rational thought implies, as its dual, quasi-emotional or quasi-intuitive thought. It is *not* subconscious thought, with which we do not know how to deal.) Until now, quasi-rationality has not (to my knowledge) ever played a central role in any economic theory. Indeed, this theory thoroughly accepts the belief that decision-making is universally an intellectual and not an emotional or intuitive process. Neoclassical price models, linear programming, decision and game theory all presume that the individual has a precisely defined objective and recognizes the move most likely to meet it.

It is utterly surprising that this should be so. A moment's reflection will reveal the plethora of situations in which a person cannot accept emotionally what he understands intellectually to be true. Many are those who act as if a dead relative were alive, who fight on when defeat is certain, or who search for a treasure they know does not exist. But we need not be so dramatic. A child jealous of a sibling may accept intellectually that both are specialists, excelling in different fields, but emotionally he may be upset if the other is superior in any field. We have already commented (page 151) that an intellectual acceptance of the fact that workers are well paid in the United States does not prevent the Soviet citizens from believing that state ownership is essential to protect the exploited. Economic planners frequently cast out projects that pass benefit-cost analysis with flying colors or accept those that fail. Such decisions are usually attributed to "political factors," which the ingenious politician has carefully weighed into his payoff matrix. The possibility that he does or does not want the project but cannot explain why invariably slips past us.

But quasi-rationality has been introduced into our theory of institutions in the following ways. First, the benefits and costs of an institution have both been taken to lie in the mind of the decision-maker (power group). The benefits consist of its projected impact on economic growth, which the power group estimates quasi-rationally, taking into account the emotional acceptance of the institution by all contestants. In addition to resource expenditure, costs include the psychological strain of value change, which the power group can cope with only by considering both emotion and reason. While benefits over costs are maximized, much more study needs to be done to measure the component parts of each and to determine precisely what are the emotional and intellectual forces at work.

This benefit-cost concept contrasts sharply with economic models in which costs are objective, based on intellectual arguments concerning technology and available resources. Economic benefits are partly subjective, as they relate to utility functions (which economists take as data), though they may also be partly objective, as they are explained by income distribution.

Secondly, our theory accepts as axiomatic that growth-sensitive power groups select optimal institutions for economic growth. They "feel" which will be more successful than others, with trial and error as the only means of testing results. The presumption of this axiom will not escape my critics, who in the tradition of the social sciences may ask for objective evidence of optimality. So far there is none. Nor is there any objective evidence that any other institutions are optimal. Each one selected is new to its setting, and experience with it elsewhere helps us but little. This is not to say that evidence will not be found in the future, for the subject should be of interest to social psychologists. But it is likely to be found in the relationships among ideology, nationalism, the value structure, and institutional effectiveness, areas which abound in quasi-rational decisions.

Thirdly, the *apparent* solution line to a conflict is subjectively derived, depending on each contestant's feeling toward the other as a person as well as upon a belief concerning his opponent's subsequent actions. The *physical* solution line is technologically derived. The physical and apparent lines are not congruous if either contestant does not fully trust the other to keep his promises. Such distrust may, of course, be written into a game model, in which the coolly rational contestant sees a payoff in a decision to renege. In our model, however, the apparent solution line may also differ from the physical because each contestant hates the other.

Finally, and most important of all, the very concept of AIE is grounded on quasi-rational thought. The contestant is not presumed to make those decisions that he intellectually accepts as optimal, for the Hammond policy tests include cues that are emotional and intuitive as well as intellectual, all of which contribute toward the selection of an optimum. Complete rationality would be the special case of zero emotion and intuition, surely not the general rule. Nor does institutional effectiveness necessarily correlate with rationality. Rather, it measures the capacity of all contestants, acting quasi-rationally, to predict the responses of other contestants behaving in like manner.

For all these reasons, AIE would introduce a quasi-rational and emotional content into models of economic growth. We are fully aware of the dangers and appreciate the vast research that needs to be done. But we are also mindful of a quotation from Max Lerner:[5]

> It is the recognition and exploitation of this possessive power of ideas that makes the genius of our age. The great intellectual revolution of the seventeenth century was the discovery of scientific method and its possibilities. That of the eighteenth century was the charting of the map of reason and the subjecting of social institutions to the test of rationality. That of the nineteenth century was the discovery of the world as process rather than as structure, with ascertainable laws of development both in the biological realm (Darwinism) and in the historical and social realm (Marxism). The intellectual revolution of the twentieth century is likely to prove the charting of the *terra incognita* of the irrational and the extraction of its implications for every area of human thought.

We now question whether a social science model of economic growth can be constructed, with AIE included as one of the independent variables. If the growth rates of various nations are subject to such a model, what gaps would remain? Before we turn to this speculation, it is well to consider briefly the kinds of macro-growth models that have already been developed. In the next three sections, therefore, we

---

[5] Max Lerner, "The Discovery of the 'Irrational': Personal and Collective," in *Ideas are Weapons* (New York: The Viking Press, 1939), p. 3; also quoted in W. G. Bennis, K. D. Benne, and Robert Chin, *The Planning of Change* (New York: Holt, Rhinehart, Winston, 1961), p. 117.

discuss the economic model, the sociological model, and a recent, promising combination of the two, the Adelman–Morris model of economic growth.

The Economic Model

Roy Harrod and Evsey Domar are widely credited with introducing dynamism to the modern theory of economic growth. Of course, economists have long recognized that growth cannot be anything but dynamic. Baumol, for example, has referred to the "magnificent dynamics" of early classical theorists such as Malthus.[6] But Harrod and Domar went further than previous writers. Recognizing modern industrial economies as having a built-in capacity to grow, evidenced by their capital accumulation and ever new technology, they postulated that, to ward off unemployment, economies *must* grow. Not only that, they must grow at a certain rate. Too much growth will mean inflation, and too little will mean depression. In other words, there is an *equilibrium* rate of growth.

It is not the duty of this chapter to present the Harrod–Domar models in all their mathematical splendor. Economists among the readers are already acquainted with them. Since I address myself to other social scientists as well, I include a simple example, just to give the general idea. Suppose that at a given moment the gross national product (GNP) of an industrial economy runs at a rate of $100 a year, of which $90 is for consumption and $10 for investment. Suppose the marginal propensity to consume (MPC) is 90 percent (i.e., people will spend 90 percent of any increment of income for consumption) and the marginal propensity to save (MPS) is therefore 10 percent. Suppose also that the incremental output-to-capital ratio[7] (IOCR) is 30 percent (i.e., $1 of newly invested capital will produce $0.30 of output per year, net of depreciation). Domar's contention is that there is an equilibrium rate of growth in output where the demand will increase by exactly the capacity of the economy to produce. Furthermore, that equilibrium rate is the product of MPS and IOCR—in the case of our

[6] William Baumol, *Economic Dynamics* (New York: Macmillan, 1959).

[7] Many economists refer simply to the "capital-output ratio." I use the term "incremental output-to-capital ratio," because this is a precise statement of what Domar used, with incremental output in the numerator and investment (or incremental capital) in the denominator.

illustration, 3 percent a year (or 0.10 times 0.30). This is illustrated in Table 7-1.[8]

TABLE 7-1

DOMAR-TYPE MODEL, TRANSLATED INTO PERIODS, WITH MPS
AT 10 PERCENT AND IOCR AT 30 PERCENT

Year	GNP	ΔGNP	Consumption	ΔC	Investment	ΔI
0	100.00		90.00		10.00	
1	103.00	3.00	92.70	2.70	10.30	0.30
2	106.09	3.09	95.48	2.78	10.61	0.31
3	109.27	3.18	98.34	2.86	10.93	0.32
4	112.55	3.28	101.29	2.95	11.26	0.33
·	·	·	·	·	·	·
·	·	·	·	·	·	·
·	·	·	·	·	·	·
·	·	·	·	·	·	·

In each year the growth in GNP is equal to 30 percent of the investment of the preceding year in accordance with the presumed IOCR. (We assume a one-year time-lag in putting the capital into production). Thus in year 1 output rises from $100 to $103 (or by 30 percent of $10). Now, the additional output ($3) is associated with an equal amount of income. Under the Keynesian equilibrium conditions, with an MPC of 90 percent, demand for consumption goods must have increased by $2.70. If the remaining $0.30 of incremental output is to be demanded, it must be for investment.

Now, how do we know that the demand for investment in year 1 will increase by $0.30? We do not, really. But *if* enterprises expect the rate of growth in total demand to continue at 3 percent (to $106.90 in year 2), then $10.30 of investment is required in year 1 to satisfy it. Thus, so long as everyone *expects* GNP to increase by 3 percent a year, it *will* do so—for both demand and capacity conditions are met. This rate constitutes, in every sense, a dynamic equilibrium. Furthermore, it goes on forever.

"Equilibrium" and "forever" distinguish Harrod–Domar models from the dynamism of earlier economists. Classical economists did not conceive of the economy as being infinite. They imagined a stationary

[8] Evsey Domar, "Capital Expansion, Rate of Growth, and Employment," *Econometrica*, XIV (April 1946); reprinted in Domar, *Essays in the Theory of Economic Growth* (New York: Oxford University Press, 1957); see esp. pp. 73-75.

state to which all was leading. Marx, an offshoot of the classical economists, conceived of socialism as the "terminal state" of the economic
system. Even Schumpeter expected his dynamic entrepreneur to fade
away as history led on to a regrettably socialist economy. But Harrod
and Domar saw no end. Infinity is now in vogue in economics.

The equilibrium rate of growth in Harrod–Domar models is, however, unstable. If by "mistake" or for another reason the investment or
consumption at any moment is not what the parameters call for, forces
are set in motion that lead farther and farther from the equilibrium
growth line. Both economists recognized this point, for one of their
objectives was to help understanding of the business cycle. The well-
known acceleration principle grew out of Harrod's model.

Harrod–Domar models are the grandparents of voluminous econometric outpourings that depend, in one way or another, on the incremental output-to-capital ratio and the concept of dynamic equilibrium.
Solow pointed out that if Harrod and Domar had assumed the substitutability of labor and capital (which they had not), then stability
could be restored to the model.[9]

The concept of an equilibrium rate of growth, of course, gave rise
to the question of whether or not it could be influenced by policy. Was
there a way in which the growth rate could be increased if society so
wished? From this happy question was generated the "turnpike
theorem," which states simply that if you take the turnpike you will
arrive faster than by the back road. If society's preference function
between consumption and investment can be influenced by monetary,
fiscal, or other policy, then (through the operation of the IOCR) it is
possible to speed up the rate of growth. It would always be possible
to return to the old set of preference functions, these theorists propose,
by getting off the turnpike at the appropriate exit.[10]

Other growth models have also been based on the incremental out-

[9] Robert M. Solow, "A Contribution to the Theory of Economic Growth," *Quar-
terly Journal of Economics*, LXX (February 1956).

[10] The turnpike theorem was introduced in a Rand memorandum, *Market
Mechanizations and Maximization*, part III (Santa Monica, Calif.: The Rand
Corporation, 1949). It is perhaps best explained in Robert Dorfman, Paul Samuel-
son, and Robert Solow, *Linear Programming and Economic Analysis* (New York:
McGraw Hill, 1958), ch. 12. A bibliography on the turnpike theorem appears in
Paul Samuelson, "A Catenary Turnpike Theorem Involving Consumption and the
Golden Rule," *American Economic Review* (June 1965), p. 486, n. 1.

put-to-capital ratio, all of them postulating some optimal path over time achievable by the specification of certain parameters and certain policy decisions. In an amusing "fable for growthmen," Phelps proposed that "under conditions of natural growth, the rate of investment is equal to the competitive rate of profits."[11] This is called the golden rule, because it results in "each generation [investing] on behalf of future generations that share of income which . . . it would have had past generations invest on behalf of it."[12]

To judge the usefulness of growth theory is, of course, a subjective matter. Clearly the Harrod–Domar models marked a turning point in economic thought (though some may argue that they are a variant of Keynesian economics, which is the real turning point), and the Solow contribution enhances their credibility. The frequent citations of the turnpike theorem and of Phelps's golden rule in subsequent economic literature reveal their popularity with the profession. No doubt the turnpike theorem may offer some guidance to policy-makers and at least some satisfaction to the intellectually curious. Beyond these points, however, the recent development of macro-growth theory has moved into ever more abstruse notions and abstract mathematics.

Occasionally a new model contributes substantially to an understanding of particular aspects of growth. Thus Fei and Ranis analyzed the agricultural and industrial sectors in takeoff, along with conditions for transfer of resources from the former to the latter.[13] Joan Robinson offered a theory of technique-switching, analyzing the factors (such as rate of interest) that affect the choice of technology.[14]

It would be overly subjective and not very useful to distinguish among these writings according to the value of their contributions to growth theory. Suffice it to say that whenever an innovation does occur it gives rise to a spate of "coattail" articles by authors eager to alter parameters and change patterns in ways more noted for mathematical niceties than for usefulness in understanding the growth process. In

---

[11] Edmund Phelps, "The Golden Rule of Accumulation: A Fable for Growthmen," *American Economic Review* (September 1961), p. 638.

[12] *Ibid.*, p. 642.

[13] Gustav Ranis and J.C.H. Fei, "A Theory of Economic Development," *American Economic Review* (September 1961), pp. 533-65; and, by the same authors, "Innovation, Capital Accumulation, and Economic Development," *American Economic Review* (June 1963), pp. 283-313.

[14] Joan Robinson, *The Accumulation of Capital* (Homewood, Ill.: Richard D. Irwin, 1956); see esp. pp. 411ff.

recent years the proportion of coattail articles to innovations has increased, leading me to believe that mathematical models of growth are
approaching their asymptote of usefulness. They will break through
that asymptote only with a significant discontinuity, and this—I believe—must arise from their combination with sociological models
rather than in the search for ever nicer economics.

The Sociological Model

Over the past two decades sociologists have debated the usefulness
of "structural-functional" models of change. In these models, the structure of a social system is distinguished from its functions. Change
emerges when functional strains become so great as to require either
destruction or modification of the structure. For example, the invention of factory technology puts strains on the functions of the handicraft household, which are ultimately resolved by a structural modification: the transfer of production to the factory.

Critics of these models have argued that the distinction between
structure and function is vague. In principle, the structure of a system
consists of those objects or roles that change but little over time and
which may therefore serve as points of reference against which to
analyze process variables, which do change in value as the system
functions. Thus the market has a structure—its physical locations and
institutionalized ways of doing business—and a process—the day-to-
day buying and selling. But the critics say that even market locations
and business practices change over time, and the assignment of variables to the two categories is necessarily arbitrary.

Despite this criticism, the structural-functional model of change has
become popular because it is practical. Even though the structure may
change, nevertheless it is useful to assume constancy while analyzing
process. The sun shifts position with respect to the stars, but one assumes constancy in analyzing movements of the earth.

Economic models of the Harrod–Domar type are structural-functional. The structure consists of two parts. First, identities are *defined*
relationships among variables, or tautologies. Gross national product
is defined as the sum of consumption and investment; investment is the
sum of its foreign and domestic parts; foreign investment is the excess
of exports over imports; and so on. These identities (tautologies) supply
a mental vision of the system, which constantly reminds the observer

that the value of no variable can change without corresponding change in the value of one or more other variables. Secondly, parameters stipulate the equilibrium conditions expected to exist among the variables. For example, consumption will be a certain multiple of the increment of investment (Keynesian principle of the multiplier), and incremental output will be a certain fraction of the investment of the preceding period. Table 7-1 is a simple model in which the only identity is $\text{GNP}_t = C_t + I_t$, while the equilibrium relationships are $\Delta\text{GNP}_t = 10\Delta I_t$ (the multiplier) and $\Delta\text{GNP}_t = 0.3I_{t-1}$ (the IOCR). So long as these relationships persist, the system will function in equilibrium.

System structure and function in sociological models are analogous to those in economics. Corresponding to the identities are the definitions of system elements, such as value, norm, actor, role, and institution, with defined relationships among them—actors play roles, institutions conform to values, and norms in one system may be values in its subsystem. Like the identities in economics, these statements apply to *any* system. The definitions are vaguer in sociology than in economics, however. This may be so because sociological variables contain so many dimensions, many of them unmeasurable, that it is impossible to tell conceptually where one variable ends and another begins. But it may also be that sociologists have not paid enough attention to their tautologies, perhaps because they have not been aware of how useful they are in achieving precise definitions of system structure.

Corresponding to the parameters in economic models are the equilibrium conditions in sociology, or forces designed to maintain the boundaries of a system. Parsons, for example, postulates a tendency toward equilibrium in every long-surviving system, for those lacking such forces would Darwinistically cease to exist. Each system contains elements of conflict, both internal (as between buyer and seller in the market system) and external (in adapting to changes in environment). Offsetting these conflicts are integrative forces that become institutionalized (such as rules for buying and selling). The equilibrium postulate simply states that the tension of conflict and integrative forces must be just so finely adjusted that the system will not fall apart.

Three principal models of change have emerged within the structural-functional framework. In the first two, alterations in system function (equilibrium conditions) eventually lead to change in structure. In the third, an equilibrium rate of change occurs with no change in structure.

1. *The differentiation model* (Durkheim, Parsons).[15] A system operating in equilibrium is disturbed by an environmental change affecting its functions. In an attempt to restore equilibrium, it alters its functional relationships in such a way that two or more systems emerge with specialized functions. The evolution from a household production system to a factory and a residual household system is an example. Developing societies become increasingly differentiated.

Analogies are found in biology. The paramecium engages in undifferentiated propagation, since one system splits into two identical ones. Evolution according to Darwin implies differentiation, with different species coming to perform specific functions that are then ecologically integrated with each other.

2. *The function-dysfunction model* (Merton).[16] A system operating in equilibrium may nevertheless generate forces productive of structural change. So long as strains (dysfunctional) and social forces to control them (functional) operate within bounds, the system remains in equilibrium. Over time, however, the strains may grow disproportionately to the controls, and change in system structure is required.

3. *Dynamic equilibrium models* (Parsons, Nagel).[17] In these models, the equilibrium conditions refer to *rates of change* in the character of system elements. (Static equilibrium is a special case where rate of change is zero). So long as the parameters are such

[15] Emile Durkheim, *The Division of Labor in Society* (New York: The Free Press, September 1933). Talcott Parsons, "Some Considerations on the Theory of Social Change," *Rural Sociology* (September 1961); reprinted in Amatai Etzioni and Eva Etzioni, *Social Change* (New York: Basic Books, 1964), pp. 83-97.

[16] Robert K. Merton, *Social Theory and Social Structure* (New York: The Free Press, 1957), part II.

[17] Talcott Parsons, *The Social System* (New York: The Free Press, 1951). Ernest Nagel, "A Formalization of Functionalism," in his *Logic Without Metaphysics* (New York: The Free Press, 1956), pp. 247-83; this article is also discussed in Francesca Cancian, "Functional Analysis of Change," *American Sociological Review*, xxv (December 1960), pp. 818-26; reprinted in Etzioni and Etzioni, *Social Change*, pp. 112-24.

that these rates of change remain within bounds, the dynamic equilibrium is preserved. Harrod–Domar models fit within this category.

Two distinct processes of change—dynamic equilibrium and dysfunctional—are implied in these models. Let us consider them separately.

Parsons declares that equilibrium may be static or moving, but no element of structure is changed:

> . . . it is necessary to distinguish clearly between the process *within* the system and the process of change *of* the system. It is very common to confuse these two things under the term "dynamic." For the purpose of our conceptual scheme the distinction derives from the concept of equilibrium and the way in which this has been used in the present work. Beyond the most general meaning of the concept of equilibrium, the meaning which is most directly applicable here is that applying to what we have called a "boundary-maintaining" system. . . . It was, however, also recognized that the equilibrium formulated in these terms could be a moving equilibrium where certain orderly processes of empirical change were going on.[18]

Parsons and Shils consider, for example, that science and religion may carry on endogenous changes in a system without rupturing its boundaries, thus contributing to a moving equilibrium.

> Where the cultural orientation gives a prominent place to achievement and universalistic orientation, this endogenous tendency toward change may be very pronounced. The obvious example is modern science, with its technological applications. . . . What is very conspicuously true of science is also true of the consequences of many religious movements, once certain processes of internal development have started. The value-orientations of modern capitalistic enterprise are similarly endogenously productive of change. Any society in which the value standards, as in a legal code (even though it is not in their formal nature to undergo development), are capable of reinterpretation will also tend toward change. Any society in which the allocations create or maintain

[18] Parsons, *The Social System*, p. 481.

dissatisfaction will be open to change; especially when the cultural standards and the allocations combine to intensify need-dispositions, change will be a certainty.[19]

Merton's concept of change, on the other hand, implies a rupture from equilibrium. Tensions occur that are too severe for containment within the system boundary, and it moves from one state to another:

> The key concept bridging the gap between statics and dynamics in functional theory is that of strain, tension, contradiction, or discrepancy between the component elements of social and cultural structure. Such strains may be dysfunctional for the social system in its then existing form; they may also be instrumental in leading to changes in that system. In any case, they exert pressure for change. When social mechanisms for controlling them are operating effectively, these strains are kept within such bounds as to limit change of the social structure. (In some systems of political theory and ideology, the workings of these control mechanisms are called "concessions" and "compromises" including the process of basic structural change.)[20]

The dichotomy between dynamic equilibrium change and dysfunctional change is analogous to the distinction economists make between dynamics and comparative statics. A comparative static model starts with a condition of static equilibrium, which is disturbed by some exogenous event, in turn leading to a new static equilibrium at a different level. The Keynesian system is an exercise in comparative statics. Suppose, for example, there is static equilibrium at less than full employment; the government (an exogenous force) increases its expenditures, which have a multiplier effect through consumption, leading ideally to a new static equilibrium at full employment. This model would appear to correspond to structural change in the Parsons–Merton sense, in that (a) one of the equilibrium conditions (relationship of government spending to aggregate income) has been changed, and (b) the boundaries of the system are therefore different (greater government spending is now included). Parsons writes as follows

---

[19] Talcott Parsons and Edward A. Shils, assisted by James Olds, "Values, Motives, and Systems of Actions," in *Toward A General Theory of Action* (Cambridge, Mass.: Harvard University Press, 1951), p. 232.

[20] Merton, *Social Theory*, p. 122.

about the comparative statics model: "The essential point is that for there to be a theory of *change* of pattern, under these methodological assumptions, there must be an initial and a terminal pattern to be used as points of reference."[21]

Merton hinted at the resolution of the comparative statics–dynamics dichotomy in the earlier citation: "The key concept bridging the gap between statics and dynamics in functional theory is that of strain, tension, contradiction. . . ." Though the kind of tension referred to here is *exogenous* in comparative static models, it becomes *endogenous* when brought about by a rate of growth whose equilibrium is in turn induced by the dynamic parameters of the model.

At first blush, the Harrod–Domar models would seem to fit this type. Investment, which is exogenous in the Keynesian model, is introduced by a static parameter; in Table 7-1, it is $\Delta\text{GNP}_t = 10\Delta I_t$. Both ΔI and ΔGNP are of the same time period (t) because the time lapse between them is irrelevant. But ΔI is then made endogenous by its dependence on the expected increase in income in the succeeding period, though the dynamic parameter $0.3I_t = \Delta\text{GNP}_{t+1}$ where ΔGNP_{t+1} refers to the expected income increment in the succeeding period.

Still, we see a snag. Merton referred to tension introduced endogenously by the parameters of equilibrium which would lead to a structural change in the system. Most economists viewing the Harrod–Domar models would see no structure change. Investment, consumption, and income continue increasing merrily forever and in the same specified ways. If there has been structural change, it has not occurred suddenly. For example, the United States in 1800 (with low income and little investment) may look considerably different from the same country now (with high income and much investment) because it occupies a different point on the same Harrod–Domar time continuum. We may define the structure as different, but the process by which it became so would conform more to the Parsons equilibrium model than to the Merton dysfunctional type.

There are, however, other economic models that conform more closely to the Merton model of dysfunction. One of these is the famous Hansen–Samuelson multiplier-accelerator model of 1939.[22] This is a

[21] Parsons, *Social Systems*, p. 483.
[22] Paul A. Samuelson, "Interactions between the Multiplier Analysis and the

static model of the Keynesian type into which a Harrod-type proportion between increment of income and increment of investment is injected. We refer to this proportion as the "relation." In this model, Samuelson demonstrated that if the relation had certain relatively low values, the model was stable, and a new equilibrium level of income would be reached asymptotically. If the relation had higher values, however, an exogenous increment of spending would lead to no equilibrium at all, because demand would explode out of all bounds. Only in a case such as the latter would an economist call a model unstable. Unstable models are usually absurd, for they tell us little or nothing of how the economic system really functions.

Now, a model of dysfunction can usually be converted into an equilibrium model through an expansion of the structure. For example, the Parsons model of differentiation assumes the classical case of the producing household which is destroyed as a system and supplanted by two new systems: the factory and the residual household. If instead we began with a broader producing-childrearing system, we might consider that that system remained intact while the differentiation of roles occurred within it according to some pattern defined by the equilibrium conditions. The problem with this procedure is that the expansion would continue indefinitely, and we would end up with a model of the entire social system, encompassing more variables than can be comprehended at once.

There is, however, a solution, to which a social-science model of economic growth might conform. This is to confine the concept of equilibrium to certain specific roles—in this case, those centering around the increase in gross national product—and to define a system whose structure remains intact with respect to those roles. Other systems may rise, fall, or change as they will (even by revolution), but the production system goes on forever. This does not mean that its character does not change. On the contrary, the production system may look totally different at two points of history. Rather, it means that we have selected production as the system whose changes we want to explain through equilibrium analysis.

In such a model, the analysis of the undifferentiated household

---

Principle of Acceleration," *Review of Economic Statistics*, xxi (May 1939), pp. 75-78; reprinted in American Economic Association, *Readings in Business Cycle Theory* (Homewood, Ill.: Richard D. Irwin, 1944), pp. 261-69.

would center around its production aspects. We would see differentiation as evolving first through father and son performing different functions and then through the putting-out system long before the threshold was reached at which employment moved to the factory. The early factories would then be simple and relatively *undifferentiated* compared to our modern production behemoths. This model conforms to Marshall's (and our) belief that *natura non facit saltum*, for we see change in a continuum.

Other systems, which appear to change their structure abruptly and discontinuously with respect to the production system (e.g., the household system, the education system, and the political system) might be shown to change continuously if equilibrium analysis were pinpointed upon one of them, while related systems, including the production, would show discontinuous change as dysfunctional elements evolve. We have now divided the social system in a different way—by roles rather than by organizations—but we are still using structural-functional analysis.

System structures, then, consist of a set of related elements (objects, actors, and roles) whose relationships to each other are expressed in two ways: (1) by identities or definitions, and (2) by parameters or equilibrium conditions. If the elements are measurable and the relationships expressible mathematically, so much the better, though this is not essential. In addition, system structure focuses upon an object of analysis (in our case, gross national product). Preservation of the system requires the following: first, that the definitions do not change; secondly, that the parameters change only over long periods and only in ways explainable within the system function. When they change, then either other parameters must change to offset them, or the equilibrium rate of change of the object of analysis must change. Thirdly, the object of analysis must never be destroyed. (In the case of GNP, the society must never cease to produce.)

The purpose of this model is to understand the continuity of change. If we were to define systems in such a way that the structures were periodically destroyed and we had no concept of what would follow, then our analysis would be of little purpose. We might show what caused the revolution but not what kind of postrevolutionary structure would be likely to evolve.

Before we turn to the conditions for a social-science model of economic growth, let us digress to consider a promising model of socioeconomic growth that has emerged recently. Unfortunately, it is a static model.

The Adelman–Morris Model of Economic Growth

The problem with purely economic models is that the IOCR is neither a satisfactory nor sufficient parameter. Social scientists have long known that economic development involves all the behavior disciplines. Economic models are widely criticized for their failure to account for social, political, cultural, and psychological forces. The number of anecdotes displaying interdisciplinary behavior in this field are legion. In response to this challenge, social scientists have attempted to create interdisciplinary models of society,[23] and a few have been aimed particularly at economic growth. Though their works are not fully fledged models, nevertheless both Banks and Textor[24] and Russett and his coauthors[25] have selected certain sociopolitical variables which they have correlated with economic development in various countries. In the same vein, Gross has proposed a complete set of social accounts, involving interdisciplinary variables, which would describe the "state of the nation."[26]

One of the most enlightening fully fledged models is the econometric study by Adelman and Morris,[27] which includes variables drawn from the economic, social, and political spectrum, as follows.

[23] The works of Talcott Parsons, referred to earlier in this book, are the best-known attempt at an integrated theory of the social system. With specific reference to the economy, Parsons has joined with Neil Smelser in *Economy and Society* (New York: The Free Press, 1956). Other theoretical formulations include Robert A. Solo, *Economic Organization and Social Systems* (Indianapolis, Ind.: Bobbs-Merrill Co., 1967), and Alfred Kuhn, *The Study of Society: A Unified Approach* (Indianapolis, Ind.: Richard D. Irwin, 1966).

[24] Arthur S. Banks and Robert B. Textor, *A Cross Polity Survey* (Cambridge, Mass.: The M.I.T. Press, 1963).

[25] Bruce M. Russett *et al., World Handbook of Political and Social Indicators* (New Haven: Yale University Press, 1964).

[26] Bertram Gross, "The State of the Nation," in *Social Indicators*, ed. Raymond A. Bauer (Cambridge, Mass.: The M.I.T. Press, 1966), pp. 154-271.

[27] Irma Adelman and Cynthia Morris, "An Econometric Model of Development," *American Economic Review* (December 1968), pp. 1184-1218. By the same authors, *Society, Politics, and Economic Development* (Baltimore, Md.: The Johns Hopkins Press, 1967).

Economic Indicators

Abundance of natural resources

Gross investment rate

Level of modernization of industry

Change in degree of industrialization since 1950

Size of the traditional agricultural sector

Level of modernization of techniques in agriculture

Improvement in agricultural productivity since 1950

Adequacy of physical overhead capital

Improvement in physical overhead capital since 1950

Effectiveness of the tax system

Improvement in effectiveness of the tax system since 1950

Effectiveness in financial institutions

Improvement in effectiveness of financial institutions since 1950

Structure of foreign trade

Social and socioeconomic variables

Character of agricultural organization

Extent of dualism

Extent of urbanization

Character of basic social organization

Importance of the indigenous middle class

Extent of social mobility

Extent of literacy

Extent of mass communication

Degree of cultural and ethnic homogeneity

Degree of social tension

Crude fertility rate

Degree of modernization of outlook

Degree of national integration and sense of national unity

Rate of improvement in human resources

Political variables

Extent of centralization of political power

Strength of democratic institutions

Degree of freedom of political opposition and press

Degree of competitiveness of political parties

Predominant basis of the political party system

Strength of the labor movement

Political strength of the traditional elite
Political strength of the military
Degree of administrative efficiency
Extent of leadership commitment to economic development
Extent of political stability

Using stepwise discriminant analysis, Adelman and Morris determined "those linear combinations of country performance characteristics that best discriminate among various groups of countries." At each step they scanned "the entire list of variables not already in the discriminant function [selecting] that variable which adds most to the explanation of the variance between group means, given the other variables already included."[28]

Dividing less developed countries into groups depending on the average percentage increase in real per capita GNP from 1950/51 to 1963/64, the authors determined that four variables were statistically most relevant to the discriminant, which distinguishes countries growing more rapidly from those growing slower. These are "(listed in the order of their statistical importance): the degree of improvement in financial institutions, the degree of modernization of outlook, the extent of leadership commitment to economic development, and the degree of improvement in agricultural productivity." They then went further to determine, by multiple regression, the variables most closely associated with each of these four. For example, the improvement of financial institutions correlated ($R^2 = 0.57$) with the change in the degree of industrialization and the extent of dualism, while modernization of outlook correlated ($R^2 = 0.72$) with the extent of dualism, the adequacy of physical overhead capital, and (negatively) with the size of the traditional agricultural sector. Carrying their investigation further, they then correlated each of the additional variables (e.g., extent of dualism) with other sociopolitical-economic variables until they emerged with a causal ordering of the model expressed mathematically and presented graphically.[29] They then attempted to explain the correlations theoretically and to throw out "nonsense relationships." Finally, the authors calculated a set of multipliers depicting the impact of each variable separately on a country's development poten-

[28] Adelman and Morris, "An Econometric Model," p. 1188.
[29] Ibid., p. 1202.

tial, by showing how increments in that variable would change the discriminant.

The Adelman–Morris model constitutes a significant advance in the understanding of all forces associated with economic growth. But it suffers from several shortcomings. First, the selection of variables and the means to measure them is subjective. Though the spectrum chosen by the authors is wide indeed, conceptually there can be no objective judgment on the appropriateness of the definitions. Secondly, the authors discriminated among countries only according to their rates of economic growth at a given time. Their model is not dynamic in the sense of showing how rates of economic growth correlate over time with rates of change in other variables selected. Thirdly, the large number of independent variables detract from the usefulness of the model for making policy. Finally, the four variables that account most for economic growth—the degree of improvement in financial institutions, the degree of modernization of outlook, the extent of leadership commitment to economic development, and the degree of improvement in agricultural productivity—do not contribute substantially to a theory of economic growth.

Relationship of Model to Theory

My criticisms of the Adelman–Morris model are exploratory only; I do not offer any improvement. Rather, I should like to point to directions in which I believe the interdisciplinary growth model needs to be developed and to the kinds of research that ought to be done. The resulting model would combine the Harrod–Domar–Solow concept of an equilibrium rate of growth with a few, selected sociopolitical indicators of the Adelman–Morris type but employing AIE as a surrogate for most of them. It would also draw on the structural-functional framework developed by Parsons, Merton, Nagel, and others.

In such a model, gross national product would be a function of the quantities of factors of production and the quality of the population as measured by such sociocultural indicators as the level of education, the stock of technology, the degree of entrepreneurial capacity, and aggregate institutional effectiveness. Though the investigator should always be open to the possibility of including more sociocultural variables, nevertheless these appear to me to be the ones with which the empirical investigation should begin, for reasons which I will detail below. First, however, I digress to consider the problem of *fusion*, which is encountered in both sociological and economic models.

FUSION

Fusion occurs when two variables overlap each other conceptually, in that part of one becomes an inherent part of the other. It is not just that one correlates with the other; it *becomes* the other. In economics, original services (e.g., labor) and intermediate product (e.g., wheat, butter, eggs) become fused into a final product (e.g., bread). As machinery depreciates, its value becomes fused into the value of its output. But not all flour is fused into bread and not all machinery into its output.

Often it is difficult to know when fusion has occurred. Suppose a municipal government supplies policemen at a cost of $50; they guard a factory for half their time and private residences for the other half. The factory produces shoes which sell for $200. What is the value added to the gross national product by the two outputs (police services and shoes)? It *ought* to be $225, consisting of $200 of shoes and $25 of police protection of residences. The other $25, of police guarding the factory, should be fused into the value of shoes, which is set by the market price. In practice, however, national income accountants cannot distinguish between police protection provided to businesses and to homes, so they arbitrarily consider all such services as final product. In the present example, they would say that value added is $250.

Fusion is even more perplexing in sociological and political models. Political stability, for example, can be subdivided into stability of the national government and of local governments. Is there *one thing*—stability—that is spread over two jurisdictions? Or are they separate things, one of which may be causal to the other? If we combine political stability and business efficiency under the rubric of institutional effectiveness, do they then become the same thing? In political science and sociology, things have a way of becoming separate concepts if they are given different names and if there are different ways of measuring them. Nor can we resolve this dilemma by finding an objective way of determining when fusion has occurred, for there is none. The depreciated machinery becomes part of its final product only because national income accountants say it does. Two items are fused if we say they are fused and are conceptually distinct if we say they are.

The problem is serious. The Adelman–Morris model might be criticized for depending on the existence of those particular variables that its authors elected to define and investigate. Had they defined or selected them differently and subdivided them differently, they might have achieved different results. Obviously, this is no criticism of the authors, for it reflects on *any* social-science model, including the one we are about to propose. In sum, if we do not recognize fusion and indulge in it, our social-science growth model becomes capable of containing an infinite number of variables, infinitely subdividable. If all are included, the model becomes unworkable, but any selection among them is bound to be arbitrary and subjective.

Unless, of course, it is related to a theory. The coming of the computer has made it possible to evolve theories out of models rather than vice versa. An econometric model has a limited number of variables, which are presumed to be conceptually distinct; all are measurable. From this fact arises the temptation to throw them into the computer, mix them in all possible combinations, and then try to explain resulting correlations. The procedure is perfectly valid in econometrics. But it is not valid for sociocultural models because of fusion. Rather, a theoretical proposition must underlie the definitions selected for concepts. *A* and *B* are fused only because the theory says they should be fused. Flour is fused into bread and depreciation into output because these concepts fit the needs of Keynesian income theories. That it does not depend on a theory is the big weakness of the Adelman–Morris model as well as of other compendiums of correlations that have been gathered.

Finally, a useful social-science growth model must contain a strictly limited number of variables. A model telling us that economic growth is related to a dash of literacy, a pinch of political stability, and a small proportion of a large number of other independent variables is not operationally useful even if the multiple correlation is high and even if a case can be made that variables are conceptually distinct. A theory helps us determine which variables to retain. For example, suppose it is shown statistically that the number of apartment houses in metropolitan areas correlates closely with economic growth. If our theory tells us that this variable is proxy for (and, we decide, fused with) the growth of a middle class (unmeasurable), which is an essential link in explaining the level of GNP, then it must be retained. If on the other hand apartment houses are only an incidental characteristic of growth, that variable can be eliminated.

THEORETICAL UNDERPINNINGS OF THE MODEL

I believe it is reasonable to propose a social-science growth model based on the following theoretical propositions. First, gross national product depends on five variables: the quantity of productive factors (subdividable as necessary into land, labor, capital, etc.); the level of education; the stock of technology; the degree of entrepreneurial capacity; and the ratings for aggregate institutional effectiveness (AIE). All independent variables are technically measurable or have proxy variables that are, and it is reasonable to consider them conceptually distinct. Some correlation among independent variables is likely, but this cannot be helped.

Secondly, the GNP function would be the same the world over, except for pre-takeoff countries. Growth is thus totally explained by the independent variables (in a statistical sense). Differences among nations in the incremental output-to-capital ratio (a partial derivative of GNP with respect to capital) would depend entirely on the other resources (e.g., quality of land, climate) and on the sociocultural variables included. If upon empirical investigation involving many countries the factor of error turns out consistently large, then the theory is imperfect, and new (additional or substitute) independent variables would need to be sought.

Thirdly, the independent variables must either change according to some specified function of time, or they must be mutually interrelated with GNP. As an example of the former, the labor supply might increase exponentially by a given percentage a year, according to population growth. As an example of the latter, investment of capital might cause an increase in GNP and be caused by expectations of further increase, as in the Harrod–Domar models. The model would then become determinate if some set of values for GNP and for all independent variables could be specified for some initial period. For any subsequent period there would be an equilibrium level of GNP and of every independent variable.

241

This outline of a theory, of course, is not very profound. It suggests simply that GNP is fully explainable by changes in economic and socio-cultural indicators and that dynamic-equilibrium analysis is possible. It mentions five variables whose investigation would seem reasonable as a first attempt, and it suggests that if the results are not good other variables should be sought. The theory does not explain the reasons for whatever parameters may be discovered (why, for example, the IOCR would turn out to be what it is). Furthermore, all the variables are subdividable into others, and much additional insight could be gained by examining the component parts. Nor would the theory discover the great secret of how growth begins. Finally, it is only a macro-theory, which ignores the many forces determining the individual's decision to save or his capacity to be an entrepreneur.

Of what use is this theory, then? Its contribution lies in the introduction of AIE, a quantifiable concept of social cohesion that is fused with many variables—such as political stability and administrative efficiency—which social scientists have already recognized as being related to growth. This fusion enables us to reduce the number of independent variables to manageable size, and possibly to open the way for significant research.

Social scientists are so often criticized for spinning elaborate theories and presenting models that have not yet been researched that I believe a word is necessary in defense. First, the outlines of a growth theory presented in this chapter are not radically new. They represent a pulling-together of the ideas that sociologists, political scientists, and economists have been developing—in ways we have discussed earlier in this chapter and in preceding chapters. Secondly, and more important, the potential research is so awesome that we must be humble before it. A gigantic, multi-year effort in many nations would be necessary before even minimal results would be discernible. Some research would not be possible because it would run counter to the perceived interests of its subjects. While waiting and before coping with these problems it seemed reasonable to outline the directions in which I believe social scientists ought to be moving if they are to further the development of aggregate growth models.

In the next section I will defend the proposition that the sociocultural variables (education, technology, entrepreneurial capacity, and

AIE) should be mutually reinforcing with GNP in a manner analogous to the relationship of capital to GNP in the Harrod–Domar models.

Sociocultural Variables and the GNP

Our theory depends on the proposition that the sociocultural variables have, like income, an equilibrium rate of growth. They are also probably interdependent, in that (for example) the rate of growth of AIE depends on the rate of growth of education, technology, and entrepreneurial capacity. They may be substitutable for each other. In the case of each variable, there would be a supply function and a demand function (other variables being held equal), and equilibrium would require that demand equal supply. In earlier chapters, we have defined the demand for and supply of institutional effectiveness as it relates to individual institutions. That is, an institution will be founded (or increased in effectiveness) if its marginal value, in the minds of those capable of founding it, is at least as great as the marginal cost to them, including both values that they themselves sacrifice and the expenditure of resources to persuade or coerce others as necessary. By the same token, the demand schedule for *aggregate* institutional effectiveness depends on its marginal product (or the increment of GNP it is believed capable of evoking) as estimated by growth-sensitive power groups, while the supply schedule depends on the marginal cost to these same groups.

We would draw demand and supply curves for AIE as in Figure 7-1.

FIGURE 7-1.

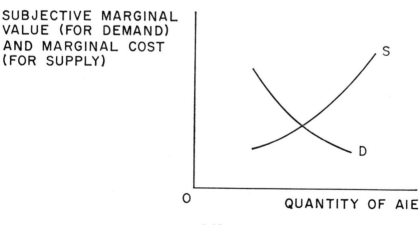

SUBJECTIVE MARGINAL
VALUE (FOR DEMAND)
AND MARGINAL COST
(FOR SUPPLY)

S

D

O

QUANTITY OF AIE

The marginal value includes the utility to the power groups of each increment of GNP which they judge will be earned by an increment of AIE. The marginal cost is many dimensional, including the values, institutions, and norms the power groups must sacrifice, as well as the costs of persuading others to join the consensus. Since different measures are implied on the vertical axis, the trade-off function among them is subjective: that is, each point represents, first, a quantity of marginal utility, and secondly, the quantity of many-dimensional marginal cost which the power group perceives to be worth the utility. If these items are not measurable cardinally, we presume they can be measured ordinally: the power groups think of them as being "more" or "less," and we assign arbitrary values.

Suppose, for example, marginal utility and marginal cost are both measured in arbitrary units from zero to one hundred. For a small amount of increased AIE, marginal utility (measured on the demand curve) will exceed marginal cost (measured on the supply curve). As increased amounts are acquired, marginal utility (demand) declines, while marginal cost (supply) rises. The equilibrium point—specifying the amount that will in fact be demanded and supplied—is represented by the intersection of the curves.

We now suggest that both the demand and supply functions will shift to the right as GNP increases, possibly in response to its level and possibly to its rate of growth. We have already discussed the reasons in earlier chapters. To recapitulate, the spread of growth-sensitive power groups throughout society (since growth-sensitivity is contagious) increases the demand function. The greater possibility of paying off recalcitrant groups as GNP increases, as well as the fact that they become persuaded to the advantages of growth, lowers the supply schedule with reference to the vertical axis, thereby moving it to the right. The more conflict resolutions become +,+, the less will be the resistance to change.

Demand and supply for the other sociocultural variables are similarly conceived. Growth-sensitive power groups perceive a demand for education when they recognize how much it contributes positively to economic growth. The "demand" on the part of those who want to be educated is construed as a reduction in the cost schedule of the power groups, for it is easier to persuade people to go to school if they want to go in the first place.

In the case of technology, the growth-sensitive power groups are the entrepreneurs demanding it, and the costs are the resources paid to buy it abroad or to develop it at home, plus the value sacrifices and risk incurred in implementing it.

The demand for entrepreneurial capacity is felt by those persons in a position to provide the institutional framework in which it flourishes. Unless he is a Robinson Crusoe, a potential entrepreneur will be developed or stifled by the extent to which the social structure encourages innovation or makes it possible. Either freedom of enterprise or a socialist framework with adequate rewards may encourage entrepreneurship. Nor are we limited to these types, for a mixed system like those found in most Latin American countries may also be effective. Which kinds of institutions are most effective will depend on ideology, as we have suggested in earlier chapters. Presumably the demand schedule shifts to the right as gross national product increases.

The supply of entrepreneurship is a matter of debate. Entrepreneurship may be innate, or it may depend on physical displacement of persons (Hoselitz) or on disadvantaged groups (Hagen), or on a number of other behavioral or psychological factors. If we believe that there is an infinite supply of entrepreneurial talent, stifled only by lack of institutional environment, then the supply schedule may be perfectly elastic (as in S_1 in Figure 7-2). In drawing S_1 we have assumed that the marginal cost of institutions is constant regardless of the quantity of entrepreneurial talent created. If we believe in the fixed supply, then the schedule is completely inelastic, as in S_2. Or it may lie somewhere in between. But most theories of entrepreneurship would accept that over time any supply schedule (except the infinitely elastic) will move to the right as GNP increases, since most of the presumed causes of this talent (e.g., physical or social mobility) correlate positively with income.

In the next two subsections, we illustrate how the equilibrium rate of growth of sociocultural forces is dependent on gross national product and its rate of increase. We select the education system and the access system. The former constitutes one of the variables in our proposed model. The latter—defined as the extent to which opportunities for political, social, and economic positions are available to members of a society—is probably one of the component parts of (and therefore fused with) aggregate institutional effectiveness. Increased access also

Figure 7-2.

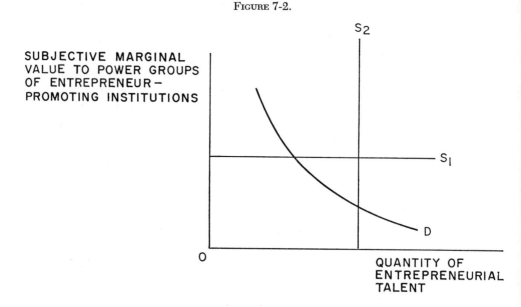

SUBJECTIVE MARGINAL
VALUE TO POWER GROUPS
OF ENTREPRENEUR –
PROMOTING INSTITUTIONS

QUANTITY OF
ENTREPRENEURIAL
TALENT

promotes the supply of entrepreneurship because it increases the capability of potential entrepreneurs to put their innovations into effect. It increases AIE because, by improving communication among subcultures and the predictability of response, it promotes higher ratings for the rules and identification criteria. The demand for access is usually incited by increased income, and its greater supply is then necessary to satisfy the consensus criterion for institutional effectiveness.

EDUCATION

What is the equilibrium rate of growth of education, as income increases over time? This question is pertinent to the oft-heard simplification that "education is the key to economic development." The implication is that millions of dollars spent on education would be the cure-all.

Veteran economic planners are more sophisticated. Education is a forceful tool to increase output, but to promote it far beyond its equilibrium rate of growth would be a waste of resources.

This hypothesis is illustrated by the experience of Cornell anthro-

pologists in the hacienda of Vicos, Peru. As part of their private, prototype agrarian reform, these anthropologists opened a primary school.
But few children came, for the (Indian) members of the Vicos community saw no reason to read and write. It was not required by their
prinicipal economic activity (growing potatoes) or by their government functions (mainly social) or by their culture norms. They neither
had books nor anyone with whom to communicate by the written
word. The Cornell anthropologists "bribed" the children to go to
school with free lunches. Education was not legitimated until their
incomes had begun to rise through changes in the structure of production and compensation.

The concept of an equilibrium rate of growth in education, dependent on income, is intuitively discerned in the historical contrast between Northern and Southern schools in the United States. At the time
of the war between the States, Southern plantation owners saw no purpose in educating their slaves or the "white trash," nor these any need
to be literate. The demand for quality education, virtually confined to
the wealthy, could be met by private schools and universities in the
North or abroad. In the North, by contrast, a growing technology required blue-collar foremen literate enough to follow instructions;
industry needed a mobile labor force. Hence more resources were
dedicated to public schooling. In terms of per capita expenditure on
public education, Southern schools long lagged behind their Northern
counterparts, and only with the changing industrial requirements of
the twentieth century did they begin to catch up.

Similar distinctions apply to segregated education today in the
United States. Many a black dropout has argued that there is no point
in continuing school because economic opportunities are denied him
on account of race. While such statements contain an element of defense, nevertheless the other element is real.

There is no universal constant relating education to income. The
parameters differ in Southern plantations, Peruvian *haciendas*, and
Northern manufacturing states. They depend on many factors, such
as type of output, kind of government, extent of popular representa-
tion, culture norms of the different social strata, and the like, all of
which we believe may be fused with the sociocultural variables (technology, entrepreneurship, and AIE) we have included in our model.

247

ACCESS

The access system, known as "civil rights" in the United States and "social justice" in many other countries, is the one by which access to positions of social, economic, and political value is or is not made available to various segments of the population.[30]

I select the word "access" because it is neutral. "Civil rights" implies a defined natural or legislated right of access on whose existence or urgency I heartily agree in practice but as a theorizing social scientist must be noncommital. "Social justice" has further subjective overtones, in addition to which it has been associated with particular movements such as the *justicialista* of Perón's Argentina.

For the purpose of our theory, access is fused with AIE. Institutions cannot be effective (by the consensus criterion) if access to them is denied those who desire it. We discuss here the relationship of access to GNP only to illustrate that even if the variables within the model (which include AIE but not access) were quantified and the theory found correct, there would still be room for research on relationships between component parts of the sociocultural variables and GNP.

Access can be quantified, though I have neither done so myself nor know of others who have. Access to specific positions, to one another's homes or to social or economic mobility, might be statistically sampled and cast in some sort of scale. It might then be plotted on a Lorenz-type curve and applied to different populations.

Some difficulty would arise in the nonhomogeneity of compared populations. Access restrictions (discrimination) are based on different ethnic and cultural considerations in different countries. In the United States, access is limited on the basis of skin color (among other things); the same is true for Panama and Brazil. In many Latin American countries, however, the limitation is based more on cultural considerations: the kind of clothes a man wears, what language he speaks (e.g., indigenous or Spanish), whether he is from country or city, and the like.

Additional questions would arise. Should access be measured purely by the number of restrictions applied or by the relative size of the

[30] In several of his newspaper columns and public speeches, Max Lerner has argued that the social system in the U.S. is characterized by greater opportunity for access than is the case in much of the rest of the world. Whether men are born equal, he finds, is not so important as whether they have equal access.

groups discriminated against. (The ratio of Indians to total population in Peru is greater than that of blacks in the United States.) If it should take account of the number of groups discriminated against, how should they be weighted? What kinds of discrimination should be counted as access denied, and how should they be weighted against each other? How should a paternalistic attitude be counted (such as the use of *tu* toward Indians in Latin America)? All strike me as questions that could be well enough answered for comparative studies to be fruitful. Even arbitrary decisions consistently applied are acceptable. I therefore assume that access can be measured and proceed accordingly.

The relationship of access to economic growth has long been recognized. Unlimited access is a prerequisite for optimum efficiency in the classical economic model. Discrimination may result in the employment of a less efficient factor of production when a more efficient would otherwise be available. Individuals with greater capacity for certain types of training may be ruled out in favor of others with less capacity. In cases of segregated facilities, there are wastes of duplication and loss of economies of scale.

But these elements of relationship are not sufficiently precise. They must be divided into those affecting supply and those affecting demand.

The desire for access comes from the groups that are discriminated against,[31] but to become effective demand it must be transmitted to the power groups. As in any demand function, demand for access has a "utility" element and a "purchasing-power" element. When the income of discriminated groups is low, the utility of access is also low. For example, low-income traditional societies are generally ascriptive, with lower classes resigned to their fates. They are not awakened to potential gratification. As income increases,[32] however, so does awareness. In fact, it builds upon itself—the more access, the greater the awareness of its utility.

Likewise, higher income provides greater "purchasing power" of

[31] I use the words "discriminated against" rather than "minority" because in some countries these groups are in numerical majority.

[32] It is assumed that the income of groups that are discriminated against increases as national income increases. This is probably so in all but isolated subsistence communities. The coefficient of relationship, of course, need not be great.

access: the capacity to stage demonstrations, to support full-time leaders, to elect political representatives (if the government permits it) or to rebel (if it does not). These are the ways in which demand is transmitted to the power groups.

Demand for access is also related to the rate of growth of income. Rapid increases in purchasing power cause strain on cultural values and customary institutions, and is probably accompanied by a more intense desire for access. Very likely the civil rights movement in the United States was spurred on not only by the high level of income but by the rate of its increase.

The demand for access is usually initiated by the underprivileged groups themselves when their income increases to the point at which they judge the cost to be within their means. They then form an alliance with those power groups who find the cost of lack of access to be disruptive to their plans for continued economic growth. These include the Department of Justice, which does not want to see Washington burned and also values the black vote, the city fathers of Birmingham, Alabama, who do not want industry to bypass them because of civil strife, and officials of the Institute for Agrarian Reform in Chile whose jobs depend on their success in implementing reforms.

The suppliers of access are the ones who would benefit by the restrictions if they were continued: whites in the United States who hold jobs from which blacks have been excluded, slave-owners in Asia and Africa, and feudal landlords in Asia, Africa, and Latin America. Their willingness to supply depends on the opportunity cost. Possibly the suppliers are converting themselves into demanders, in which case they are on both sides of the fence. This situation would occur if feudal landlords were becoming industrialists. They might then require the cooperation of the unprivileged groups in a common venture, and wish, for example, to employ them in a growing industry rather than as feudal peons, and access may be the price. In the United States, the shortage of skilled labor (and excess of unskilled) has called for blacks to fill the gap. The supply of civil rights has increased over the past decade, even though to many that increase has been far from enough.

The advantages of granting access thus correlate positively with the level of income. Greater opportunities reduce the number of privileged positions from which it is "necessary" to exclude the unprivileged group. But they also correlate with the rate of increase in income. As that rate increases, the suppliers become more culturally flexible, they are more apt to turn into demanders, their horizons become wider, and they are more willing to apply social experimentation.

Let us illustrate with one kind of access—agrarian reform in Latin America. Such reform would provide the hacienda peons with access to landowning, social mobility, and possibilities for higher income. At the behest of the Alliance for Progress, all Latin American countries that had not done so previously have now passed agrarian-reform legislation. Its implementation, however, is slow. The frequent outbreaks of violence indicate clearly that demand is greater than supply.

It is hard to tell whether the demand for agrarian reform is affected more by the level of income or by its rate of increase. As incomes rise in countries where the feudal hacienda system is prevalent, peasants whose fathers neither knew their nationality nor in a lifetime traveled more than a few miles from their birthplaces suddenly hear of the marvels of the city and find the transportation to move. Their contact with political leaders interested in championing agrarian reform and the greater communication between the lower classes in city and country lead to a steady increase in demand.

The power group finds itself in an ambivalent position. As landowners, it is opposed to agrarian reform, for its own land would be confiscated. As industrialists, however, it is in favor. Manufacturers recognize more and more that inefficient agriculture leads to shortage of food supply, and higher food costs in turn lead to demands for higher wages. While industrial output in Latin America is increasing at an annual rate of approximately 6 percent, long-term agricultural output in the 1950s and 1960s has scarcely kept up with the population growth of over 3 percent. Though the immediate impact of agrarian reform on production is often negative, nevertheless over the long run the abolition of feudalism would doubtless provide greater elasticity of farm output.

But the clarity of interests is muddied by the fact that industrialists and landowners are often the same people. Landowners are the major economic group capable of seizing new industrial opportunities; if others do initiate industry, the successful ones become landowners with their profits. Furthermore, the increase in population and migration from country to city tend to dampen the upward push of wages on the inelastic agricultural supply.

One may conjecture that *if* the rate of increase in income were higher, the capacity to supply access would be increased. In the first place, the shift in dominance of interest away from agriculture and toward industry would be put into perspective, and members of the power group would think of themselves more as industrialists than as landowners. In the second place, the absorption of unemployment in the urban slums would release the upward pressure on wages, forcing the new industrialists to face the desirability of agrarian reform.

The relationship between the increment of income and the supply of agrarian reform is illuminated by the case of São Paulo, Brazil, a rapidly industrializing state whose income in the last two decades has increased more rapidly than that of Brazil as a whole. Late in 1960, São Paulo approved an Agrarian Revision Law, whose passage was made certain by the dominance of industrial groups. Forced land purchases were to be financed by rural property taxes. The rest of Brazil was not ready for such reform, however, and the federal Congress approved a constitutional amendment transferring the jurisdiction over rural property taxes from the states to the municipalities. The state was therefore forced to finance its reform with sales and consignment taxes, which not only reduced its ability to carry out the reform but also relieved the burden of the property-owners.[33] Had the rate of income increase elsewhere in Brazil been as high as in São Paulo, we may conjecture that the reform might have been more successful.

[33] Inter-American Development Bank, *Social Progress Trust Fund, Second Annual Report*, 1962 (Washington, D.C., 1963), p. 201.

CHAPTER 8

The Landing

IT IS now time to retrench. We have argued for a social-science model based on the presumption that economic growth is infinite. Yet it is unbelievable that growth should continue forever. The absurdity of the notion is evident if we ponder the exponential rates of growth implied by the Harrod–Domar and successive models, for such might also be the equilibrium rates of our own proposed social-science model. While such a model might do for the time being, nevertheless we cannot propose that it would be valid forever.

But what are the limits to growth? Were the classical economists right in predicting a stationary state? Is Rostow justified in assuming that the "age of mass consumption" is the last stage currently visible? If a society takes off, will it also land? Surely the theory of institutions should help us grapple with these questions.

We see three potential constraints, any one of which might serve as the ceiling to growth. They are the following.

1. Man's inability to achieve beyond a certain level of institutional effectiveness. Let us call this the effectiveness constraint.

2. A limit to the quantity of goods and services the earth is capable of producing. Classical economists saw this as the only constraint. We label it the supply constraint.

3. A maximum level of economic output that people want. Beyond a certain point, growth will not remain a dominant goal. We call this the demand constraint.

THE EFFECTIVENESS CONSTRAINT

The limited effectiveness of big-power diplomacy (e.g., Soviet-American) clearly constrains economic growth in more developed countries, just as the inadequacy of institutions does in the less developed. In each case, institutional effectiveness is low because opposing parties diverge on fundamental values, are unable to predict each other's actions, and fear and mistrust each other. To agree on institutional ideology, they must form consensus on a dominant goal, which we have presumed to be economic growth in the case of less developed countries.

If growth remains a dominant goal in the more developed countries, man will ultimately discern that both international wars and civil disturbances frustrate his progress, and he will seek institutionalized means of resolving these conflicts on a predictable basis. There is no optimism in this statement, for we have no way to predict how much bloodshed will occur in the meantime.

Limited effectiveness is also implied in relations between more and less developed countries. If the dominant powers first select a coercive international order in which the less developed do not willingly accept the degree or type of participation permitted them by their "superiors," the cost of final consensus will be high indeed and might never be paid. The theory of institutions would predict only that *if* economic growth remains a worldwide dominant goal, *ultimately* consensus institutions must emerge on an international basis.

Unless man blows himself up in the meantime, time and ingenuity are both infinite. It is hardly probable that the effectiveness constraint will be the one finally to stop growth.

THE SUPPLY CONSTRAINT

The supply constraint would appear to be a more likely candidate. For years we have supposed that technology had an infinite capacity to overcome the law of diminishing marginal productivity. This law applies when one factor of production exists in limited quantity, and we have presumed that the capacity of earth was not really limited but could be indefinitely increased through inventions.

Population increase may seem to be the immediate challenger to infinite supply, at least on a per capita basis. But the technology for population control is known. The problem lies in its social acceptance. If society does not select population control, the reason is either that it prefers more population to increased output per capita or that its institutions are not effective enough to make the choice. In the former case, growth stops because of the demand contraint, in the latter because of the effectiveness constraint. The supply constraint operates only where corrective technology is not known and cannot be found.

The pollution of resources would appear as the next challenger, since continued economic growth might destroy the earth. The problem is twofold: first, technological, and second, one of social acceptance. The technology must be one of recycling inputs and of converting noxious waste into nonnoxious. Ultimately it resolves into recycling alone; otherwise some natural resources would be totally exhausted into nonnoxious waste and would not be renewable. We would be on no sure ground if we were to predict that man does not have the ingenuity to solve this problem, even with infinitely continuing growth. If we did so predict, we would be back with the classical economists who foresaw that the stationary state would come about because of diminishing returns.

The recycling technology will be more costly than most are disposed to think. The current popular tendency is to believe that pollution will be resolved by gimmicks, such as improvements in automobile engines, and that economic growth will continue merrily with little change in pace. But it will require the abandonment of much technology and the discovery of new. It will also require that automobiles (and other products) be reconverted into their inputs—not that iron be returned to the ground but that it become steel sheets ready for reuse. Cans would once again become aluminum or other alloys, while plastic would turn into the chemical compounds of which it is composed. No research has come to my attention that would estimate how costly this might be. However, a conservative guess might be that 45 percent of gross national product is essentially polluting (mining, construction, manufacturing, transportation, communication, and power), and that the cost of recycling or conversion into nonnoxious materials might be 50 percent of original cost to produce. On that basis, the cost of any given volume of gross national product would increase by a fifth to a quarter. It is hardly likely that the increase would be less; most probably it would be even more.

Let us suppose, ultimately, that consumers are willing to pay the cost. Still more is implied. New pricing institutions must be found, and these will surely run counter to the productionist ideology so strongly embedded in the United States. Prices are now determined through comparison of *private* cost with *private* demand. Social (as opposed to private) cost covers the sacrifices (such as pollution) suffered by others than the producer. There are, to be sure, public goods; also taxes, which cover some social costs, are debited in private profit-and-loss statements. But by and large the pricing system is a private one. Institutions would therefore have to be established through which the user of any product would be charged its full cost: to manufacture, recycle, and convert nonrecyclable waste into nonnoxious form. There are many ways in which this could be done. The original purchaser or producer might be taxed, and with the proceeds the government might contract out the recycling or disposal. Or the consumer might be required by law to submit his waste for appropriate treatment, paying its cost at the time of disposition. (But how would this be done for automobile exhaust?) Whatever the institution selected, it does not stretch imagination to suggest that a great social upheaval will occur. Ways of doing business must be drastically altered, and the sanctity of private initiative will be severely threatened.

Other decisions must be made and institutions formed to make them. Even if the technology is invented for most products, there will be some that cannot be fully recycled or whose waste cannot be made fully nonnoxious. Should these be prohibited? Or will society determine that the pollution they cause can be overlooked? In some products, the cost of recycling may be low for (say) 70 percent of waste, but then it will rise sharply. Is there a tolerable level of pollution up to which the more expensive or impossible parts of recycling may be passed by? This is the sort of decision to which economists would apply marginal conditions: the value of the marginal product forgone must equal the value of the marginal increments of purity in air and water preserved. But who shall make the decision, which does not lend itself at all to the private pricing system to which we have been accustomed? The United States will find itself going through the same trauma now experienced in takeoff countries. In each case, new institutions must be selected to resolve new conflicts in a context of less than full consensus on social goals.

The supply constraint would stop growth if we could not find the technology to recycle; the effectiveness constraint would stop it if the technology could not gain social acceptance. But we now see that the two are linked, for the level of tolerance is influenced by both technology and acceptance. Despite overwhelming obstacles of which politicians seem not to have dreamed as yet, it would not be safe to predict that either the supply or the effectiveness constraint will be the ultimate slower of growth. We may predict, if we will, that thousands will die of smog in Los Angeles and New York or of mercury poison in drinking water before our society acts. It is quite another thing to predict that the technology can *never* be found or that the social will can *never* be mobilized.

The demand constraint will slow down growth if society decides that increasing material wealth is not wanted. But demand is not independent of supply, for it may well be that people will decide that if they cannot have it, they do not want it (sour grapes). Even this reaction would be attributable to the supply constraint. As, however, the true cost of production (including pollution) dawns upon large segments of society, it is possible that values will be so altered that consumers will question whether objects should be wanted at all, *even if they did not cost so much.*

Let me summarize and repeat, for the idea is an important one. Before the effectiveness and supply constraints directly slow economic growth, they may lead to a reexamination of values and a decrease in growth sensitivity. This in turn may lower demand by *more* than would be required by the effectiveness and supply limitations, which would thereby gain some slack. Hence the demand constraint by itself would bring economic growth to the zero rate. Indeed, any other conclusion would be a slur on man's ingenuity either for technological progress or for social organization.

At first blush, it seems optimistic to predict that landing will occur because man does not *want* growth rather than because he cannot have it. Upon reflection, however, we find the runway perilous. We have already mentioned the institutional problems of recycling. These cannot be avoided simply by scaling down demand. Antipollution is now a value of upper-income people who may already have what they want. The level of output must be significantly higher than it is now and distribution of income significantly different, before all social sectors will consent to stopping growth. (The redistribution of income will also require institutional change.) The higher level of output will create enough pollutants to do intolerable damage unless new technology is put into effect.

Still other changes in the social order are necessary. Growth-*de*-sensitized individuals and groups must replace the growth-sensitized. Values are upset. New conflicts arise, and old institutions are incapable of handling them. Landing is thus symmetrical to takeoff; in many ways it is the mirror image.

The signs of landing are found mostly on university campuses in the United States, which we have already referred to in Chapter 3. Any similarity between campus unrest in the United States and in less developed countries reflects the similarity between takeoff and landing; it does *not* reflect unanimity among restless students everywhere on ultimate values. In the United States, the signs of landing include the following beliefs.

1. That social ills, such as the Indochina war, racial prejudice, pollution, and inequities in income and power distribution are caused by the materialistic ethic, which thereby becomes less popular with the present university generation than with previous ones.

2. That those values that have most promoted economic growth in Western countries, such as competition and *im*personal (affectively neutral) relationships, have an increasingly inhuman quality.

3. That the products of modern society, such as ticky-tacky suburban houses, are too standardized, and are devoid of creative distinctions.

4. That employment opportunities are increasingly limited to narrow functions in large organizations, where the employee has little individuality or sense of personal creativity; that once settled in such employment he finds little opportunity to change, for in doing so he would jeopardize commitments, such as those to children's education or to socially expected standards of housing, even if he were individually willing to restrain consumption.

5. That levels of consumption beyond a certain minimum become undesirable frills, and commitment to income beyond a certain amount is worship of false values.

6. That it is increasingly appropriate for college seniors to graduate with "no plans" for work or to accept simple or handicraft jobs which in an earlier age would have been looked down upon as "menial." In 1971, Harvard College's Office of Graduate and Career Plans announced that 18 percent of the Class of 1970 had "no plans" (as against 4 to 6 percent in 1964-1967); candi-

dates for graduate school had dropped from 74 percent in 1966 to 46 percent in 1970, and manual trades were becoming more popular.[1]

Charles Reich, whom some have hailed as spokesman for the new generation, writes of the swing away from economic motivation as follows:

> We need not dispute the general thesis that consciousness is determined by a person's working conditions and basic interests. But the interests of a person should not be defined in narrowly economic terms; they could, conceivably, include a person's needs beyond the economic, once the latter have been satisfied. Throughout most, if not all, of the history with which Marx was familiar, economic situation and "interest" have perhaps been largely identical. But in an affluent society, where everybody's economic interests are or can be satisfied, other aspects of interest may become dominant in the formation of consciousness— interests such as status or personal liberation. Marx simply was limited by the evidence and the historical situation of his times. It is by no means inconsistent with Marx to suggest that new interests become dominant when, perhaps for the first time in history, the economic ceases to be of primary concern in men's lives.[2]

In 1970, the President's Commission on Campus Unrest reported a youthful tendency away from those beliefs and traditions associated with production:

> The subculture took its bearings from the notion of the autonomous, self-determining individual whose goal was to live with "authenticity," or in harmony with his inner penchants and instincts. It also found its identity in a rejection of the work ethic, materialism, and conventional social norms and pieties. Indeed, it rejected all institutional disciplines externally imposed upon the individual, and this set it at odds with much in American society.[3]

[1] *Time Magazine,* March 22, 1971, p. 12.
[2] Charles A. Reich, *The Greening of America* (New York: Random House, 1970), p. 309.
[3] Governor William W. Scranton, *Campus Unrest,* Report of the President's Commission on Campus Unrest (Washington, D.C.: U.S. Government Printing Office, 1970), p. 62.

The President's Commission also reported what might be interpreted as a tendency toward institutional *ineffectiveness*: a belief on the part of the young that organization *per se* limits self-expression. For organization is selective: it promotes those activities that further its goal, discouraging those that are alien. But such selection contradicts the right of dissenters to be heard:

> At the same time, they try very hard, and with extraordinary patience, to give each of their fellows an opportunity to be heard and to participate directly in decision-making. The new culture decisional style is founded on the endless mass meeting at which there is no chairman and no agenda, and from which the crowd or parts of the crowd melt away or move off into actions. Such crowds are, of course, subject to easy manipulation by skillful agitators and sometimes become mobs. But it must also be recognized that large, loose, floating crowds represent for participants in the new youth culture the normal, friendly, natural way for human beings to come together equally, to communicate, and to decide what to do.[4]

Whether or not the mass meeting is institutionally effective (according to our three criteria) will depend on goals and the degree of consensus upon them. The mass meeting would clearly be ineffective as a means for a corporation to decide its production schedule. But if the goal is not to promote output but a certain kind of relationship among people, then the mass meeting may indeed be effective. The ways in which university students organize themselves may therefore be a clue as to whether they are becoming growth-desensitized.

Indeed, the above observations would lead one to believe that the conflict over economic ideology in landing countries has a different dimension from that in takeoff. In takeoff countries, it is a conflict of appropriationists versus productionists. In landing countries, the discrepant views of society may be over whether material possession is so emphasized as to engulf other values, such as life, human warmth, and earth, or whether on the other hand material product serves to emancipate man from drudgery so that he may embrace the other values. The new student culture would appear to believe that the former is the way society *is*, while the latter is the way it *ought to be*.

[4] *Ibid.*, p. 66.

The similarity between youth movements in more and less developed countries lies, therefore, not in substance but in tactics. It may also lie in what Erikson has called the revolt of the dependent:

Out of the combined revolutions of the oppressed and the repressed, of the proletarians, the unarmed, and the mental sufferers there seems to have now emerged a *Revolt of the Dependent*. That to be dependent means to be exploited is the ideological link betweeen the developmental stage of youth, the economic state of the poor, and the political states of the underdeveloped. This, at least, could partially explain the astounding similarity of the logic used in the patterns of confrontation both by privileged youth and by the underprivileged citizenry. . . .[5]

Though the "revolt of the dependent" may be common ground for university youth in the United States and nationals of less developed countries (young or adult), nevertheless the dependence is related to a different goal-reorientation in each case: growth-sensitizing in take-off countries and growth-desensitizing in those that are landing.

There is no consensus on growth-desensitization among the university youth of the United States. Many who hold the beliefs enumerated above will lose them as they cope with a social system whose structure the beliefs threaten. Nevertheless, if growth-desensitized individuals do pervade society and move into positions of power, a new institutional ideology must be formed.

This ideology, as well as the economic and political ideologies it depends on, will require a new set of dominant goals to replace economic growth. It is not yet clear what they will be, though the phrase "quality of life and earth" has been applied to them. Social scientists are already at work trying to define them and to measure them.

The author of *Institutions of Economic Slow-down* (Princeton University Press, 2022) will be concerned with a fascinating world in which landing is as confounding as takeoff, and in which some nations are still taking off while others are landing. The dilemmas of international organization will surge out of the relationships between big powers on the one hand and less developed on the other more than out of diplomacy among the superpowers, and they will be much more

[5] Eric H. Erikson, "Reflections on the Dissent of Contemporary Youth," *International Journal of Psychoanalysis*, LI (November 1970), pp. 11-22.

perilous than the difficult problems we now face at home. The simultaneous occurrence of different historical eras will confront a technology of fast verbal communication but—alas!—less rapid communication of values.

A Postscript on United States Policy
Toward Latin America

IN RECENT YEARS, public statements by U.S. government officials and others speaking for the government have emphasized that the United States does not wish to impose its own cultural values or institutions on others through foreign aid or other diplomacy. One such statement comes from the Peterson report:[1] "This country should not look for gratitude or votes, or any specific short-term policy gains from our participation in international development. Nor should it expect to influence others to adopt U.S. cultural values or institutions."

Curiously enough, the same report—on different pages—specifies several U.S. cultural values and institutions that our aid policy ought to promote in less developed countries. These citations include the following:

In the most successful countries, the value of encouraging private initiative has been amply demonstrated. . . . Furthermore, a dynamic private sector has resulted in greater internal savings, more effective use of domestic and foreign resources, and rapid economic growth [p. 18].

[A major area of concentration for the proposed U.S. International Development Institute would be] support of social development, designed to assure popular participation through organizations such as cooperatives, labor groups, trade associations, and civic associations and through community development programs [p. 29].

The first of these assertions is false. The rate of economic growth in the Soviet Union has been persistently greater than in the United States. So has it also been in Mexico, where approximately half of national capital is owned by the government. Conversely, in Bolivia and Haiti private enterprise has grossly failed to equal the virtues at-

[1] *U.S. Foreign Assistance in the 1970's: A New Approach*, Report to the President from the Task Force on International Development (Washington, D.C.: Government Printing Office, March 1970), p. 2.

tributed to it here. If the authors would reply that Bolivia and Haiti are not "dynamic," then their statement is a tautology.

In Table A-1, I attempt to show that the entire Alliance for Progress is designed to inculcate into Latin American countries the cultural values and institutions of the United States. In the left-hand column are selected statements from the Charter of Punta del Este, the basic document of the Alliance.[2] In the right-hand column are references to U.S. institutions and values as reflected in specific events in the socio-political-economic development of the United States. A strong similarity between the New Deal (and its offspring institutions) and the Alliance is evident.

TABLE A-1

Alliance for Progress	*U.S. Domestic Counterparts*
1. "That comprehensive and well-conceived national programs of economic and social development, aimed at the achievement of self-sustaining growth, be carried out in accordance with democratic principles."	1. Policies for economic growth as conceived under the Employment Act of 1946 and implemented through the Council of Economic Advisers and the Joint Congressional Committee on the Economic Report.
2. "That national programs of economic and social development be based on the principle of self-help. . . ."	2. Community action programs under the Office of Economic Opportunity; requirement that state and local government participate in poverty programs such as the work-training programs; tradition of state's rights and local autonomy over education. etc.
3. "That in the preparation and execution of plans for economic and social development, women should be placed on an equal footing with men."	3. Interpretation of the equal-protection clause of the Fourteenth Amendment to mean equality of economic opportunity for men and women.
4. "That the Latin American countries obtain sufficient external financial assistance . . . in order to supplement domestic capital formation and reinforce their import capacity. . . ."	4. The economic development of the United States and its capacity to import was based in part on European capital, and the United States was on balance a debtor country before World War I.

[2] Organization of American States Official Records Series H/XII.1, *Alliance for Progress*, official documents emanating from the special meeting of the Inter-American Economic and Social Council at the ministerial level, Punta del Este, Uruguay, August 5-17, 1961 (Washington, D.C., 1961).

Alliance for Progress	*U.S. Domestic Counterparts*
5. "That institutions in both the public and private sectors, including labor organizations, cooperatives, and commercial, industrial, and financial institutions, be strengthened and improved. . . ."	5. The National Labor Relations Act (1935) and subsequent labor legislation; the development of the Cooperative movement in the United States; the key roles played by U.S. commercial, industrial, and financial institutions such as commodity exchanges, banking system, private industry.
6. "Improvement of human resources and widening of opportunities by raising general standards of education and health . . . technical education and professional training with emphasis on science and technology. . . ."	6. Federal aid to education; special promotion of scientific education after 1958; public health programs and insurance.
7. "Wider development and more efficient use of natural resources. . . ."	7. Conservation policies with respect to public lands, forests, wildlife, and fish, soils, and water resources.
8. "The strengthening of the agricultural base, progressively extending the benefits of the land to those who work it, and ensuring in countries with Indian populations the integration of these populations into the economic, social, and cultural processes of modern life. To carry out these aims, measures should be adopted, among others, to establish or improve, as the case may be, the following services: extension, credit, technical assistance, agricultural research and mechanization; health and education; storage and distribution; cooperatives and farmers' associations; and community development."	8. The integration of Indian populations corresponds closely to the Federal programs for promoting civil rights in the United States (equal opportunities for colored populations in an integrated society). Every one of the services cited has been provided, in one way or another, by the U.S. Department of Agriculture or by other agencies of the Federal Government.
9. "More effective, rational and equitable mobilization of and use of financial resources through the reform of tax structures, including fair and adequate taxation of large incomes and real estate, and the strict application of measures to improve fiscal administration . . . measures for the	9. The income, corporate profit, and property tax structures of the United States; the use of monetary and fiscal policy to control inflation; the institutional structure (mostly private) for assuring the smooth flow of private savings into investment.

Alliance for Progress	*U.S. Domestic Counterparts*

maintenance of price stability, the creation of essential credit facilities . . . and the encouragement of private savings."

10. "Improvement of systems of distribution and sales in order to make markets more competitive and prevent monopolistic practices."

10. The Sherman and Clayton antitrust laws, the Federal Trade Commission, and the activities of the antitrust division of the Department of Justice.

11. "The American republics consider that the broadening of present national markets . . . is essential. . . . The Montevideo Treaty and the Central American Treaty on Economic Integration are appropriate instruments. . . ."

11. The United States itself constitutes an integrated community of fifty states which provide broadened national markets.

12. "National measures affecting commerce in primary products should be directed and applied in order to: (1) avoid undue obstacles in the expansion of trade in these products; (2) avoid market instability; (3) improve the efficiency of international plans and mechanisms for stabilization; and (4) increase their present markets and expand their area of trade at a rate comparable with rapid development."

12. Support prices and other measures to avoid instability of markets for agricultural output; encouragement of the production of minerals (oil, lead, and zinc) through import quotas; stockpiling (though ostensibly for strategic materials only) operated so as to stabilize markets.

13. "To encourage, in accordance with the characteristics of each country, programs of comprehensive agrarian reform leading to the effective transformation, where required, of unjust structures of land tenure and use . . . so that . . . the land will become for the man who works it the basis of his economic stability, the foundation of his increasing welfare, and the guarantee of his freedom and dignity."

13. The system of private, family farms in the United States, on which presumably is founded the political and economic security of the farming community.

Hemispheric Destiny and the "Special Relationship"

We have seen, in other contexts, that institutions transplanted from the United States to Latin America have served the latter area with mixed instructions and deficient effectiveness. This deficiency may well have retarded economic growth. If growth in the Americas is indeed a concern of the United States—either because it is in our interest or for humanitarian reasons—we should pause before further promoting the transplant of our own institutions.

Let us digress to consider the intellectual and emotional basis for transplants. The overall orientation of U.S. policy toward Latin America is based on the concept of hemispheric destiny: that the countries of Latin America and the United States are bound by a common history and a common goal. Frank Tannenbaum wrote of this union as follows:[3]

> Don Federico de Onís, for so many years the leading influence in Hispanic studies in the United States, likes to say that he can always recognize an American in Paris but cannot tell whether he comes from New York or Buenos Aires, from Chicago or Caracas. There is something about his bearing—the way he holds his head, his swinging arms and long strides, the innocence and optimism reflected in his every gesture—which marks him as a child of the New World. This is one way of saying that Americans North and South are in some measure interchangeable, that their history has moulded them in a similar if not identical crucible. The familiar list of differences between the United States and Latin America is only partially true. Four centuries of a common heritage have given all of us "something" marked as American rather than European. It is discernible in our prose and poetry, in our politics, in our attitude toward the outside world, in our popular heroes and folk tales, in the stories we tell our children, and in the moral issues that trouble the grown-up.

In 1969, at the request of President Nixon, Governor Rockefeller visited all Latin American republics except three that would not re-

[3] Frank Tannenbaum, *Ten Keys to Latin America* (New York: Alfred A. Knopf, 1962), pp. 3-4. Originally published in Tannenbaum, "Toward an Appreciation of Latin America," in Herbert L. Matthews, ed., *The United States and Latin America* (Englewood Cliffs, N.J.: Prentice-Hall, for the American Assembly, Columbia University, 1959), p. 8.

ceive him. The rioting and bombings that occurred in connection with this trip were symptoms of the deep ideological divisions within the countries. Upon his return, Rockefeller asserted that the United States has always maintained a "special relationship" with Latin America, and he recommended that that relationship be preserved.[4]

Historically, the United States has had a special relationship with the other American republics. It is based upon long association, geography and above all, on the psychological acceptance of hemispheric community. It is embodied in the web of organizations, treaties and commitments of the inter-American system. Beyond conventional security and economic interests, the political and psychological value of the special relationship cannot be overestimated. Failure to maintain that special relationship would imply a failure of our capacity and responsibility as a great power. If we cannot maintain a constructive relationship in the Western Hemisphere, we will hardly be able to achieve a successful order elsewhere in the world. Moreover, failure to maintain the special relationship would create a vacuum in the hemisphere and facilitate the influence in the region of hostile foreign powers.

"Special relationship" is but a synonym for hemispheric (or common) destiny, a term Rockefeller has used on other occasions. For example:[5]

Of his coming meetings with Latin American leaders, he [Rockefeller] said, "I think the most important thing is to listen to them, to find out what their reactions are, what they feel the possibilities are, their hopes, their aspirations, their fears and then blend this into common goals and common programs."

He kept stressing the need for taking advice rather than giving orders so "that *together we—this country and they—can find roads that will lead to common best interests and a common destiny.*"

The concept of hemispheric destiny is questionable not only as a value but also in terms of whether it has ever existed historically. Pos-

[4] Nelson A. Rockefeller, *Quality of Life in the Americas*, Report of U.S. Presidential Mission for the Western Hemisphere, reprint (Washington, D.C.: Agency for International Development, 1970), p. 26.

[5] *New York Times*, February 16, 1969. Italics added.

sibly de Onís's characterizations of the "American in Paris" would apply to all Americans (North and South) with enough resources to go to Paris, but they certaintly do not apply (say) to Ecuadorian Indians. Furthermore, overall U.S. policy has always been oriented more toward Europe than Latin America. When our goals for one have conflicted with those for the other, Latin America has always been sacrificed. This has been so for three reasons. First, our ethnic origins lie more in other European countries than in Spain and Portugal. Secondly, Europe's more advanced stage of economic development has led us to closer trade and mutual investment flows with her than with Latin America. Thirdly, the political, economic, and military influence of European governments causes us to listen harder to her statesmen than to those of Latin America.

Some might argue that the contrast with Europe is not valid; the real comparison should be with Asia and Africa. Here, however, we would enter into endless and fruitless discussion concerning our economic and diplomatic transactions with Japan, Indochina, Liberia, Israel, and oil-producing countries in the Middle East. It seems we have a "special relationship" with everyone. Indeed, in trade negotiations our government has consistently rejected the philosophy of world compartmentalization. If, for example, more developed countries are to reduce tariffs unilaterally in trade with less, we have strongly stated that we would prefer reductions to be universal, by *all* more developed to all less developed. Our European partners, by contrast, have (until 1971) preferred the special relationships: Britain with the Commonwealth, Europe with Africa, and the United States with Latin America.

On October 31, 1969, following Rockefeller's trip to Latin America, President Nixon announced that "in world trade forums [the United States would] press for a liberal system of generalized tariff preferences for all developing countries, including Latin America."[6] Ten days later, in a gesture toward the special relationship, while proposing *global* preferences before the Organization for Economic Cooperation and Development, he nevertheless said that, if the other industrial nations did not agree, the United States was prepared to offer preferences to Latin America alone.[7] Even so, universality was again the theme in

[6] Address of President Nixon before the Inter-American Press Association, reprinted in the *New York Times*, November 1, 1969.
[7] Tad Sculc, *New York Times*, November 10, 1969.

the section on the Western Hemisphere in his foreign policy statement of 1970.[8]

> The U.S. will press for a liberal system of *generalized* tariff preferences for *all* developing countries. We are working toward a system that would eliminate discrimination against South American exports that exist in other countries. Through the Organization for Economic Cooperation and Development and the United Nations Conference on Trade and Development, we are pressing other developed nations to recognize the need for a genuinely progressive tariff preference system.

The present argument is not intended to criticize the Nixon administration for vacillation in its Latin American policy—others have done that—but only to use it as illustration of what might be said about all recent administrations: that the special relationship is one of lip service only. At the time of writing (late 1971), the European Economic Community and Japan have just offered preferential arrangements to all less developed countries, but the Nixon administration has made no effort to introduce any such legislation in Congress.

The Battle for Ideology

Despite the tenuous evidence supporting hemispheric destiny, the United States has frequently called upon this concept to promote specific institutions in Latin America. In order to clarify the conflict, in Table A-2 I have listed general classes of institutions favored by holders of the different economic and political ideologies discussed earlier in this book.

Any association of institutions with ideologies is intuitive and hazardous. Often ideology is imputed from the kinds of institutions a person favors. Research needs to be done to determine a person's political and economic ideologies independently from his institutional preferences. His view of how society functions, such as how it creates and distributes wealth and political power, should be examined. This ideology should then be correlated with preference for institution-types. Lacking this kind of research, however, I believe the classifications in Table A-2 constitute a reasonable working hypothesis.

---

[8] President's Report on Foreign Policy for the 1970s, *New York Times*, February 19, 1970. Italics added.

TABLE A-2

INSTITUTIONS SUPPORTED BY DIFFERENT IDEOLOGIES IN LATIN AMERICA

Category	Productionist	Appropriationist	Third
Business organization	Private enterprise.	Nationalized enterprise.	Many nationalized enterprises; private initiative under benevolent government direction.
Agriculture	Private farming; no confiscation.	State farms; confiscate private property.	Mixture of collective and private farming under state direction; some confiscation.
Labor	Unions totally independent of government (or else no unions at all).	Unions fully controlled by government.	Union–employer relations carried out under benevolent direction of the Ministry of Labor.
Elections	Free elections, though possibly manipulated to exclude mass participation.	Free elections postponed until socialist government is firmly in power.	Free elections with special effort to ensure mass participation and to educate masses to nationalist cause.
Foreign investment and foreign aid	Welcomed as source of needed capital and technology.	Manage without it.	Permitted only under government control to ensure conformity with nationalist goals.
Nationalism	Elitist type, to protect the national interests of producers; not xenophobic except for Communist countries.	Popular nationalism based on support for socialist institutions; xenophobic outside Communist orbit.	Popular nationalism based on support of third ideology; xenophobic in fearing foreign influence from whatever source.
Government	Source of law, order, and stability; economic policies to promote employment and development based on private initiative.	Promoter of interests of the proletariat and regulator of the economy.	Promoter of economic and institutional development with government firmly in control.
Military	Final protector of political stability when democratic processes fail.	Guarantor of the integrity of socialism.	Deemphasized as much as is politically feasible; excluded from government decisions.

In Latin America United States policy has persistently promoted the institutions in the "productionist" column. We have supported private enterprise through many policy statements, such as those cited from the Peterson report. In agriculture, our aid programs have helped reforms of the colonization type and steadfastly ignored those of confiscation. In labor, we have financed the American Institute of Free Labor Development, an organ of the AFL/CIO whose objective is to help Latin American countries form strong unions. We have put our weight behind free elections, failing however to criticize violations of their spirit, such as physical threats to opposition candidates and exiling of losers (e.g., the Dominican Republic, 1966 and 1970). Our favor for foreign investment is expressed in the investment-guarantee program as well as our many policy pronouncements. We have opposed nationalism that smacks of being directed against the United States. The year-to-year program guidelines of the Agency for International Development continue to stress stable governments to promote development policies based on private initiative. Finally, we have eagerly recognized and supported military governments that have prevented left-wing parties from assuming control (e.g., Brazil in 1964, Bolivia in 1971).

The struggle between productionist and appropriationist institutions (Table A-1, second column) in Latin America is fierce. It has split the Christian Democrat party in Chile and caused it to lose the 1970 election, it has brought violence and massacres to Colombia, it has caused demonstrations threatening to government stability even in Mexico. Sometimes these upheavals have caused a productionist government to fall to another one which promises greater resistance to the appropriationists (e.g., Argentina, 1970). In all these struggles, the United States has favored the productionist over the appropriationist institutions and lent its support in the ways already indicated.

Nevertheless, two countries—Mexico and Venezuela—appear to have achieved political stability grounded primarily on third-ideology institutions (those listed in column 3). Once they had demonstrated their capacity for independent strength, or the ability to resist foreign pressures regardless of source, the United States began to view them more tolerantly. Indeed, it would appear that we are not so much in favor of productionist institutions *per se* as we are opposed to appropriationist institutions. If the third ideology can win, we would be moderately happy. We see no current threat from Mexico or Venezuela.

The problem is one of polarization. As third-ideology institutions form, they bear (to our eyes) such close similarity to the appropriationist that we oppose them indiscriminately.

But Latin American countries are *torn* by the productionist–appropriationist split. Far more than lack of capital, this dissension constitutes their most serious cause of underdevelopment. *It underlies the inefficiency of government and business enterprise.* It obscures institutional goals in ways we have already discussed, and it divides groups —such as unions and industrialists—that must cooperate in the successful division of labor. The United States ought to favor third-ideology institutions if they and they alone can heal the rifts.

There is strong reason to believe that the productionist ideology cannot win in Latin America. Rather, the choice seems to lie between the appropriationist and the third, for the following reasons.

First, there is a strong historical predilection toward appropriationism. Peoples who have *not* developed economically find it satisfying to adopt an ideology that explains their failure in terms of exploitation by others and not of their own lack of achievement. This tendency would lead toward either the appropriationist or the third ideology.

Secondly, the narrow power base, wide disparities in income and wealth, and years of oppression by self-seeking dictators lead to the appropriationist conviction that the unfettered individual seeking his own gain detracts from rather than promotes the welfare of others. For these reasons, the appropriationists are far more likely to gain the allegiance of the uncommitted masses than are the productionists.

Thirdly, however, and partly offsetting the above, is the fact that the power base in Latin America has been strongly influenced by West European and North American cultural traditions. Their land and capital holdings and their political control give them a strong influence over institutions, even though numerically they are in a minority.

For these reasons, if the power base is overthrown there is a strong chance for victory by the appropriationists (e.g., Cuba). If appropriationist institutions do not follow a revolution, it would be because their supporters could not agree among themselves and had to call on the old power base for help (e.g., Bolivia). If the power base is not overthrown, then it must—if development is to occur—cooperate with the large mass of potential appropriationists. The only cooperation conceivable would be through institutions of the third ideology.

The United States is a powerful contributor to the struggle, far more so than our statesmen are aware. Frustrated over the many reverses that are inevitable when defending a lost cause, these statesmen are blind to their robust capacity to prolong and deepen the struggle. They seem to believe that ideology and efficiency have nothing to do with each other. Again we quote from the Peterson report: "Each nation must fashion its own policies and institutions to meet its own needs. If the goals are economic development, *the issue is one of efficiency, not ideology*" (p. 18; italics added).

The phrase in italics can be interpreted in two ways. One, consistent with our analysis in Chapter 5, is that the *choice* of ideology is unrelated to efficiency (or effectiveness). But this generous interpretation is not consistent with the report's other pronouncements in favor of private enterprise. Rather, the Peterson task force probably believed that consensus on ideology (or lack of it) has nothing to do with efficiency. If so, it has been the purpose of this book to show how sorely they were wrong.

Summary and Conclusions

The following propositions summarize and conclude this appendix.

1. Latin America is beset by deep popular divisions and civil wars (cold and hot) that debilitate her institutions.

2. Independent strength, or the development of national institutions capable of resisting foreign pressure, is today the only means available for Latin America to defend her political, social, and economic integrity.

3. The major division on economic institutions lies between holders of the productionist ideology, who favor capitalism, and holders of the appropriationist ideology, who favor socialism. Each believes that its institutions alone are workable and just.

4. But workability and justice depend not so much on the intrinsic character of institutions as on whether there is consensus upon them. Strong institutions will emerge only as a product of national consensus on ideology, or a vision of how society does function and ought to function. The institutions will conform to the ideology selected.

5. By supporting productionist institutions in Latin America, U.S. policy has deepened and prolonged the conflict, reducing the probability of institutional strength through compromise (third ideology). The longer the conflict persists, the greater the probability of appropriationist victory.

6. The United States cannot select the third ideology for Latin America. Nevertheless, because it is nationalist, dignifying, and compromising, that ideology holds a greater probability of winning without bloody revolution than either of the other two.

7. Since U.S. policy can do little to promote the third ideology, its object should be to avoid impeding its natural selection. The greatest problem for the president of the United States will be to check those forces within his own country that believe a productionist victory alone is compatible with U.S. private and national interests.

INDEX

acceleration principle, 225
access system, 248-52
Adams, Richard, 185
Adelman, Irma, 235ff
Adelman-Morris model, 235-38
Adler, John H., 211
Agency for International Development, 202, 272
aggregate institutional effectiveness, 215ff; contagion of, 216; defined, 216; demand and supply of, 243ff; and empathy, 218-20; introduced, 83
agrarian reform, 251; in Chile, 134; in São Paulo, Brazil, 251; legitimacy of, 51; in Peru, 247
agricultural credit agencies, 197
agricultural price supports, 113
AID, *see* Agency for International Development
AIE, *see* aggregate institutional effectiveness
Albania, 91
Alger, Horatio, 27, 156
Alliance for Progress, and agrarian reform, 251; comparison with U.S. institutions, 264-66; and planning, 197
American Institute of Free Labor Development, 272
amoral familism, 218
apparent solution line, 43, 177, 221
appropriationist, 148
Arabic language, 169
Argentina, football with Peru, 65; takeoff, 16; under Perón, 167, 248
Aristotle, 52
authoritarian institutions, 21, 172

Banfield, Edward, 218
Banks, Arthur S., 235
Bantu languages, 169
basic principle of institution theory, 20
Bauer, Raymond A., 125
benefit-cost principles, in institution selection, 20, 27; in project analysis, 201, 210, 213
Beuchner, John, 86
biased institutions, 21, 173
Birmingham, Alabama, 250
black power, 98
Bolivia, ideology in, 28; revolution in,

273; since revolution, 189; under Paz, 167
Boulding, Kenneth E., 34, 38, 144
boundary, 175
Brazil, 167
Burma, 93

Canada, 169
capital absorptive capacity, 33, 60, 211
capital-output ratio, 200
Castro, Fidel, 167, 188
centralized institutions, 21, 172
Chile, agrarian reform in, 134, 250; Christian Democratic party, 272
China, 91, 101
Christian Democratic party, in Chile, 272
Cicero, 52
civil rights, 248
Civil Rights law of 1964, 63
coercion, law of, 139-44
coercive institutions, 17
collective bargaining, 131-32, 219
Colombia, 153, 272
communication, cross-cultural, 122-23
comparative static model, 231
complex institutions, 136
Comte, Auguste, 20
conflict, defined, 13, 33; degree of, 73; intensity, 73
Congo, 169
consensus, 62
consensus criterion, introduced, 14; defined, 39-40; in Nicaragua, 107; measured, 80-83; and taxes, 95
consensus institutions, 17
consensus society, United States, 99
constructive conflict, 23, 51-57
convergence theory, 186-87
Cornell University, 98, 247
corporaciones de fomento, 197
corporation, 89
corruption, 181-83
Coser, Lewis A., 52
cost, 21. *See also* benefit-cost
Crockett, Joseph P., 64n
cross-cultural communication, 122-23
Cuba, ideology in, 28, 273; revolutionary conditions in, 188; under Castro, 167, 188
Czechoslovakia, 49

279